TECHNICAL FILM AND TV FOR NONTECHNICAL PEOPLE

by Drew Campbell

ALLWORTH PRESS
NEW YORK

06 05 04 03 02   5 4 3 2 1

Illustrations © 2002 Kis Knekt

Published by Allworth Press
An imprint of Allworth Communications
10 East 23rd Street, New York, NY 10010

Cover and interior design by Mary Belibasakis

Page composition/typography by Integra Software Services, India

ISBN: 1–58115–229–9

Library of Congress Cataloging-in-Publication Data:

Campbell, Drew.
Technical film and TV for nontechnical people / by Drew Campbell.
p. cm.
Includes bibliographical references and index.
ISBN 1-58115-229-9
1. Motion pictures--Production and direction. 2. Cinematography. 3. Television--Production and direction. I. Title.
PN1995.9.P7 C32 2002
791.43'023--dc21
2002001506

Printed in Canada

For Abby,
who loves without question

TABLE OF CONTENTS

ACKNOWLEDGMENTS

Hollywood can be an unfriendly place, but all of the following people have willingly and unhesitatingly extended a helping hand to a poor writer (who really wants to direct). Since my Oscar speech has to be just forty-five seconds, please allow me to thank them here.

My thanks to cinematographer David Safian, gaffer Tim Speed, editor Gary Durrett, and Renaissance woman Mieke Kramer for their technical advice and suggestions.

My thanks to industry mavens (and fellow Brunonians) Stephen Kay, Toni Kotite, Julie Warner, Laura Linney, and Nina Jacobsen for supporting me and helping to assure the success of this book.

To the cast and crew of *Disclaimer Date*, thanks for all your hard work and talent. I'll have a final cut done next month— I promise.

Thanks to the excellent folks at Keslow Camera, who gave invaluable demonstrations and advice.

My thanks also to everyone at Universal Studios: Pat Moloney, Sam Hatcher, Chris Durmick, Chris Williams, Catherine Forester, Denise Wilson, Yvonne Smith, Mike Gename, Frank Masi, and everyone else in production and show development who supported me and looked the other way when I scammed off the copier.

Many thanks to those who offered up their friendship, both in and out of the industry: Sue Bennett, Tisha Goldstein, Martha and Michael Maxim, Mark and Bridget Horton, Drew Dalzell, Jeff Folshinski, Ann Farthing, and of course, my friend and illustrator, Kis Knekt. Thanks to you, too, Ann Marie, for all your support.

And of course, to my family: Mom, Dad, Jim, Heather, Alec, and Colin, who seem to keep opening the door every time I show up. Much love to all.

<u>FLY THAT STINGER TO THE MIDGET ON THE PLATYPUS:WHY THIS BOOK</u>

"Fly that stinger to the midget on the platypus!"

Someone actually said that to me. And expected me to understand.

It was my first day on a movie set, and I was feeling good. I had spent over twenty years in live theater as a technician, designer, director, and actor, and I knew my way around backstage. I knew a Leko from a fresnel from a hole in the ground, you betcha.[1] I knew how to use a parametric equalizer to wring feedback out of wedge monitors, and I wasn't afraid to do it. So when I got to L.A. and plunged into the world of television and film production, I figured that my knowledge would translate, and it would take me no time at all to become Mr. Lighting, Mr. Sound, or Mr. Whatever You Need.

So here I am, day one, 9:00 A.M., and this stressed-out person is shoving me towards the set with this frantic command: "Fly that stinger to the midget on the platypus!"

Do what?

Let me tell you, it had been a while since I had stood slack-jawed and clueless like an inbred hillbilly cousin, staring at a pile of cables and lights like I had never seen electricity in all my born days. This guy had rendered Mr. Technical speechless in one swell foop. Of course, my first thought was that this was one of those hazing things they do to the new guy, so I looked around for the telltale signs of snickering technicians, huddled in clusters by the coffee machine, waiting to see if I would take the bait. I suppose it's only fair, I thought. I've sent an intern out to get polka-dot paint once or twice myself.

---

[1] And so do you, if you read my first book, *Technical Theater for Nontechnical People*, (Allworth Press, 1999).

But, no—all I saw was an experienced and professional crew, rushing to get the first shot set up before the sun got too high in the sky and made everything look flat. These guys were serious. So, I did the only thing that you can do when you land in a foreign country. You learn the language, word by word. I swallowed my pride, looked this guy in the face and asked, "What's a stinger? What's a platypus? How do I fly them? And where do I find the midget?"

Do you need to know what this sentence means? Let's say you're an actor, just starting to work in film. Or an eager production assistant, determined to learn everything you can about television. Or an aspiring filmmaker with lots of ideas and no idea what to do with them. Or let's say you're like me, a theater veteran, trying to understand how film and TV can be so much like the stage and yet so different.

If you are any of these things, then, yes, you do need to know that to "fly in" something means to bring it onto the set, a "stinger" is an extension cord, a "midget" is a small, 200-watt lighting instrument, and a "platypus" is a clamp with broad, flat jaws used to mount a light on a scenic wall.

This book exists to help you distinguish between what you need to know and what you don't need to know. Don't get me wrong: Knowledge is power, and the more you know about the craft of filmmaking, the more you can bend it to your will. But if your brain is like mine, you run the risk of information overload, the dreaded "Etch-a-Sketch" effect, where your brain just gives up, turns upside down, and shakes, thereby clearing all information—both essential and not—from your mental screen.

Do you need to know that the Panaflex 35mm silent camera has a pellicle reflex system? Unless you want a career as a camera assistant, the answer is no. Do you need to know the difference between deep focus and shallow focus? Yes, you do, because it affects everything from the actor's performance to how big a parking space the grip truck will need. (And yes, you do have to know what a "grip truck" is.)

But if the four-decibel difference between axial and displacement magazines really fascinates you, then get a subscription to *American Cinematographer* and move on to more detail-oriented books. (You might look up some of them in the bibliography in the back of this one.)

If, however, you want to act, direct, produce, get a PA job, be a production manager, hire a crew for your music video, or get a training film made, this book is for you. Right now, a Hollywood conversation may sound like so much gibberish, but take heart. Grab that stinger, that midget, that Nagra, that redhead, that quarter silk, and that finger solid. We'll have you shooting the martini in no time.

Chapter 1:

WHO DOES WHAT: THE POPULATION OF A SET

When I made my first real film, as opposed to the video experimentations that I used as a rationalization for introducing myself as a "filmmaker" at parties, I made an arrangement to do a shoot at a local restaurant. I assured the nervous owner that it was a small, no-budget production with a skeleton crew, a fact I knew to be true, having spent some time on large feature film sets. Just the essential people—no frills, no entourages, no paparazzi. I reminded people repeatedly that we were a small, hardy troupe of players, not a bloated Hollywood production. Think of the troupe of players in *Hamlet*, I said, not the legions of workers from *Singin' in the Rain*.

So I show up on the morning of the shoot, virgin producer-director-writer that I am, my crew showing up in ones and twos, and within an hour, the nervous restaurant owner has gone straight into hysterics. There are thirty-one people standing in his tiny bistro.

"I thought you said this was low budget!" he screamed.

I assured him that the budget was strictly limited to the credit limit on my Visa.

"But why are there all of these *PEOPLE?*" he cried, bug-eyed and rampant.

Why, indeed.

I thought back to this moment recently while working a professional commercial shoot. The production brought in no less than ten different trucks requiring that an entire city block be cleared for parking. Besides the lighting truck, the grip truck, and the camera truck, there was a wardrobe truck, an art-department truck, and a truck specially designed to create food props. This was all in addition to the requisite catering truck and a production trailer that could have housed a family of nine.

Because I was working on the lighting for the shoot, I spent most of the time up in the grid work looking down on the action. The soundstage was ablaze with people. Everywhere you looked, there were moving bodies, and most of them were in a terrible hurry. Lighting equipment filled every corner of the room and there were two complete 35mm-camera setups. Money was being spent like rain.

From my vantage point, high above the center of the action, I looked down into the center of the set, and there, at the center of this hurricane of activity, brilliantly lit from all sides like an Impressionist still life, looking for all the world like a precious artifact, was the object of all this attention—a bowl of oatmeal.

Actually, a series of bowls of oatmeal, because every few minutes the oats would become mushy or tepid or cool or whatever oatmeal does under movie lights, and a props person would sweep it away and leave another, perfectly formed, delicately steaming bowl in its place. I believe the cast and crew got a warm, filling breakfast several times over. Regularity was not a problem on that set.

Why does it take so many people to run a set? Why does a caterer have to feed a small army just to shoot a cereal spot or a music video or a public service announcement, let alone a feature film?

I believe the answer is this: The number of things that can go wrong on any given shoot is so incomparably huge, so vast in detail, that you literally have to parcel out the responsibilities to a squadron of folks just so you can get through the shoot and into the editing studio without anyone saying, "Oh no, we forgot about the [insert detail here]."

Filmmaking is an art that rests on detail. And the filmmaker's defense against detail is to create safety in numbers. That is one reason why a film shoot has so many people—with so many eyes on the set, someone is bound to notice that the spot of sunlight on the wall has moved between shots, or the actor's tie has come loose, or the sound of the motorcycle outside ruined the take.

Another reason why we need so many people is that we have a very demanding master—the camera. When a shoot is in full swing, the whole idea is to keep the camera rolling as much as possible. Anything that delays the camera is a delay to the whole process. Again, the defense is to have a person on set, somebody *right there* who knows exactly what to do to solve the problem, remove the block, or answer the question. An electrician *right there* who can refocus that light, a soundman *right there* who can adjust that microphone, a script supervisor *right there* who knows if the actor put his glasses on before or after his line, and yes, a props person *right there* who makes sure that the oatmeal is steaming on cue.

Multiply the number of possible problems by the number of people needed to solve them, and you get a whole bunch of folks standing around a set, waiting for their moment to jump in.

So who are these people?

Basically, the population of a set is divided into fourteen categories. Let's look at the categories and then meet the folks.

Producing Department: The Bill-payers
Directing Department: The Visionaries
Camera Department: Keepers of the Beast
Lighting Department: Feeders of the Beast
Grip Department: Movers and Shakers
Sound Department: The Dialogue Catchers
Art Department: Making the Walls
Prop Department: Phasers to Falcons
Wardrobe: Dressing the Cast
Makeup and Hair: Preening and Prepping
Catering and Craft: Feeding the Multitudes
Drivers: Moving the Show
Teachers, Doctors, and Other Helper-Types: Keeping us
Learned and Healthy
The Talent: The People in the Frame

See what I mean? A whole lotta people, and these are just the ones on the set. Wait till we get to postproduction. Another whole town of people is waiting when these people are done.

PRODUCING DEPARTMENT

Somebody once said that all you needed to be a producer was a phone booth and a stack of nickels. Of course, these days, it's a cell phone and a clear signal, but make no mistake, the ability to talk fast and smooth is still a job requirement for a producer. The producer stays with the film, commercial, or TV show from the idea stage (when it is called a "concept" or a "package"), through preproduction (when it is called a "project"), production and postproduction (when it is called a "show"), and then through distribution and marketing (when it is called a "film," "commercial," or "TV show").

The Producer

The producer is the one in charge—the *capo di tutti capi*—for one simple reason. She's the money. Or at least she represents the money, because every good producer knows the folly of investing her own hard-earned cash in a film. She is in charge of staying on budget and on schedule. She also may operate as a liaison between the show and the production company or studio.

The film is the producer's baby. She raises the money, buys the script, hires the crew, chooses the cast, approves the budget, signs the checks, accepts the Oscar, and, with any luck, makes the profit.

People who come to film or TV from the theater are often surprised at the difference in power structure between the producer and director. In theater, the director tends to be a much more powerful decision maker, both on larger items like designs and casting and on smaller, more daily decisions like props and acting styles. The theatrical producer concerns himself more with large decisions, like choosing a play and raising money. In film, the producer is much more visible during the production process and much more involved in daily decision-making.

In the theater, there is generally a moment, somewhere between casting the stars and starting rehearsal, when the producer backs off and lets the show run on its own. The pieces are in place; everyone knows what to do. Now, it's time to see the crew sail its own boat. Generally, if the producer is in the rehearsal hall, something is going wrong.

There is no such moment in film. The producer is omnipresent, heading the ad hoc corporation that grows up around a film and, generally, micromanaging it. Most producers make a surprising number of artistic decisions—they generally do it at a distance by choosing cast members, hiring directors, and buying scripts, but they involve themselves much more deeply in the creative process than their theatrical counterparts. Actors and designers accustomed to getting notes only from the director may find themselves startled to get direction and approvals from the producer just as often. Little wonder that successful directors and actors try to become producers of their own movies. It is the only way of gaining any control over the finished product.

Again, *the producer makes decisions.* Which star do we cast? Which script? Which version of the script? Do we shoot in Los Angeles or Toronto? Which format do we shoot in? Which revision of which annotated rewrite of the script based on the notes from which story editor?

If it involves money (and it always involves money), it is the producer's call. The director may decide that he needs an extra day on location, but no one is booking the hotel until the producer says yes.

There is a gaggle of different producers and an unwritten code about what the titles mean:

Producer. The trend these days is for producers to travel in packs. It's rare to see a single producer on a film anymore, because everyone wants power, and this is where it is. A producer credit can bestow visibility and money on its recipient, so it is sometimes offered as a negotiating point with people who may only be tangentially involved with a show. The title "producer" is generally bestowed on the people who are really driving the project, on a day-to-day basis, from concept to completion.

Executive Producer. Either someone who arranged financing for the film and wants a vanity title or someone who is barely involved but has a recognizable name that will help the show raise money. Sometimes it's a studio head who has championed the film.

Associate Producer. This title is sometimes given as a reward for someone like a production manager or 1st AD who worked above and beyond the call to get a film done. Sometimes it's given to a writer or director who negotiated for a producing credit, or as a way of assuring certain production team members that they actually have some power in the production.

Line Producer. Large-budget shows will have someone between the producer and the production manager whose job it is to manage the budget. Besides riding herd on overruns, they also make sure that enough money is provided for each area. Unlike the producer, the line producer does not make artistic decisions. This is the realm of the creative but exacting money manager.

The Production Staff

Under the producers is another group of people who monitor budgets, create schedules, and otherwise keep a show running.

Unit Production Manager. The UPM puts together the budget (with the line producer on big shows) and makes the whole shoot happen. He hires crew, rents trucks, handles locations, and does everything necessary to put the right people in the right place with the right tools at the right time. He is brought in during preproduction, and his planning can make the difference between a smooth shoot and a nightmare.

Production Coordinator. While the UPM is generally out in the field, the production coordinator works out of the production office to coordinate logistics, particularly lodging, transportation, and shipping of critical items like film and dailies.

Production Assistants. The time-honored way of breaking into film and TV. *PAs* run errands, type schedules, carry equipment, post signs, and anything else that needs to be done. Their mating call is, "I'm on it!" For years, they were famous for making coffee, but in this day and age, they keep track of the closest Starbucks and which actor gets the no-fat, no-foam, triple grande vanilla latte.

Location Managers and Scouts. "Let's just keep going!" says Thelma. "What do you mean?" says Louise, as the crowd of police cars forms up behind them, cutting off all hope of escape.

"Let's just keep going!" repeats Thelma, gesturing to the sheer cliff ahead of them, beyond which there is only air and a thousand-foot drop to oblivion. Louise jams the car into gear and over they go, leaving their lives behind them, frozen midair in female-empowered jubilation, silhouetted against endless miles of striped canyon.

Callie Khouri's script for *Thelma and Louise* may have ended with the triumphant, suicidal plunge of two determined feminists, but it wasn't going to end up on-screen until someone found a photogenic cliff. That person was a location manager or a location scout. (On small shows, the location manager scouts, as well, while big shows have two different people.) His job is to scour the world in search of the perfect place for a suicide, a murder, a love affair, a heist, or whatever else is called for in the script. Once a place is found, a delicate negotiation begins with the owner, the neighbors, the local government, and anyone else who might have a stake in whether or not a film is allowed to shoot.

When a film comes to town, the effect is somewhere between traveling gypsies and a gold rush. A shoot can mean dozens of people may be tramping across lawns, bright lights may be on in the middle of the night, traffic and access to homes and businesses may be affected, and, in some cases, a '66 T-Bird may be tossed off a cliff.

The arrival of a film can make people cranky. During the shooting of *The Bridges of Madison County*, one neighboring farmer got so incensed that he ran his mower nonstop next door, ruining take after take until the film crew found a way to placate him.

In Los Angeles, film locations inside the city limits are posted at City Hall, and one man in need of therapy has made a career out of disturbing them. He is known among location managers as "Weedeater Man." When the film is setting up in the morning, Weedeater Man stands across the street and cranks up his gas-powered weed trimmer nice and loud. When it becomes apparent that he is going to stay all day, the location manager crosses the street and pays him off. He tosses the weedeater in the trunk and heads home, another day's work (and another pissed-off crew) behind him. (If you are the Weedeater Man and you are reading this, *get help*, you idiot.)

It is the location manager's job to solve problems like these. After the scout has dug up the place and the producer and director have agreed to it, the location manager is responsible for getting permission to use the place, negotiating with any open palms, and planning the logistics.

For the record, Thelma and Louise's cliff is on Potash Road, off Route 279, nineteen miles south of Moab, Utah.[2]

DIRECTING DEPARTMENT

The phrase, "But what I really want to do is direct," is so far beyond cliché that it almost doesn't bear mentioning. EVERYBODY wants to direct. I want to direct. Directors are Hollywood's favorite sons and

---

[2] For hundreds of these bits of location trivia, check out *Shot on This Site*, by William Gordon (Citadel Press, 1995).

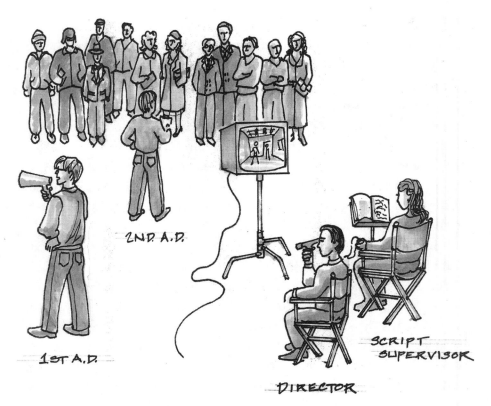

The directing department.

daughters, even though they still serve at the pleasure of the producers. In Hollywood, the director is seen as the Great Artist.

The Director

While the producer wields control over the big decisions like casting, script, and budget, the director controls all of the shot-by-shot, moment-to-moment decisions. Of course, he has input in those pre-production issues, but he doesn't become a deity until we are on the set. He will choose where the camera goes, how it moves, and what it sees, and, because everything that happens on a set happens for the camera, that makes the director a powerful person.

The director has a mental image of what he wants, and it is his job to communicate that image to the cast and crew. Their job is to turn that image into celluloid or videotape. Success depends on the clarity of the director's image and his skill at communicating that image to others.

But what, exactly, does a director do?

Directors are visual storytellers.

In *Jurassic Park*, a small group of humans find themselves on the wrong side of the evolutionary tracks when they are trapped on an island full of marauding dinosaurs. The early scenes of the movie set up the fact that the most vicious of these dinosaurs are velociraptors: lean, mean, killing machines of the highest order. When it becomes clear that the electric fences that contain the dinosaurs have been turned off, the desperate human party sets off across the compound to restore power (and, therefore, safety) to the park. As they walk along the trail, the camera tracks along beside them, watching them through the steel bars of the raptor cage. The actors talk nervously as the bars of the fence ripple by in the foreground. After they have gone a little ways, however, the camera reaches a gaping, jagged gash in the solid, steel enclosure. The party stops and looks straight at the camera, through the obvious evidence of the raptor's escape. The camera frames the quavering, oh-so-edible humans in the ripped girders of the raptor cage. The message is clear: These people are dino-lunch.

This is what directors do. Besides helping the actors discover the right style of performance for their character, the director manipulates the camera to tell a story through visual imagery.

The director has several assistants that help him move things forward.

First Assistant Director

The 1st AD works with the UPM to set up the shooting schedule and then executes it. His specialty is knowing how long it will take to get a shot and making sure he's right. He is the whip-cracker on the set, much like a stage manager in the theater. The 1st AD position is not a job for someone training to be a director. Despite the name, it is an entirely different career path. It is a people-management job, not an artistic one. It is also not a job for someone who wants to be liked all the time. The AD's job is to push people.

Second Assistant Director

The 2nd AD supports the 1st AD, but, while the 1st AD can generally be found close to the camera and the actual shooting, the 2nd AD will be more involved in logistics and paperwork. They also help move extras around in crowd scenes. Second ADs grow up to be 1st ADs.

Second Second Assistant Director

Why not the 3rd AD? Why do we park in driveways and drive on parkways? Some questions are not meant to be answered. 2nd 2nd AD is a position very similar to the production assistant in the producing department. As a matter of fact, some people (I'm not mentioning any names) will list a PA job on their resume as a second second assistant director.

Script Supervisor

My brother's wife has an astounding skill. Every time my brother loses his keys, his wallet, the magazine he was just reading, or anything else, he asks her where it is. She pauses, cocks her head, purses her lips slightly, and then, unfailingly, pinpoints the missing object, usually within inches. When asked about her prodigious talent, she shrugs. "I just pay attention," she says.

She would make a great script supervisor.

Was the actor's top button closed in the previous shot or not? Did he stand up while saying his line or after? How full was that glass the last time around? These questions may sound like mundane detail on the set, but once you get to the editing suite, they can make the difference between a usable shot and one that ends up on the (now proverbial) cutting-room floor. **Script supervisors** help maintain **continuity**, the consistency of the images from shot to shot and from scene to scene. This is a huge job, particularly because films are rarely shot in sequence.

Besides noting this type of minutia, "script supers" also keep track of what shots have been filmed, which lenses or filters were applied, which takes were flubbed, and piles of other information that will serve the editing team in postproduction. A good script super will shoot dozens of Polaroid pictures to document everything (although many are now switching to digital cameras).

CAMERA DEPARTMENT

Lots of people think life on a movie set is fascinating, fast-moving, exciting, or laugh-a-minute. It isn't. More than anything else, for most people on the set, filmmaking is catastrophically boring. Movie sets are the only place I know where you can be stressed out and bored at the same time—stressed out because money is being spent at a terrific rate, every little detail matters, and the tiniest mistake can ruin hours of effort and thousands of dollars of investment; bored because, let's face it, most people on the set sit around for hours, if not days, waiting for their turn to do whatever it is they do. I have learned more good card games on a set than in my grandmother's parlor, and that is saying something. Contacts are made, nails are filed, gossip is exchanged, poker is played, cigarettes are smoked, romances bloom, and a great deal of betting goes on, covering everything from pager races[3] to the time the shot will actually be made.

There are two exceptions to this rule—that is, there are two people on a movie set who are always busy, always occupied doing what they are there to do. They are the director, who is always busy communicating his vision; and the cinematographer, who is always busy creating it.

Life on the set revolves, literally, around the camera. It is the center of a vast sea of activity, roughly divided into what is "in frame" (and, therefore, important for what it looks like) and what is "out of frame" (and, therefore, important for what it does). This prominent position puts tremendous stress on the men and women of the camera crew. It is also the reason that camera crew positions are highly prized and difficult to get.

Director of Photography

Yes, his official title is "cinematographer," but even the people who publish *American Cinematographer* don't call him that. You also won't hear him called the "director of photography," even though that's what it says on his contract. In old movie credits, he was referred to as the "cameraman," but these days, the man or woman behind the camera is called the **DP**.

The DP is in charge of choosing the film stock, assembling the camera package, lighting the set, and getting the shot, all with the help of a rather extensive crew. He gives orders to three groups of people— the camera crew, the lighting crew, and the grips. The director should be giving the DP guidance in all of this, of course, but it is the DP who

---

[3] For the uninitiated, pager races are played with cell phones and beepers. Each participant puts his pager, set on "vibrate," in the middle of a table. When the referee calls "Go," each player picks up his cell phone and dials his pager number. The first person to vibrate his pager off the table wins.

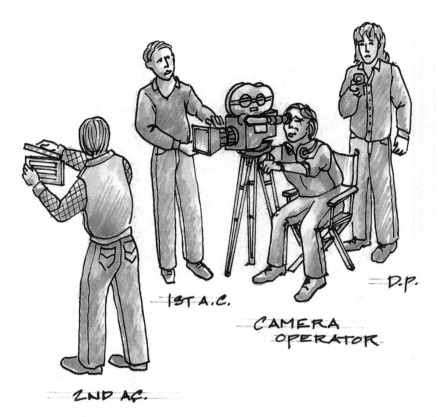

The camera department.

ultimately decides how best to capture the image that the director wants.

The DP is assisted by a small camera crew. These crews often stay together for years and go with the DP on every project he does. They tend to be very close-knit, which is a plus, considering how easily miscommunication can ruin film stock. They are so blended together that they are often, without a trace of sarcasm, called the "camera family."

Camera Operator

A self-evident title. On a small show, the DP may run the camera himself (sometimes the director will even do it), but on shows of any size, there needs to be someone who is concentrating exclusively on maintaining the composition in the viewfinder.

First Assistant Camera

The 1ˢᵗ AC keeps track of lenses and focus. Sometimes called the **focus puller**, she usually sits on the other side of the camera from the operator.

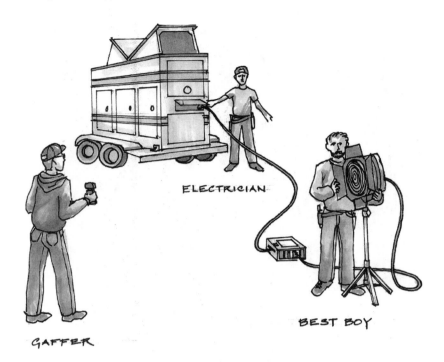

ELECTRICIAN

GAFFER

BEST BOY

The lighting department.

In some camera setups, this may not be possible, so you will see her holding a **remote focus unit** and watching the monitor. The 1st AC also "checks the gate" after every shot for dust and hair (see "Getting the Shot," chapter 12).

Second Assistant Camera

Sometimes called the "clapper/loader," the 2nd AC loads film magazines and operates the slate, a.k.a. the clapper, before every shot. He also helps the 1st AC clean and set up the camera and anything else the camera crew needs. Look for a person walking around with a bunch of colored tape rolls hanging off his belt.

LIGHTING DEPARTMENT

To the old-timers, electricians are "sparkies." If you spend any time at all on a movie set, you will probably find yourself waiting for the lighting crew more than for anyone else—not because they are slow, but because lighting is both time-consuming and deeply critical to the filmmaking process.

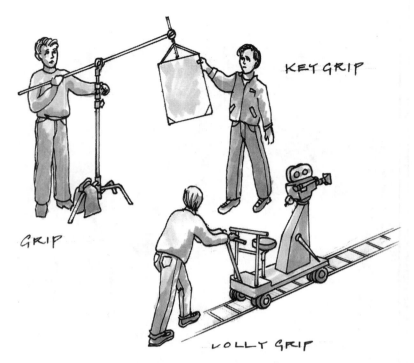

KEY GRIP

GRIP

DOLLY GRIP

The grip department.

Gaffers, Best Boys, and Electricians

The **gaffer** is the head of the lighting crew, but, more than that, he is here to help the DP get the right amount of the right kind of light. The DP-gaffer relationship is about two people looking at the same problem—lighting—from two different perspectives. DPs are primarily photographers. Gaffers are primarily electricians. DPs talk about f-stops and shutter speeds. Gaffers talk about amperage and watts. But they are trying to achieve the same thing—the right amount of the right kind of light on the set.

Back in the old days, gaffers used to call down to the union hall and hire whoever was around that day to work on a shoot. They did have some standards, though, so they would tell the union steward to send the union hall's most qualified up-and-comer, the "best boy," along to be the gaffer's assistant. Hence, the gaffer's assistant is referred to as the **best boy** (the grip crew has a "best boy grip," as well, but the term seems to be more common in the lighting department).

Under the gaffer and the best boy come the electricians, who are responsible for the lighting instruments, cable, generators, and anything else electrical on the set.

GRIP DEPARTMENT

The DP's other right hand is the **key grip**. Grips have a wide range of jobs on a set. They move scenery, certainly, but they also set up a particular collection of gear known as "grip equipment." If a lighting instrument is spilling unwanted light onto a piece of scenery, it is the grip's job to place **flags**, **fingers**, or **scrims** to block or reduce the light. You might think that this would be the electrician's job, but in Hollywood, things aren't always what you think.

Grips also handle the cranes, dollies, and track that the camera rides on. Of course, the camera crew handles the camera itself, but the grips will lay track, set up the crane, and assemble the dolly. There is even one grip, the **dolly grip**, who is charged with moving the dolly during the shoot.

WARDROBE DEPARTMENT

Wardrobe means clothes: period or contemporary; bought, made, or borrowed; uniforms, ball gowns, or rags. The wardrobe department sews, alters, fits, dyes, and accessorizes. By the way, when speaking about the entire process, we say that costumes are *built*, not sewn. Saying a costume is sewn is like saying a set is hammered.

Costume Designer

The costume designer is responsible for designing or purchasing all the clothes for the film, following the direction of the director and the production designer. He will have several assistants to shop, draw, measure, and dress the actors throughout the production. He is also assisted by a **wardrobe supervisor** and **dressers** who handle the costumes during the shoot.

In many cases, a star will negotiate her own costume designer or dresser into a production. This can be quite successful, or it can lead to the star looking woefully out of place amidst a carefully designed palette of costumes.[4]

Makeup

The **key makeup artist** is in charge of this area and everyone in it, including assistant makeup artists, hairstylists, and body makeup

---

[4] I'm not mentioning any names. Batman.

artists. The key makeup artist designs all the makeup as well. A touch-up artist is always available on the set to touch up an actor's makeup. This is a constant battle, as actors live their lives under the glare of hot movie lights. A touch-up artist might also be called upon to apply (sing it with me now) Blood, Sweat, and Tears.

If there is a lot of special prosthetic makeup, like battle wounds, werewolves, Grinches, or people made up like apes, a special makeup designer will be hired.

As with costumes, a star will often bring his or her own makeup artist into the show.

ART DEPARTMENT

The art department is responsible for the sets and everything on them, including dressing and greenery. (But not props. See Prop Department, below.)

Production Designer

The production designer is responsible for the "look" of the film. His job is conceptual and integrates several departments—sets, costumes, and props—to create an integrated whole, an environment where the film can take place. He must also decide which scenes will be shot at existing locations and which will be done on the soundstage.

Production designers have an army of help to create their masterpieces.

Conceptual Artists. When a film takes place in a world very unlike our own, a conceptual artist may be brought in to dream up spaces, objects, or creatures that would exist there. Like Syd Mead on *Blade Runner*, Ralph McQuarrie on *Star Wars*, or H. R. Giger on *Alien*, these artists help the production designer to get a handle on what a replicant, an X-wing fighter, or a carnivorous alien looks like.

Art Director. The art director plans and executes the sets, while following the overall look created by the production designer. Art directors on smaller films are expert shoppers and will strive to keep up to date on rental houses, thrift stores, and estate sales. On larger films, the art director will have a staff to shop for him, and he will concentrate more on creating the sets on paper.

Set Designers. These designers create the construction diagrams that the various shops will use to create the sets and props. In addition, if the film relies on miniatures, the set designer will produce drawings for them as well.

Set Decorators. Set decorators choose all the set dressings, from furniture to frying pans to velvet Elvis paintings. There is always at least one on-set dresser who maintains the set dressings throughout the shoot.

Greensmen. If it is growing and green, the greensmen are in charge of it on the set. They are even in charge if it only appears to be growing, since they handle fake greenery, as well. (Actually, a film shot on a soundstage will almost always have fake greenery, as real plants aren't fond of being fried by movie lights all day long.)

Storyboard Illustrators. Storyboards help the director to show the rest of the production team what the shot will ultimately look like. Some directors, like Ridley Scott, draw these themselves (Scott is famous for his "Ridleygrams"), but most shows employ at least one storyboard artist to create the comic-book-style drawings that show composition and camera movement.

PROP DEPARTMENT

The *propmaster* is distinguished from the set dresser because "props" refer to specific items mentioned in the script, like the "neuralizer" in *Men in Black*, or the tacky alarm clock that wakes up Bill Murray in *Groundhog Day*. If some of those props are guns, there may also be (and should be) a weapons expert on the set.

It is important to remember that props aren't always what they seem. The most famous story comes from the original *Star Trek* series, where the propmaster was sent out to find futuristic saltshakers for a scene in the mess hall. When he got back, the art director wasn't satisfied, saying that the shakers were so futuristic that no one would recognize them. "But," he said, in a moment of inspiration, "these would make great medical instruments." That's right—when Dr. McCoy is scanning the internal organs of some alien species, he is using, yes, a saltshaker.

Some propmasters specialize in the preparation of food. This surprising specialty is in wide demand for **product shots**, those beautifully lit scenes (like the oatmeal I was talking about earlier) that show off the relevant item in all its splendor. Food prop people have a huge bag of tricks to make food look its best, none of which make the food taste any better. From Vaseline on apples to varnish on lobsters, they bring a hardware store's worth of materials to a set, all to make food look as tempting as possible.

CATERING AND CRAFT

The film industry is unlike any other that I know of in that it consistently feeds its own people. In fact, food on a set is considered such an entitlement that I have seen crews refuse to continue with a shoot simply because the food was bad.

All sets serve lunch, and most will serve a light breakfast, as well. If the shoot stretches into the evening, dinner will probably appear, although this gets into the realm of pizza more often than not. Everyone knows you can tell the budget of a film by its food, but it is an unwise producer who scrimps in this area.

Caterers are pretty self-explanatory—they serve meals—but some people may be confused by the term "craft services."

Craft services refers to the person who provides snacks between meals. In my experience, the crafts person is almost invariably an actor who discovered that a few trips to Costco was the only investment needed to start a company. Not that crafts services isn't an art. On the contrary, a good crafts person can almost single-handedly preserve morale on a stressed-out set, just by showing up at a propitious moment with a tray full of pizza snacks.

DRIVERS

As you might expect, the teamsters union has a lock on the American film business. All trucks for any reasonably sized production will be driven by a teamster, and, yes, you will pay him to sit in his truck all day long. You got a problem with that? The guy who coordinates trucking on a large set is called the **transportation captain**.

TEACHERS, DOCTORS, AND OTHER HELPER-TYPES

Federal law has strict rules for children on sets, including what times of day they can be on the set and the number of hours they can work. The law also mandates that any production shooting on a weekday must have a teacher who conducts classes for a specified number of hours. If you are including children in your show, or if your own children are becoming actors, make sure that you contact Actors' Equity to confirm that your show is in compliance. Like the fire marshal, representatives of the board of education do have the power to shut down your set if they see children being mistreated. And rightly so.

Medical personnel are not necessarily required to be on a set unless stunts are being done. Any large show filming in a remote location will bring a doctor or nurse to keep everyone healthy. If dangerous stunts are being done, an EMT and ambulance should be standing by. If large pyrotechnic effects are in use, the firemen will be there, as well. Most locations in Los Angeles and New York will require at least one off-duty policeman, especially if you are impeding traffic (including pedestrians) in any way.

THE TALENT

The word "talent," when used to describe people on a set, refers to any living being who is actually seen on-screen. Generally, the "talent" is an actor, but it also refers to extras, stunt people, stand-ins, and animals (but not their trainers). Anyone the camera sees is "the talent." And, as you can see from the above list, unless you are shooting *Gandhi*, part II, with 300,000 extras, the talent is pretty well outnumbered.

Chapter 2:

THE LANGUAGE OF FILM: SHOTS, CAMERA MOVES, AND TRANSITIONS

With a hundred years of development behind it, the language of film has become relatively stable, the efforts of experimental filmmakers aside. The shots themselves are the nouns, marking out the story in blocks of time and narrative. The transitions between them are the verbs, establishing relationships between people, places and events. The camera movements are the adjectives, amplifying and describing the action by providing speed and changes in perspective.

Like our spoken language, the language of film continues to develop and diversify, sometimes splitting into styles that benefit one part of the population (younger, older, more academic, more sexual, more corporate) in particular. Nevertheless, the basic building blocks of film have been standardized so that people in every aspect of the industry can understand and communicate.

Here, then, are the basic shots, transitions, and camera moves used in the business today, including some technical names for shots that you will only see on call sheets.

SHOTS

On the set, a shot is often called a "setup" because each one involves a particular arrangement of lighting, camera, and grip equipment. A common crew question is, "How many setups are we doing today?"

Establishing Shot

Often used at the beginning of a scene, the establishing shot gives the viewer the overall layout of where the scene is taking place. Generally, it does not show the talent directly—it shows the outside of the lonely warehouse, crippled airliner, speeding train, or car caught in traffic. The implication is that the scene to follow is happening inside. It is often shot by the second unit or pulled from stock footage. Lately, as the pace of movie editing has increased, the establishing shot has fallen on hard times and is sometimes omitted.

Master Shot

As opposed to the establishing shot, the master shot shows the room where the scene is actually taking place. It usually includes the entire set and all the actors and extends from the beginning of the scene to the end. It can be a butt-covering shot—a guarantee that, come hell or high water, the crew has shot every line in the script. It is often the first shot completed, on the theory that if the crew lights the entire set at the top of the day, most of the lighting for the other shots will already be in place when we move in closer. Continuity people must pay close attention during the master shot, as they will need to match every element— blocking, props, and line deliveries—with the close-ups later.

Wide Shot

This is a loosely defined, catchall term that refers to any shot that isn't a close-up. The term is sometimes used interchangeably with "master

The wide shot.

shot," but this can lead to confusion, as a master shot is a more specific thing—a shot that covers everything that happens in a scene. A wide shot just means that it isn't a narrow one.

Two-Shot, Three-Shot, Four-Shot, Etc.

These terms all refer to shots with said number of people in them. In other words, a **two-shot** is a shot with two people in it. Note that this number refers to the speaking characters. A shot with the lead actor, the lead actress, and a stadium full of extras in the background is still a two-shot. In practical usage, only two- and three-shots are really used. Any more than three people, and it's a wide shot or a master.

Over-the-Shoulder

This is the shot you see when two people are talking to one another and the camera is shooting over one of their shoulders. The **OTS** shot (yes, we use the initials on this one, too) can be "clean" or "dirty." This is not a G-rated versus an R-rated shot. It refers to whether the foreground actor's shoulder does (dirty) or does not (clean) appear in the frame. The clean shot is considered more intimate because it puts the viewer closer to the actor, without an intervening body. The dirty OTS adds some emotional distance and increases the sense of voyeurism. "Is this shot clean or dirty?" is a good question to ask if you are involved in an OTS shot. The answer will tell you a little about how intimate the director wants the shot to be. Sometimes, an editor will start a

The two-shot.

The dirty over-the-shoulder shot.

scene with dirty shots, then move into clean shots as the intimacy grows and we "get into the actor's head."

Close-Up

The close-up (usually abbreviated C/U on a shot list but never called that out loud) is a shot of one person, seen from the waist up or closer. If the camera shows more of the body, it is called a ***full body shot***. If the camera zooms in on a particular facial feature (like the eyes or mouth), it is called an ***extreme close-up***. (Unlike the close-up, the

The close-up.

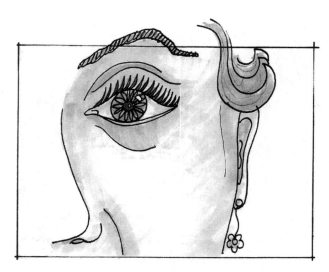

The extreme close-up (ECU).

extreme close-up is generally referred to, even out loud, by the abbreviation "ECU." These distinctions exist to make you crazy.)

Aerial Shots

Usually shot from a helicopter, the aerial shot gives a vast sense of space and environment. This shot serves as an introduction to an environment. If the location of the film is significant, it may open with an aerial shot, like that of *Groundhog Day*, which begins with the actors leaving Philadelphia; or *The Birdcage*, which relies on the carnival atmosphere of South Beach in Miami; or *Working Girl*, which tells the story of office women, lost in the concrete canyons of Manhattan. Each one of these films begins with an introductory helicopter shot as a way of placing the film firmly in a specific place.

Of course, the aerial shot is a staple of sports broadcasting, where the shot from the blimp circling overhead adds to the spectacle of the match.

Other Ways of Describing Shots

Any of the shots we have talked about so far may also fall into one or more of the following categories.

POV. A **point-of-view** shot mimics the viewpoint of a character in a scene. When Rosanna Arquette drops a nickel into the binoculars at

Battery Park to spy on Madonna in *Desperately Seeking Susan*, the director cuts to a POV shot—a shot of Madonna in the distance, as she would be seen by Rosanna Arquette. The POV shot pretends to be what the character herself is looking at.

MOS. It is not always necessary to record sound with a shot. Sometimes a shot will have music, or dialogue from another scene, or merely sound effects that are added later. In this case, the shot is **MOS**, or shot without audio. Depending on who you ask, MOS means either "minus optical stripe," meaning there is no sound track on the film, or "miz out ze sound," meaning that your cinematographer hails from Eastern Europe.

Pickups. Sometimes a long take will only be partly usable because the actor flubs a line halfway through. If the first part of the scene was usable, the director may decide not to double back and do the whole thing again. He will ask the actor to start in the middle and do the scene from there to the end. This is called a **pickup**, and it is important that it be communicated and recorded as such on everybody's notes. Otherwise, there may be an uncomfortable moment later, when you discover that the take you thought was "perfect" doesn't include the first half of the scene.

Martini. Harkening back to a romantic age when working Hollywood ended the day with a dose of chilled gin and vermouth, the last shot of the day is called the **martini**.

CAMERA MOVEMENTS

Any camera shot that does not move is called a **lock-off**. Once the camera gets moving, though, the possibilities are endless.

Dolly Shots (or Tracking Shots)

A **dolly shot** is a shot in which the camera is mounted on a dolly. (That will be twenty-five cents for that valuable piece of knowledge.)

Dolly shots can be complicated and time-consuming to set up, mostly because they require more attention to lighting. With the camera moving, the audience sees more of the set from different angles, which necessitates lighting things more carefully. Also, dolly shots require track, so the shot must be carefully designed to avoid getting the tracks themselves in the shot.

Modern filmmaking, however, seems to rely on dolly shots more and more. Watch any high-budget Hollywood film and you will see the camera constantly moving, ducking, and weaving like an NFL running back on almost every shot. No doubt about it—American filmmakers are in love with their dollies.

For a look at one of the most famous dolly shots of all time, rent Orson Welles's *Touch of Evil*. The first three minutes of the film are one long dolly shot that travels almost a quarter of a mile, introducing a string of characters in a Mexican border town, then blowing two of them up to kick off the story. Then, for a good inside joke, rent *The Player*, Robert Altman's tribute to Hollywood nastiness. The first *eight* minutes of this one are one long dolly shot following (among other things) two men as they walk across a Hollywood studio lot, discussing the three-minute shot in *Touch of Evil*. See there? Now you're an insider.[5]

Panning and Tilting Shots

Panning and tilting shots, like dolly shots, are moving shots, but in this case the camera stays rooted to one spot. **Panning** means the camera is moving from side to side. **Tilting** means the camera swings up and down. The camera can also move up and down on the hydraulic arm attached to the dolly. This is called "arming down" and "arming up."

Panning shots are often used to reveal landscapes, particularly if the intended effect is to impress the viewer with the scale of the land. Westerns do it all the time. Robert Zemeckis's film, *Cast Away*, uses long, slow pans to reveal the great, shapeless ocean that surrounds the shipwrecked Tom Hanks in every direction.[6]

---

[5] For another dolly thrill ride, watch Hitchcock's *Rope*, which is one continuous dolly shot from beginning to end.

[6] This shot is also an interesting illusion—by panning around in a slow circle, Zemeckis causes us to lose track of how much ocean we have seen. Because the shot is long and slow (and Tom Hanks actually moves when the camera's back is turned), we think we have seen all the way around the island when, in fact, Zemeckis has only shown us three sides, concealing the fact that the movie was shot on a peninsula in Belize.

Panning is also used to connect an object and the person looking at it, as when the camera pans from the giant diamond to the thief who is considering stealing it. Pans can also follow a person's point of view as he scans a crowd or follows a passing car—in short, they imitate a person turning his head from left to right.

Zooming Shots

Back in the 1960s, when zoom lenses came into wide usage, the sudden zooming shot (known as a **crash zoom**) was often used to show a character's shock, or surprise, or realization. Nowadays, the effect is considered dated, especially when it is used to parody the earlier style, as in the *Austin Powers* movies.

The sudden zoom was replaced in the 1980s by the dolly-zoom effect. Originally invented by Alfred Hitchcock to simulate Jimmy Stewart's vertigo in the film of the same name, this shot involves zooming the camera lens out while simultaneously dollying in (or vice versa). The net effect is a disorienting change in perspective, while the size of the subject remains essentially the same. Like the crash zoom, the dolly-zoom effect is used to show a character's strong reaction. Look for it in *Angels in the Outfield, Ever After,* and many other films.

Crane Shots

Crane shots are used to take the camera up in the air. Like all moving shots, they require considerably more time to set up, because they reveal more of the set. Check out the classic crane shot in *Notorious,* where the camera cranes down from high atop a swirling party scene to focus on the tiny key that Ingrid Bergman clutches behind her back.

Crane shots are great if you need to move the camera up and down several stories. If you need a more contained move, you will generally use the smaller and more convenient jib arm. Among other things, **jib arms** have become a staple of modern concert footage. If you see a shot where the camera appears to fly out over an audience, you are probably watching a jib-mounted camera. Jibs have a limit on how high they can go, however, so if you see a shot coming down several stories or more, you are probably watching a crane in action.

Steadicam Shots

Besides the practical advantages of the **Steadicam** (or **floating camera**) shot, such as the ability to go through doors and up stairs, it also provides a sense of immediacy that is missing in a dolly shot. A floating camera shot[7] is much steadier than a standard handheld shot, yet it still retains a small amount of jitteriness that translates into dramatic tension. This effect has been used in every horror movie since the darn thing was invented, as well as in TV dramas like *ER* and *NYPD Blue*. To see the effect vividly, watch *The Brady Bunch Movie,* when Mike Brady goes to the police station and encounters the cops from *NYPD Blue*. Director Betty Thomas shot Mike Brady with a tripod, while shooting the cops with a ducking and weaving Steadicam. The contrast between the stodgy Brady and the hard-bitten cop is shown to great comic effect with the two camera styles.

TRANSITIONS

When we talk about transitions, we are talking about how we move from scene to scene. Each type of transition gives a specific message to the audience about the style of the film and how the passage of time is being handled.

Cuts

When one scene ends and another picks up immediately, it is called a cut. From the audience perspective, it means that no time has passed between the two events. That other thing happened; now this is happening. A cut implies continuous time. This type of transition is listed in a script as "CUT TO." When two storylines are told at the same time, with the editor cutting back and forth between them, the viewer understands that these two sets of events are happening simultaneously (and are destined to collide sooner or later). This technique is known as **crosscutting** or **parallel editing**. When a single scene is taking place in two different locations, such as when two characters are talking on the phone, the two locations are said to be **intercut.**

---

[7] Remember that Steadicam® is a brand for one type of floating camera rig. There are others. The word "Steadicam," however, has become so ubiquitous that most people use it to describe any similar rig.

Dissolves

A *dissolve* means one of two things: either time has passed or we are going inside the mind of the character. If no other visual clue is given, the audience will assume that some amount of time has passed. A screenplay denotes this transition as "DISSOLVE TO." If we are going inside the mind of a character, to a dream, flashback, flash-forward, or fantasy, we must be given some sort of clue early in the sequence (unless the filmmaker wants us to be surprised later: "It was all a dream!").

Wipes

A *wipe* is a transition where one shot is replaced by the next in a side-to-side, sliding motion, as if a screen were being pulled over the previous shot. Wipe transitions were used heavily in serial action films in the thirties and forties. Lately, they have been used to give a film a period or nostalgic flavor. *Star Wars* used wipe transitions to make the film seem more classic, more epic, and a bit of a throwback to earlier, simpler films. In terms of time, the wipe can be interpreted as "meanwhile . . ."

Iris In, Iris Out

An *iris* transition is like a wipe, only circular. That is, the new picture appears in a circle that either grows from the center of the screen (iris out) or collapses inward from the edges (iris in). This transition, made popular in musical comedies in the '30s, tells the audience that you are doing broad comedy or parody, or both. In semi-modern film, look for it in Mel Brooks's *Young Frankenstein*.

Funky Video Transitions

In the world of video editing, hundreds of different, highly stylized transitions have become available through digital editors. You can wipe, iris, box, page-turn, shatter, or anything else you can imagine. These effects are used in popular video all the time as a quick and dirty way to liven up video. They imply that the video in question is fun and offbeat. As far as time, theme, and audience interpretations go, all bets are off.

Chapter 3:

THE FIRST BIG CHOICE: FILM AND VIDEO FORMATS

The first big choice that a producer makes when starting up a new project is the *format*. Film or video? What size film? Which video format? There are more options than you can shake a stick at, so let's dive in. The first question is the most important:

FILM OR VIDEO?

People are always asking me, "Should I shoot in film or video?" and the answer is always, "Yes, absolutely."

I wouldn't exactly say this is Sophie's choice—a decision between two horrible choices, both too terrible to consider—but the fact is, there is no easy answer, especially in this age of exploding technology and monumental change. In fact, this chapter may be out of date by some time next week, so read it with some indulgence, won't you?

The film versus video decision used to be a lot easier. You shot film if you had the time and the money. Otherwise, you shot video. Video became the territory of the news media, low-budget sitcoms, and porn. Hollywood producers knew that, in general, "real life" went on video, while "acting" went on film. The viewer became conditioned to particular kinds of images in particular contexts, and life was good.

Two things happened: video quality kept getting better and better, and the industry started mixing up formats and confusing the issue. One of the most popular and well-funded shows on television, *Survivor*, is shot on video. Offbeat films like *The Blair Witch Project* and *Natural Born Killers* mixed film and video together. Mike Figgis's *Time Code* became one of the first feature films shot entirely on digital video. Music videos threw formats together like chopped salad, and the implied meanings of video and film "looks" became jumbled.

Of course, the budgetary issues haven't changed much—film is still more expensive than video. To some extent, these two categories of formats also produce different working styles—in film, all activity is oriented towards the moment the camera starts rolling. In video, the camera can literally be rolling all the time. But the decision to commit to film or video is mostly an artistic one—what kind of an image do you want?

I am fully aware that this does not answer the question.

With the above caveat in mind, therefore, let's look at the issues to consider when making decisions about format.

Except, I have to give one more caveat.

There are at least six different film formats in common use and perhaps twice that many for video. The question is not just film or video, but what type of film? What type of video? Film and video are not just formats; they are families of formats.

We're going to look into each individual format in the next chapter but, with both of the above caveats in mind, let's dig into the big picture of film versus video.

We don't have to dig very far before we reach the big land mine.

Cost

Film costs more than video. Period.

Sure, your brother's colonic therapist knows somebody who works at Kodak who can slip you the leftover film stock from *Rocky*, Part Seven. Yes, you can get a deal on processing because the lab tech has a crush on your star. Okay, you got a slammin' deal on a camera package because you pulled the rental manager from the jaws of a great white shark.

Right. You got yourself a deal. You're a player. You're the man. Your money's no good here. Got it.

Film costs more than video.

Film costs more than video not only because the stock is more expensive but also because there are more steps to the process—three, to be exact. The film must be:

1. Shot

2. Processed

3. Transferred to video

Technically, step three is optional. You can still edit your film using the actual film, a flatbed editor, and a razor blade.

But, *why?*

Why waste your money on working prints of your footage, dredging up a working flatbed editor, and beating the bushes for an editor who actually remembers how to use it? To the few remaining film schools that feel it necessary to subject their students to editing on a flatbed, I say, listen up. We have entered the new millennium, and we now edit films on computers. Thank you, Apple. Thank you, Avid.

If you are reading this in a war-torn, third-world country and all you have is a flatbed Moviola, then bless you. You have my deepest respect. All you other film students, though, tweet! Out of the pool.

In order to edit your film, however, whether on a fully tricked-out Avid editing system or a Mac in your bedroom, you need to transfer it to video. Hence, step three.

If you shoot on video, you can load it into your computer and start editing right away. So it's cheaper.

How much cheaper? Well, there's the rub. You can shoot a film for $10,000 or $10 million. The same numbers apply for video, but it will look different. In order to figure out your production budget, I suggest that you explore some of the film budgeting books I have listed in the bibliography. Here are some general rules, however: A low-budget 35mm-camera package costs around $1,000 a day to rent. A high-end DigiBeta camera is half to two-thirds of that.

But here's the real difference: Film stock costs about a dollar a foot, including processing. Thirty-five millimeter cameras shoot ninety feet per minute. Therefore, film stock costs about ninety bucks a minute. Digital Betacam video—a very high-end format—costs about thirty dollars for a one-hour tape or around fifty cents a minute.

So, that's $90 a minute versus 50¢. And we still have to transfer it. Plus, if you shot something you don't like, you can always rewind and record again over the same piece of tape. Um, don't try that with your film, okay?

Beyond the stock and the camera rental, however, most of the costs of the shoot—lighting, scenery, talent, and so on—are pretty much the same.

Resolution (Width)

Imagine a photograph. A face, perhaps. Now, imagine creating a stone mosaic that depicts that photograph. The mosaic is made up of small colored stones, laid out to represent the shapes, lines, and colors of the face. If the stones were, say, the size of baseballs, you would be fairly limited in the amount of detail you could depict. A smoothly shaped eyebrow might become a stair step of rocks. The gentle fade of the pink cheek fading into the tan forehead might be a hard-edged boundary between red and brown. The hair might be a big black blob instead of individual curls (let alone individual hairs). The only way to really view the design is to step way back and let your eyes blend it all together. The whole thing might look chunky and primitive.

Now, imagine creating the same mosaic with stones the size of quarters. While you still couldn't create truly smooth curves or color fades, you could do a much better job of recreating the photograph. With sand, you could create even smoother lines, more natural fades, and smaller details.

The difference between these mosaics is the difference in *resolution*. Resolution refers to the number of points of light and color that are used to create a design; the more points of light and color (known as *pixels*), the higher the resolution and the higher the level of detail.

Regular video comes in a wide range of resolutions. A normal Beta video image contains about 350,000 pixels. That's a lot, for video, and it gives a very sharp, accurate image compared to normal VHS video, which contains about 150,000 pixels.

Neither of these formats, however, can hold a candle to film. One frame of 35mm film has about 16.7 million pixels. With that kind of resolution, film can create an image that is much closer to what the lens really sees. Colors fade more smoothly, curvy lines are really curvy, and fine detail, like hair, is clearly rendered.

Resolution (Depth)

There is another scale of resolution that we can understand by looking at one of those mosaic rocks. Let's say that we are making a mosaic out of quarter-sized rocks and we come to a place where the cheek is a warm pink. The artist has collected several different pink rocks of varying shades, from a pale, almost white, pink to a deep, rich red. Let's say the artist has collected five possibilities.

Next to this artist is another artist who is a good bit more industrious. Before he even started his mosaic, he gathered hundreds of thousands of stones in every shade of every color of the rainbow. His selection of pink rocks is hundreds strong, some so close in color as to be almost indistinguishable.

Now, whose mosaic is going to be closer to the original photograph? The guy with four pinks to choose from or the guy with a hundred pinks to choose from? This is a type of resolution as well, known as *bit depth*. All those colors can be represented with electronic ones and zeros, known as bits. The only thing you need to know here is, more is better. More bits means more colors to choose from.

Film is capable of greater bit depth than video, which means that film can more accurately depict subtle differences in color, all of which add up to a more pleasing image. Film is vastly superior to video when it comes to resolution in both width and depth.

High Definition Television (HDTV)

The resolution difference is fading, however, now that **High Definition Television (HDTV)** is gaining popularity. Driven by powerful new digital chips, these cameras are approaching the resolution of film, although the two are still clearly distinguishable. As the technology progresses, however, expect this difference to narrow and, someday, go away entirely. On that day, celluloid will begin to go the way of the vinyl record, and there will be a sea change in the industry. It won't happen all at once (there are too many film projectors in theaters around the world), but it will happen. Oh yes, it will happen.

Range of Light

The last area of comparison between film and video has to do with the amount of light available to shoot. Video requires more light than film, which means that film will look better when exposed under low light. Furthermore, video can only shoot in a fairly narrow range of light levels. Let's say you are shooting a scene of two lovers lying before a fire. On video, you would probably get a pretty nice image from the lovers' faces and clothing, but the shadows under them would turn complete-ly black. There is just not enough light there to be picked up by the video. The flames of the fire behind them would be blown out—that is, they would show up on the video as bright white areas without definition.

Film picks up a much wider range of light intensities. When shoot-ing on film, you might see the detail of the bearskin rug under the lovers, even though it is in shadow. You might also see a host of colors in the flames, instead of a big, white blob. With its wider tolerance of light levels, film shows off detail that video cannot pick up.

FILM FORMATS

Each format comes complete with its own set of statistics (such as size and aspect ratio), as well as its own set of pluses and minuses (such as res-olution and price). Every format has its champions and detractors, as well. Let's look at what sets each format apart from the others.

Size

The biggest determiner in choosing a film format is the size of the film. Everything else sifts down from that initial decision. The size of the film determines the cost of the shoot at a basic level. It also can determine creative options, crew size, quality of the output, where you can show the film, and much, much more. Let's break it down. By the way, "mm" stands for millimeter, so 8mm film is eight millimeters wide—about the width of a pencil.

8mm. With the advent of home video, the old 8mm camera has gone the way of the dodo. You don't even need the projector anymore, what with all the photo shops that will transfer all your home movies to videotape. Have we lost anything? Well, maybe. Eight millimeter, and its fancier cousin Super 8, did offer a cheap and available format for fledg-ling filmmakers to practice on before graduating upwards. Today, most film students practice on video before doing their final projects on 16mm. Personally, I believe that there is no replacement for the tactile nature of film stock and no better way to learn the black art of expo-sure (see chapter 4) than to load that film loop into the family movie camera and start plugging away. Steven Spielberg's first films, at age eight, were 8mm war films starring his extensive collection of toy soldiers. M. Night Shyamalan, director of *The Sixth Sense*, made over forty short films, many of them on 8mm, before making his phenomenal freshman feature.

Make no mistake: I have no sentimentality for the lousy picture quality, the rough sound, the expense of processing, and the pain of setting up a projector and screen every time you want to see the movie. But I do lament the simplistic learning tool that has gone away.

For those of you who insist that Super 8 lives on, more power to you. You are purists, and there is always a place for the person who prefers his art hand-washed and raw. Certainly, there is no other scale of filmmaking that puts the artist so personally in touch with his canvas.

16mm. For years, 16mm was the film size of choice for documentaries, experimental films, student films, festival films, pornography, and any other film that was below the Hollywood radar, either because of subject matter or because of budget. In recent years, however, digital video has taken a big chomp out of the 16mm pie. Hey, would you like to shoot an hour of footage for $5,000 or $10? The resolution may not be quite as good as 16mm film, but $4,990 buys a lot of food for the crew. As more filmmakers move to digital video, the problem escalates as the prices for 16mm film go higher. Some labs have stopped processing it (although you will have no problem getting it done in L.A. or N.Y.C., at least as of this writing), some festivals have stopped accepting it, and it has become a smaller and smaller niche. The thinking is, basically, hey, if we're going to do film, then there is an expectation that we will have a certain quality on-screen and that level of quality is only achievable with the industry-standard 35mm.

16mm is still the instrument of choice for film-school projects. Super 16mm, a film stock that achieves a wider image through having sprocket holes only on one side, lives on in professional shows because it is almost exactly the same aspect ratio as the up-and-coming HDTV format. Anything shot on Super 16 today can be transferred to HDTV in the future without losing any of the image.

Of course, a 16mm shoot still holds some financial appeal when compared to a 35mm shoot. When it comes to the camera package, film stock, and processing, it is about a quarter of the cost.

35mm. The workhorse of the entertainment industry and, interestingly enough, the same size that is in your basic household still camera, 35mm film is best described as the middle-of-the-road film. Like Baby Bear's bed, it is not too small or too big. It is small enough not to cost an arm and a leg to process, but big enough to give an acceptable level of resolution when projected on a large screen. Thirty-five millimeter is the definition of an industry standard. If you are working on a mainstream film or a shot-on-film TV show, you will be working in 35mm. Guaranteed.

One nice thing about shooting a 35mm film on a tight budget: If you are making your film in Los Angeles or New York, you can feed off the industry table scraps through *short ends*. Short ends are pieces of film left over from larger shoots done by people with more money than you. See, the most expensive thing on a large-scale production is time, and no one wants to waste it by ever having the film run out during an important shot. Rather than risk earning the hatred of every single person on the crew, the 1st AC will replace a reel of film well before it is completely exposed, just to be sure he doesn't have a *runout*. That leftover film is called a short end, and there is a brisk trade on short ends in Hollywood. There are a few small companies that buy it, check it to make sure it is still usable, and then sell it to small filmmakers on a budget. The downside is that you have to shoot shorter scenes (plus, you are constantly reloading), but the price is truly excellent.

70mm. While 35mm is by far the industry standard, people have been pushing its limits almost from the beginning. In 1976, a new theater opened at the National Air and Space Museum in Washington, D.C. that had the largest movie screen in the world—over five stories high. Nowadays, we see them all over the place, but at the time, IMAX screens were novelties—very impressive and very expensive novelties. The idea with an IMAX screen is to completely fill the visual field of the viewer. That is, everywhere you looked, you saw screen. Without any visual reference points like the walls, seats, or exit signs, your sense of motion could be controlled completely through a visual image. If the screen was filled with an aerial shot diving through a canyon, your brain was fooled, and you got the sensation that you yourself were flyin' down through that canyon. The illusion was particularly juicy with flying shots, so it was no wonder that the first successful IMAX film was called *To Fly*.

The first problem with a large screen is, once again, light. It takes a lot of it to fill a screen that big, and if you try to push that much light through a 35mm negative, you risk melting it down. The second, more sinister, problem is resolution. If you blow 35mm up to a screen five stories high, you can start to see the grain of the film—the little pieces of silver that make up the image.

A larger screen means a larger negative, and that's where 70mm came in. A negative that is twice as wide actually has four times the surface area, which means you can push four times as much light through it without causing a meltdown. Plus, a 70mm negative has to be enlarged only half as much as a 35mm negative to fill the same size screen, which helps get rid of the graininess.

Of course, a format that is twice as big means a bigger camera, more film stock, more processing, and a host of other "mores," not to mention one big ol' projector. Consequently, 70mm is really only cost effective when the film is guaranteed a long run in a single location, like a specialty theater in a tourist area. DPs love 70mm because of the clear, bright image, but don't look for Hollywood to be switching over to it as a standard. It is a specialty format for specific uses where there is a guaranteed audience and venue. It is still used occasionally for effect photography where crispness is essential. Eventually, however, the images are downgraded to 35mm for distribution.

One interesting quirk of most 70mm film formats: It is a "sideways" format; that is, the images are printed on the film sideways, with the top and bottom of the frame against the sprocket holes instead of the sides. This means that the film enters both the camera and the projector from the side, instead of from the top, like all the other formats. Looks a little strange when you first see it.

3-D Film. Any of the above sizes can be used for 3-D film, but the most common are 35mm and 70mm. The three-dimensional effect is created by projecting two films simultaneously onto the same screen. The two films are shot by a camera with two lenses set the same distance apart as your eyes. Two projectors then shine the images through polarizing filters, which line up all the beams of light in the same plane. One projector puts out only horizontal beams and one puts out only vertical beams, each of which looks normal to the naked eye. Audience members are given special glasses with polarizing lenses, however. One lens only admits the horizontal beams while the other only admits the vertical ones. Thus, your left eye only sees the left film, while the right eye sees the right one. By screening two slightly different images, your eye is fooled into believing that the images are actually 3-D.

Some 3-D formats only use one piece of film and a projector with two lenses. In this case, the frames of film alternate between horizontal and vertical polarization. This guarantees that the two images will be in sync. Those clever engineers . . . In any case, 3-D is complicated and expensive enough that you won't see it outside of semipermanent installations, like theme parks.

Formats of the Future

As I said, 35mm film has been the industry standard since the 1920s, but not for lack of trying new things. The standard 35mm, widescreen image is a terrible compromise in many ways, and those brave souls who are ever trying to bring us better quality images, God love 'em, have never given up (and, hopefully, never will) trying to improve it.

One of the more visible attempts was made by Douglas Trumbull, who first became famous for his groundbreaking special effects in *2001: A Space Odyssey.* Not only did Trumbull increase the size of the image; he also increased the speed of the film, creating the 60–60 format—a 60mm-wide film played at 60 frames per second.

The first public showing of the format began, hopefully enough, with spectacular opening credits and bold, breathtaking images on the screen. Unfortunately, moments into the picture, the film snapped inside the projector and then melted, showing the audience the familiar wash of oily colors that comes from film disintegrating. The theater went dark and voices were heard backstage. A light came on behind the screen, and a workman was seen walking back and forth in silhouette. He walked towards the audience and pushed up against the screen, showing the outline of his face where he was poking his face against the movie sheet, trying to see the audience. After a few moments, the workmen got the film going again, and the demonstration continued. The gag, of course, was that the film had been running the entire time, and all the action described above was just a scene in the movie, made possible by the incredible resolution of the format.

So, why didn't 60-60 take over? Well, let's do the math. A 35mm frame has 689 square millimeters of film, while a 60mm frame has

2,025 square millimeters of film, almost three times as much. Plus, the film is moving over twice as fast, all of which adds up to seven times as much film going through the camera every second. Seven times as much film, seven times as much processing, bigger cameras, bigger projectors . . . the list would (and did) give producers hives. Nope—if you are going to upgrade the technology to that extent, you have to have a very compelling reason and a public that is hungry for change. Right now, people seem to be pretty happy with 24 frames-per-second, 35mm motion pictures, so that's how it will stay, at least until someone comes up with a cheap upgrade or a new killer technology—something on the order of adding color to film or stereo sound to TV.

The most likely future change seems to be the growth of digital film-making and projection. As of this writing, the quality of digital images is rapidly approaching the quality of 35mm film images. There are also substantial reasons for studios and exhibitors to switch over to fully dig-ital projectors, especially with the modern-day method of distributing pictures. Up until the invention of the summer blockbuster (some peo-ple say it was *Jaws*), films opened first in New York and Los Angeles, then, a few days or weeks later, in large cities like Chicago and Boston. As the weeks rolled by, the films came to smaller and smaller towns until, at last, the small theaters in out-of-the-way towns got them in. This method of distribution meant that you needed, at most, a couple hun-dred prints of the film, and they could be shipped via regular trucking services and the mail. This was in the days before national advertising. Nowadays, studios stuff all their advertising into one national mega-campaign that tries to get everybody excited to see the film on opening weekend. Unfortunately, that means you need to have the film available all over the country on the same day. Large-budget films like, say, *Jurassic Park III*, open simultaneously in thousands of theaters across the coun-try, to say nothing of the rest of the world. Suddenly, you need thou-sands, not hundreds, of copies of the film, and they need to be shipped overnight, to prevent them from being shown prematurely. That's money, honey. Not only that, but this style of distribution is also vulner-able to any number of snafus. When the first *Jurassic Park* opened, the lab got behind and didn't get all the prints out the door in time. Turns out there was a little theater on Long Island that got gypped and couldn't open the film on time. Problem was, the theater was just down the street from Steven Spielberg's house, and Mr. Spielberg, the director of the film, was understandably ticked that his own neighborhood theater couldn't show his film on time.

The other problem with standard prints is well known to anyone who has ever seen a print that has been playing for quite some time. The prints invariably pick up scratches and dust with repeated viewing, not to mention a break or two.

Now imagine a world where a theater owner just points a dish at an orbiting satellite on opening day and downloads an electronic copy of the film right into his projector. Boom. Done. Crank up the popcorn maker and let's sell some tickets. Distribution costs drop, delivery snafus disappear and, because the image is stored and projected digitally, it will look as good in six months as it looks now.

So all we have to do is buy all new digital projectors for the 25,000 movie screens in the U.S. and we're on our way to the land of Seamless Digital Distribution. Those projectors are currently running around $100,000 apiece, which is still cheaper than normal distribution, so it's doable. The real sticking point is who will foot the bill—the studios (who get cheaper distribution costs) or the theaters (who get better image quality and guaranteed delivery).

Stay tuned.

Aspect Ratios

The aspect ratio is the ratio of the width of the image to its height, with width always listed first. A 4:3 ratio means that for every four inches of width, there are three inches of height. You see this aspect ratio every day—it's your television screen. Legend has it that the original inventors of the television screen tried to make it as close as possible to the "Golden Mean," an arithmetic ratio that the Greeks considered to be a perfect numerical relationship. (The front entrance of the Parthenon, for example, is built on the Golden Mean; so next time you are in Athens, imagine the Parthenon as a really big TV.) Your basic 27" television screen, for example, is around 21.3" wide and 16" high, which, if you remember your high-school math, comes out to something like four by three. Actually, though, the 4:3 ratio was already in use when television first appeared—by the film industry.

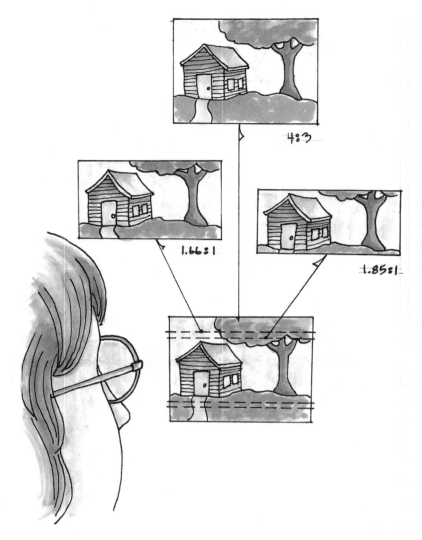

Aspect ratios.

After futzing around with different aspect ratios for a few years, the Academy of Motion Pictures Arts and Sciences (yes, the people who give out the Oscars) gave their stamp of approval to the 1.33:1 ratio back in the '20s. That's "one point three three to one" and, if you do the math, you will find that it is extremely close to 4:3. I guess television people don't like decimals, because they tend to use "four-three" when talking about their screens. In the film world, the 1.33:1 ratio became known as the "Academy" ratio, a term still used today.

When television came along, the engineers adopted the Academy aspect ratio and, for a time, both the television screen and the movie screen were the same shape. The situation started getting complicated when television spread across the country like bad gossip. Suddenly, theaters were seeing drops in attendance as everyone stayed home at night to gaze at the little gray screen. The movie producers had to do something to make the theatergoing experience more compelling, so they started messing around with the technology, and the aspect ratio was the first thing in their sights.

The producers figured, if they could make a wider image, one that stretched out to the edges of the audience's peripheral vision, it would be more exciting to watch. They tried it several ways. Perhaps the most extravagant attempt was the Cinescope process, which actually used three cameras to shoot three shots of every scene—a left, a right, and a center. When projected with three projectors that were locked in sync with one another, the movie screen could be almost three times as wide, immersing the audience in a HUGE! GIGANTIC!! ENORMOUS PICTURE!!! (if you believe the advertising of the time) that would LEAVE YOU BREATHLESS!!

It's safe to say the Cinescope was pretty impressive, but it was also pretty expensive to produce. What's more, it required three projectors in every theater that played the film. It died an early death, along with 3-D films, another attempt to make the theatrical experience better than watching TV.

What eventually did stick was a solution that seems like a step backwards.

The key to making a wider image on the screen was a higher aspect ratio. It didn't mean that the film had to be bigger; it just meant that the ratio of its width to its height had to be bigger. So, filmmakers started cutting off the top and bottom of each frame and then, using a slightly bigger lens, blowing up the remaining part of the image when it was projected. The result was a picture with a wider aspect ratio (and a lot of wasted film on the top and bottom of every frame).

Yes, that's right. The big advance in technology in the film industry was cutting off the top and bottom of the film and blowing the image up bigger. The more they threw away, the wider the image got. They went to 1.66:1, then 1.75:1, and 1.85:1, all collectively entitled "widescreen." Of course, because the film was being enlarged more, the image quality suffered some and the resulting projected image was a little grainier than it would have been otherwise, but producers didn't care. The image was wider and, like they say, wider is better. This change happened in the '50s, but we are still using the same technique today.

There are ratios that are even wider than 1.85:1, but these depend on another technology that grew out of the desperate search for TV-killers: **anamorphic lenses**. Normal camera lenses are round—they have no top or bottom—and the image they project on the film is the same as the image that comes to them from the outside world. Anamorphic lenses "squeeze" the image on the horizontal axis, while leaving the vertical axis unchanged. When working in the anamorphic process, a special lens squeezes the image as it is shot. The entire surface of the film is used and nothing is thrown away. Then, when the film is projected, another lens "unsqueezes" the image, spreading it out across the screen with a ratio that is considerably larger than Academy. In fact, with anamorphic lenses, you can get images upwards of 2:1, and without the graininess of normal widescreen techniques using "spherical" lenses.

So why doesn't everyone use anamorphic lenses? Three reasons: One, they are painfully expensive; two, they are more difficult to focus; and three, TV.

First, the pain. Anamorphic lenses are much more expensive, because they're much harder to produce. They are also harder to use, because they have to be *perfectly* aligned on the horizontal axis or the actors start looking like Picasso paintings in his Truly Strange period. Finally, they are a pain because every single screening room, editing bay, postproduction house, and movie theater has to be fitted with special lenses. People still use anamorphic lenses all the time, but generally, the projects are high budget and high visibility, and the producer or director involved has a lot of clout. Otherwise, few people want to mess with it. It is easier to mask off the top and bottom of the image and be done with it.

And then there's TV. Remember how I said that the original Academy ratio was 1.3:1 and all we did was throw the top and bottom away? Well, in this day and age, a film will generally be seen on more than one medium. After a theatrical run and a video release, a film may find its way to television, which is 4:3 or 1.33:1 or Academy or whatever you want to call it. Bottom line: You can just put the top and bottom back on the image and use the whole thing. Poof. Done. When a film is shot with this strategy in mind, it is called "TV protect," meaning that the camera operator "protects" the top and bottom of the image, keeping them clear of equipment and crew.

That's why you will often hear a DP say something like, "Let's make sure that we protect the top of the frame." You might see this format listed like "1.85:1 widescreen, TV protect."

Anamorphic films (and films that were not TV-protected) have to suffer one of the entertainment industry's greatest indignities when being prepared for television viewing: *pan-and-scan*. In order to make a widescreen image fit on a TV screen, the machine that dumps it onto video cuts the edges off the image. It doesn't always work to cut the same amount off each side, as sometimes the important part of the image is off to one side. Pan-and-scan technology was invented so the technician could at least tell the projector which chunk of the image to put on the video. The projector could be panned back and forth over the image and programmed for what to keep and what to throw away. Filmmakers have wrung their hands for years, as chunks of the image are lost in the pan-and-scan process. If you want to see a good example of the problem, rent *The Graduate* and take a look at the last scene as Dustin Hoffman and Katherine Ross sit in the backseat of the bus after he has stolen her from her wedding. In the original film, they both sat quietly, he on frame left and she on frame right. The director, Mike Nichols, deliberately set them with a cavernous space between them. They do not touch or hold hands. As the bus pulls away from the church and the euphoria of their escape dies away, their faces begin to register the doubt and discomfort that is already taking hold in their minds. We watch them realize the enormity of what they have done as reality sets in. As they slump down slightly in the bus seats, without looking at each other, we are treated to a vision of their future. These kids don't have a chance.

Compare that to the experience of watching the scene on pan-and-scan. Because the image is too wide for the TV screen, the camera must cut back and forth between them, first Hoffman, then Ross. We lose the sense that they are both staring forward, both going through the same mental process simultaneously. The cutting back and forth almost creates the illusion that they are looking at one another. The tremendous physical gap between them is lost altogether, along with the impact of the ending.

The good news is, with the growth in the size of television screens, as well as the wider acceptance of DVDs, more filmmakers are releasing their films in widescreen versions, leaving the top and bottom of the screen black, or "letterboxed," in order to show the entire widescreen image. If you are given the choice, get the widescreen version. Otherwise, you are missing almost a third of the movie. (Of course, if you are checking out my story about *The Graduate*, get the "unletterboxed" version so you can see what I mean. Then get the widescreen version and watch it again. It's a classic—you should see it at least twice.)

With any luck, the appearance of high definition television will relegate pan-and-scan to the artistic torture chambers of the past. High definition television has a 16:9 ratio, which is within a few decimal points of 1.85:1 widescreen.

VIDEO FORMATS

Video comes in lots of flavors, but they mostly line up in a nice hierarchy by quality and expense. You won't find many people making decisions between video formats based on aesthetics. More expensive is more better.

Let's talk for a second about how video is structured. A video image on a television is created by an electron gun at the back of the TV tube. It scans a light-sensitive screen very quickly, from side to side and top to bottom. Each time it crosses the screen, it excites a line of sensitive cells that promptly glow, producing the image. The cells are put together in groups of three—one red, one blue, and one green. These primary colors mix together to make the colors that you see on the screen. In the **NTSC** standard that America uses, the gun completely redraws the screen thirty times per second. It does it in two passes, however, doing all the odd lines first and then all the even ones. Each pass is called a field, so there are two fields in each frame. That's why we say that video runs at thirty frames per second but has sixty fields. That distinction will become important during postproduction.

Different parts of the world use different video standards for a video signal. North America uses NTSC, which stipulates a 4:3 aspect ratio, 525 lines of resolution, and thirty frames (or sixty fields) per second. The rest of the world is roughly split into two standards: the **PAL** standard and the **SECAM** standard. Both of these standards have 625 lines of resolution and fifty fields per second, but they handle color and sound slightly different. If you are sending a tape to a foreign country, consult a postproduction house to find out which standard is in use. Western Europe and Australia use PAL, while Eastern Europe and France use SECAM.

Trying to play an NTSC signal through PAL or SECAM equipment won't burn anything up—it will just look very strange. Conversion between formats is easy, but it requires a special tape deck. Any postproduction house can do it for you.

VHS

The normal, vanilla videotape that we rent, pass around, and record on is called VHS. Some people refer to it as "half-inch" tape, because that's how wide the actual tape is. While everyone agrees that, compared to virtually any other format, VHS is a low-quality, grainy format that does not stand up well to being copied, it will undoubtedly hang on for a while because of the millions of VHS machines around the world.

The story of the adoption of VHS as the consumer standard is the story of marketing prowess overcoming technical inferiority. When consumer video first appeared, there were two competing standards: VHS

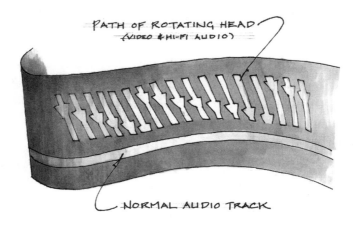

The anatomy of videotape.

and Beta. Although Beta was acknowledged as the superior format with better resolution, the makers of VHS decks were able to produce the decks more cheaply. That, combined with an aggressive campaign to have new films released on VHS, eventually pushed Beta out of the consumer market. Beta's technical superiority was eventually proven by the fact that it became the format of choice for professional taping and broadcast.

All formats eventually give way to better technology, however, and VHS is slowly giving way to DVD and digital recording. For the moment, however, it is still the distribution medium of choice when you want to make your tape as accessible as possible.

A word about VHS and audio: The normal audio track on a VHS tape runs alongside the video track. The video head actually spins at an angle to the forward direction of the tape, producing stripes of video information like a slanted picket fence. (Of course, these stripes are invisible to the naked eye.)

The head spins this way to create a higher apparent tape speed. Higher tape speed means that more tape is passing under the head per second. The video head needs more tape to pass by because it is trying to lay down a phenomenal amount of information, and it needs somewhere to put it. It's kind of like the way you can park more cars on a street if you use diagonal parking rather than parallel.

The audio track, however, is laid down in one long, straight line, like a string of parallel-parked cars. Audio information is far less dense than video, so it can be laid down this way, but, because videotape moves so slowly, these audio tracks do not produce high-fidelity sound. Lower tape speed means less tape to record on, which means lower quality.

Enter Hi-Fi (high-fidelity) VHS. In Hi-Fi VHS, the audio head spins along with the video head, enjoying the same fast tape speed. The audio information is mixed in with the video information, producing higher quality, but with one restriction: You can't change or remove the audio track without also destroying the video. A standard VHS audio track, on the other hand, can be changed or removed without disturbing the video.

Usually, a Hi-Fi VHS deck will have both Hi-Fi and standard audio heads, so they will play whatever kind of VHS tape you throw in them.

S-VHS

Basically a higher resolution form of VHS, S-VHS is convenient for lots of uses. It is sharper and more colorful than its predecessor, but S-VHS decks can still play the old VHS tapes. It became a good format for industrial and training videos that needed better-than-consumer quality but were not ready for a true pro format. S-VHS worked wonderfully for professional wedding videographers, in-house training videos, low-budget filmmaking, and so forth. Unfortunately, it never became cheap enough to replace VHS in the home and is now going to the Island of Lost Formats as it is replaced by digital alternatives.

Three-Quarter Inch

For many years, the professional format of choice was 3/4" tape. With more tape to record a signal on, a 3/4" tape could record more information than the 1/2" version used in VHS. This greater capacity meant that the picture had a higher resolution and sharpness. Like VHS, the three-quarter format eventually spawned a higher-quality version known as 3/4" SP. And, like S-VHS, both are rapidly being replaced by digital formats. Don't throw away that 3/4" deck, though. A great deal of professional material has been archived on this format.

Betacam

As I mentioned earlier, the war between VHS and Beta for the home video market is legendary and is still used today to describe any technological face-off where an inferior format wins through superior marketing. Today, Beta is still in constant use in Hollywood, particularly when copies are going to be made. A copy of a VHS tape looks faded and fuzzy—more so with each successive "generation." Beta tape can be copied onto VHS tapes with little loss of quality. Therefore, when making a master copy of your program, put it on Beta. Then, when you are ready to slam out a copy for every agent in town, the copies that you make from your Beta master will look sharp and colorful.

Beta spawned a higher quality version known as Beta SP a few years back, which is used a great deal by news cameramen. Even with this upgrade, however, Beta's dominance of the market is being challenged, by the growth of . . .

DIGITAL VIDEO

No question—digital is the wave of the future in all forms of media. Now that your computer has replaced your typewriter and your CD player sits where your record player used to be, the next digital frontier to cross is video.

Digital Betacam

The wave of the future. Digital Betacam, or **DigiBeta**, is the highest-quality tape in general usage at the moment. While other high-tech formats are used in specialized applications (such as instant replay for sports), DigiBeta represents the highest quality that most people need and most production houses are prepared to deal with. In addition, there is another digital beta format, known as Betacam SX, which is aimed at news reporters.

DV

The DV format (formerly known as DVC, or Digital Videocassette) is the basis for a group of formats designed for consumer and "prosumer" applications.

Sony came out with a version of DV called DVCam, while Panasonic's version is called DVCPro. The two formats are not compatible, but there is one piece of common ground. The DV format is used to make smaller, consumer-oriented tapes, known as miniDV. This gets a little confusing because miniDV is not a format; it is a style of cassette. However, you can usually stick a miniDV tape into either a DVCam or DVCPro deck.

In video, it's all about resolution, and all these formats have higher resolution than any format that was being used on any video system ten years ago. The bar has been raised—like, to Mars. DVCam and DVCPro tapes are a shade better quality than miniDV, but the main difference has to do with dropouts. MiniDV is notorious for occasionally having a missed frame or two, causing portions of the frame to suddenly go all blocky and distorted. The effect only lasts a heartbeat and is hardly a problem for home video or a low-budget shoot (where you can just shoot it again and spend another seventeen cents on videotape), but for news gathering or a higher-budget shoot where you can't take chances on losing a critical shot, MiniDV is not reliable. Not yet, anyway. What MiniDV does do, however, is put digital video quality into the hands of every soccer parent, high-school drama program, or ultra-low-budget video shoot. With the advent of video-ready computers, you can create a reasonable, fully digital camera and editing package for under $3,000, and a high-class one for under $10,000. That may sound like a major chunk of change, but ten thousand can buy you a better quality studio than two hundred thousand could have bought you ten years ago.

DVCam is a viable professional format, although it is still not something that a first-class network would use. It is perfect for music videos, low-budget features, local commercials, and professional wedding videos.

DIGITAL VERSUS ANALOG VIDEO

The best way to understand the difference between analog and digital media is to go back to the original analog device—the record player. The record player was simple: a groove was cut into a wax (later, vinyl) disk. The groove changed shape depending on what kind of sound was being recorded—deep for loud sounds, shallow for softer sounds. A needle was dragged across these grooves and the changing depth of the grooves caused the needle to bounce up and down. A magnet on the end of the needle moved up and down through an electrical coil, sending a constantly changing voltage down a wire into your stereo. That constantly changing voltage was amplified and used to drive a speaker, creating sound. Brilliant, really, in its time. This same idea was later translated to magnetic tape. Instead of a record needle bobbing up and down, a magnetic tape head was used to rearrange metal particles attached to a plastic (later, Mylar) tape. Louder sound, more pieces of iron pointing in the same direction, more order. Softer sound, more chaos. Another magnetic head could read the pattern put down by the first one and create a constantly changing voltage based on the constantly changing pattern.

The same idea was eventually translated into video. The patterns of light and dark seen through a lens were recorded magnetically in the same way. Of course, a picture carries a lot more information than a sound (which is where that picture-is-worth-a-thousand-words thing came from, I guess), so the tape had to be a lot wider. That's why a cassette tape is 1/8" wide and a videotape is 1/2".

The problem was, all that constantly changing voltage was susceptible to noise and interference. All you had to do was put a scratch in the record, for example, and the whole thing was kaput. In video, the problem is copying. The process of picking up and laying down those magnetic particles is not exact. Every time you make a copy of a tape, some of the information gets lost, causing the image to get fuzzy and colorless. In some formats, like VHS, just two or three "generations" can render an image downright ugly.

Once you enter a digital format, you can, for all practical purposes, kiss these problems good-bye. Rather than describing the sound or picture as a stream of constantly shifting voltages or metal particles that may or may not be pointed in the right direction, digital formats break everything down to a series of numbers. When you record, and subsequently read, this series of numbers on a tape, the loss of information is almost zero. Hence, you can make copy after copy after copy without losing anything.

Chapter 4:

PAINTING THE FRAME: LIGHTING AND CINEMATOGRAPHY

Film *is* light. Everything that the audience experiences is transmitted through light beams that flash through the lens, imprint themselves on the film, and are later revealed through projection on a screen. Even the audio in film is light—imprinted on the film as an optical sound track and recreated in the theater by an optical reader.

Today, although audio has become a digital medium, light remains central to the process.

DPs are primarily photographers. They just take twenty-four pictures every second. They are concerned with how much and what type of light the set will need, what type of film stock is most appropriate, and what kind of processing is required. It is a highly artistic position requiring vast technical knowledge. In my opinion, it is, along with screenwriter and composer, one of the three great underappreciated positions in the film industry. Actors act, directors direct, but the image you see on the screen is put there by that quiet little man or woman by the camera. I say "quiet" because I have never met a DP who was loud or obnoxious. I'm sure they are out there, but until I meet one, I will always imagine the DP to be a studious, meticulous man or woman with a rich inner life and a gift for visualization. Because that's how the good ones are.

HOW LIGHT REVEALS THE STORY

The most basic skill in cinematography is a deep understanding of light, in all its moods, shapes, and technical complexities. Good DPs are masters of light, and light reveals the story in four specific ways:

Time and Place

Every moment of the day, light is shifting and changing all around you. One of the most spiritual things you can do is sit in one place, all day, and just watch the light change. When Impressionist painter Claude Monet painted the haystacks in his fields, he had to work feverishly, tossing half-completed canvasses to his assistant, to keep up with the changing light as the sun passed over and then set. His canvasses are masterpieces; each one is unique, though they all show the same subject, sometimes only minutes apart. When his wife was dying, he sat heartbroken by her bedside, painfully aware that he could not, even in his moment of grief, ignore the shifting shades of the light on her face. Light is constantly moving and changing throughout the day. Take a look around the room right now and see where the light is. Is there sunlight on the walls? Where are the shadows? If it is night, is there a moon? Streetlights? How are the lamps arranged? Take note of the fact that the light in this room is unlike any other light in any other place at any other time. It is totally unique to this place and this moment. The color, angle, and quality of light all reveal time and place. I'll ask you to look around again, at the end of the chapter, to see how things have changed.

Mood and Atmosphere

Lighting creates a mood and an atmosphere in which the scene can take place. We use two words because mood is about a character's feelings, while atmosphere is about a place. If the scene is somber, the lighting can reflect that. If the characters are in a lighthearted mood, the atmosphere of the scene can be lit to express that. For example, when Luke Skywalker dreams of the adventure he is missing, he does so with the romantic orange of a double sunset on his face.

Of course, a DP can choose to work against the mood of the scene in the script, but she does so at her peril. Playing the chatty comedy of *When Harry Met Sally . . .* amidst the foreboding light of *Sleepy Hollow* may get you interesting notices in the independent film press, but it will probably give you fits at the box office. These films may represent extremes, but the concept holds true—the mood and atmosphere of a script must be reflected in the lighting. The gritty, futuristic terror of *Alien* is played amidst grimy, jittery fluorescent lights that suggest the ship could fall apart at any moment. The playful fantasy of *Ever After* is lit in warm, romantic light that sweeps us into another world where princesses are discovered in the scullery. The shadows of *The Godfather* trilogy seem to evoke the shadowy minds that live in the world of organized crime, while the triumphant award ceremony at the end of *Star Wars* is lit like a victory parade. There is no one simple way to create lighting, and there is certainly no "right" way. Lighting can express any emotion, revealing character as clearly as the spoken word.

Movement

As I said earlier, lighting changes over time, so one of the primary types of movement that can be conveyed by lighting is movement through time. When Michelle Pfeiffer wakes up in Jeff Bridges's apartment the morning after they make love in *The Fabulous Baker Boys*, the light is completely different from the warm romantic candlelight that accompanied their romantic interlude the night before. It is harsh and uncompromising and, combined with Pfeiffer's bold choice to get a really bad makeup job, it tells a clear story: the mood is broken, reality has intervened, and last night was, well, last night. There has been movement in time as well as movement in story.

Compare that with Zeffirelli's *Romeo and Juliet*, where the lovers wake in a cloud of pink sunrise, full of love and hope for their future. In this operatic version of Shakespeare's story, the light practically sings along with the dialogue, until Romeo lies dead in the chilly gloom at the bottom of Capulet's tomb.

Focus

It is the director's job to tell the audience where to look, but the DP can always help out. Watch *The Natural*, when Robert Redford steps up to the plate, unsure of his abilities and taunted by the crowd. He looks up at the stands and sees a mysterious woman in white. Inspired by her presence, he sends the ball over the outfield wall. The woman in white (played by Glenn Close) stands out from the crowd as if she is from another dimension, partly because of her white dress and partly because she is lit like an angel amidst a crowd of brown, unremarkable people. DP Caleb Deschanel literally carved her out of the crowd with very specific lighting, forcing us to look at her as something different from the rest. Lighting can help us decide what is important and what is background.

TALKING TO A DP

Knowing how to talk to a DP is a very useful skill for anyone in film and TV, but especially directors. Here's what a DP wants to know from the script and from the director:

1. *When and where does the shot take place?* What time of day is it? What time of year? What part of the world? What sort of a place are we in? Is this suburbia or the Garden of Eden?

2. *Where is the light coming from?* A fireplace? The sun? The moon? A burning cigarette? The glowing eyes of an ancient idol?

3. *What is the mood of the characters?* Moods are about emotions. Loving? Terrified? Determined? Hopeful?

4. *What is the atmosphere of the place?* Atmosphere is about adjectives. Forbidding? Welcoming? Romantic? Cold?

5. *What is the story that the shot is telling?* Is this a shot that shows our hero in a moment of utter despair or glorious triumph? Are we close to the actor, reading the thoughts in her head? Or are we far away, taking in the environment around the actor and forming our own conclusions? This question leads to three specific concerns that the DP must determine, under the director's vision: Where do we put the camera? What lens do we use? And how does the camera move?

All these questions influence the lighting. It often helps to give the DP specific visual references, such as paintings, photographs, or other films.

THE BASIC DECISIONS

Creating lighting means solving a puzzle, fitting together such technical considerations as film stock and lens with story considerations like location, mood, and action. Despite the fact that film (and, thus, film lighting) is essentially about emotions, it rests on some fundamental technical realities. Having defined the five major artistic elements above, the DP must decide six very practical things before proceeding:

1. F-stop

2. Depth of Field

3. Film speed (ISO or ASA)

4. Shutter Angle

5. Camera Speed

6. Color Temperature

F-Stop

The f-stop determines how much light is coming through the lens. Although it is expressed as a single number, it is actually a ratio. F-stop is the ratio of the length of the lens to the diameter of the *iris*, the opening in the lens that determines how much light will reach the film.

If you want less light, you close up the iris. This is known as "stopping down." If you want more light, you open up the iris. This is known as "opening up." (They can't all be fancy terms.)

If, for example, you have a 50mm lens (meaning it is 50 millimeters long)[8] and you have your iris set with a 25mm opening, you have an f-stop of 2. If you stop down the iris to 12.5mm, then your f-stop has risen to 4.

If you prefer not to do math, don't sweat it. In actuality, no one ever talks about the size of the iris—they just talk about the "f-stop." The only reason I mention the ratio breakdown is that people are often confused because the higher the f-stop, the lower the number that is printed on the lens. (Note that in the example above, when we reduced the size of the iris, we got a higher f-stop number.) This leads to such confusing statements as, "We're at f-stop 2. Let's go down to f-stop 4." Remember, a *bigger* f-stop number means a *lower* f-stop, which means *less* light is hitting the film.[9]

| 2 | 2.8 | 4 | 5.6 | 8 | 11 | 16 | 22 |

---

[8] The "length" of the lens is actually not its overall length. It is the "focal length": the distance from the center of the front lens to the plane of the film. Whatever.

[9] In real life, the crew would say "f/2" or "f/4."

The f-stop scale is a strange set of numbers, but they make sense if you remember that they are representations of this ratio. In the f-stop series:

Each successive f-stop gives you about half as much light as the one before. That is, setting the camera at f/2.8 will allow only half as much light in as setting it at f/2.

Depending on the film stock and the look he is going for, the DP will probably specify a particular f-stop he wants to use, then have the gaffer light the set to that level of brightness.

DPs and gaffers will often communicate in f-stops. A DP might tell a gaffer, for example, to "light the set to a four," meaning, "light the set so I can shoot at f-stop 4."

F-stops are broken down into thirds, so when the gaffer says, "Five point eight and a third," he means that the light is just a little brighter than f/5.8; that is, it is one third of the way to f/4.

You will occasionally hear camera crews talking about a "t-stop," as well. T-stops are f-stops that are calculated for a particular lens, whereas f-stops in general are an overall measurement that is shared by all cameras. T-stops are slightly more accurate, but they follow the same concept.

Depth of Field

Before we can understand depth of field, we need to understand what it means to be "in focus."

The primary way that the audience knows what to look at in a shot is by looking at what is in focus. Out of focus equals, "Don't look at me." The focus on a camera is always set at a specific distance from the camera. If the focus wheel is set at ten feet, then anything that is exactly ten feet away will be in focus. But what about something ten feet, six inches? Or nine feet, six inches? How close do you have to be to ten feet to be in focus? The answer is, predictably, it depends.

When the camera assistant twirls the focus knob, the individual pieces of glass inside the lens move back and forth very short distances. This miniscule adjustment causes the light beams coming from an object to converge at a particular point inside the lens. These light beams will converge in different places depending on how far away they are. The light beams coming from the actor's face ten feet away will converge in one place, the beams coming from the car across the street will converge somewhere else, and the ones coming from the distant skyline will converge in another place altogether. The relationship of the various pieces of glass inside the lens to one another determines whether these focal points are in front of, on, or behind the film. The ones that converge exactly on the film are the ones that will be in focus. As the pieces of glass inside the lens move back and forth, so do the focal points. If you want to focus on the actor's face, you twirl the focus knobs and move the lens back and forth until the beams of light from the actor's face converge precisely at the plane of the film. To us, standing on the outside of the camera, the convergence of the beams produces a sharp image, one that is "in focus." The beams coming from the car or the building do not converge precisely at the film plane, producing images that are fuzzy and "out of focus."

Of course, your eye adjusts its focus, as well. It just does it really quickly, using only one lens. Rather than moving two lens surfaces around to get different points of focus, the human eye has a soft lens that can change shape to adjust focus. That's why some people have to squint to see objects very close or very far away. When you squint, you are actually pushing in on this lens, changing its shape and, by extension, the focal length of your eye. Your eyes do this instantly whenever you look up from something close at hand towards something far away. Within a few months of your birth, your eyes had trained themselves to switch back and forth instantly from close objects to faraway vistas with tremendous precision. Cameras are a bit clunkier than your eyes, so even a veteran focus puller misses a shot now and then.

So a lens keeps light beams coming from a certain distance— whether five inches, five feet, or five miles—focused on the front of the film. There is a little wiggle room, however. Objects directly in front or behind this distance may also be in focus, depending on the **depth of field**. This critical term refers to how much you can move in front or behind the point of focus and still be seen sharply. If the depth of field is large (known as **deep focus**), you may be able to move towards or away from the camera a fair distance and still be in focus. In a deep focus shot, an actor walking down the street may be in focus, along with the storefronts behind him and the parked cars in front. If the depth of field is small (*shallow focus*), then even moving your head could take you out of focus. In some extreme cases, your eyes may be in focus but the tip of your nose may not. This effect is very much in vogue in commercials right now. If you are an actor, it is worth asking about the depth of field.

Focus is handled on the set by one of the camera assistants, known as the *focus puller*. Focus is so important that the person doing it may have no other job, at least not while the camera is rolling. Home videographers will set the focus by looking through the lens and twirling the focus wheel until it looks right. With millions of dollars of production money on the line, a focus puller is considerably more scientific. He will attach a tape measure to the camera (most cameras have a little hook specifically for this) and pull it out to whatever he wants to be in focus. (Your face, for example.) He will then set the focus on the lens to this distance. The distances marked on your consumer camera lens are approximate, and you must always adjust it using your eye as a guide. On a first-class movie camera lens, these distances are tightly calibrated. Ten feet means ten feet, and if it doesn't, that manufacturer is going to hear about it. The image will still have some depth of field, however, and, to figure that out, the focus puller needs two pieces of information. Depth of field depends on two factors: f-stop and *focal length*.

Why F-Stop Matters. The higher the f-stop, the deeper the focus. Translation: If you want deeper focus, you must have more light.

Why?

Physics. Accept that and move on.

The movie *Citizen Kane* is renowned for its use of deep focus. Hypertalented DP Gregg Toland kept Mrs. Kane sharp in the close foreground while also focusing on the little Citizen playing with his beloved sled, Rosebud (oops, gave it away), in the extreme background. The entire film is packed with brilliant deep focus shots. Toland was nominated for an Academy Award but lost to *How Green Was My Valley*, a film that was, ironically, shot in black-and-white.

Toland played every focus trick in the book, but one of the most common was flooding the set with light. With lots of light to play with, Toland could "stop down" the lens, letting in less of the available light and gaining more depth of field.

Why Focal Length Matters. The length of the lens is an even more powerful way to determine depth of field. This is even more physics, so here's the nugget: Longer lens means less depth of field. A long telephoto lens produces a very shallow depth of field. Filmmakers use this effect to great advantage to remove unwanted things from a shot. Let's say a star is standing on a street corner surrounded by scads of people walking by, but the filmmaker wants us to see only her, to live only in her little world. One way is to put the camera down the block and use a long lens. Once she is in focus, the actress will be sharp, but the people in front and behind will drop out of focus and, thus, will not command attention. Any time you see a film image where actors are in focus but objects just behind them are out of focus, you are probably looking through a long, or ***telephoto, lens***. Take a look at the beginning of the old *Mary Tyler Moore Show*, with Mary tossing her hat amidst the crowded streets of Minneapolis, to see a great example of this.

A short, or ***wide-angle lens***, on the other hand, will produce a giant depth of field. *Citizen Kane* is full of these, as well. Toland probably used a 25mm or shorter lens to capture Citizen and Mrs. Kane in the shot mentioned earlier. If you are being shot from very close by, you probably have a great deal of depth of field to work with.

Depth of field is something you can talk to the camera assistant about. Focus pullers use the DP's bible, *The American Cinematographers Manual*, to look up their depth of field, based on the lens and the f-stop, and it is all quite scientific. A particular f-stop plus a particular lens gives you a particular depth of field. Not negotiable. If you are an actor, make sure that you understand what kind of depth of field you are being shot with. One other bit of trivia—two thirds of the depth of field is behind the point of focus; one third is in front. You always have more room to move back than forward. Why? Physics.

Film Speed

One of the primary artistic considerations that a DP will make is the type of film stock used on the production. Film stocks come in a huge variety, and the DP will make his choice based on the style of film, the shooting conditions, past experience, and, in general, what kind of a "look" the director wants to achieve. All types of film have unique qualities, but, for now, let's look at one defining aspect of a film stock—its speed. "High speed" film stocks require less light to be properly exposed. They can be used in lower light situations, meaning fewer lighting instruments or less natural light. These film stocks are more sensitive to light, but they also can appear grainier. Slower stocks require more light, but they have less visible grain. The speed of a film is listed as its ASA or ISO. ASA 100 film is on the slow side—you would only use it in a brightly lit studio situation or outdoors on a sunny day. ASA 500 film is more sensitive—you could use it indoors with less light or for night scenes.

F-stop, depth of field, and film speed form a holy trinity of light which the DP must worship, or be damned when the dailies are shown. They each tug on one another in a constant balancing game. A slower film means a higher f-stop, a higher f-stop means less depth of field, more depth of field requires a lower f-stop, which may mean switching to a faster film, and so on, and so on.

But wait. Like Ginsu knives, there's more. Before we can turn to the light meter to determine our f-stop, there are a few more pieces of information we need to clarify:

Shutter Angle

The shutter is the little door that opens between the lens and the film. When it is open, light is hitting the film and imprinting the image. Still photographers use "shutter speed," the amount of time the shutter is open, to control the amount of light that hits the film. The slower the shutter speed, the longer the light is allowed to hit the film. A slow shutter speed, like 1/15, allows a lot of light to hit the film. A fast speed, like 1/500 of a second, allows less light in.

DPs don't have the option of adjusting shutter speed. A film camera shutter is a half-moon shaped piece of metal that rotates in sync with the entire camera mechanism. Under normal circumstances, the film moves at twenty-four frames per second, so the shutter covers and uncovers the film twenty-four times every second. This gives a shutter speed of around 1/50. Period.

A DP can control the **shutter angle**. Normally, the shutter is a perfect half-circle, meaning that the shutter angle is 180 degrees (a half-circle). If, however, the DP needs more light on the film, she can make the shutter angle smaller, creating a shutter that is less than a full half-circle, like a big piece of pie. Because there is less shutter going by, the film is exposed for more time. Likewise, a larger shutter angle (meaning that the shutter is more than a half-circle) puts less light on the film.

Larger or smaller shutter angles do not affect depth of field directly. They do, however, allow the DP to use larger or smaller f-stops, which affect depth of field quite a bit. Bigger shutter angles also tend to make moving objects or people look more jittery and less fluid. When taken to extremes, such as in the opening sequence of *Saving Private Ryan*, the effect can be disorienting and almost nauseating. Smaller shutter angles, of course, make people look blurrier.

Some really sophisticated cameras allow the shutter angle to be changed while the camera is running, something that you may want if you need to change the exposure during a shot. This might be necessary if, for example, you were panning from a dark area to a brightly lit one. Changing the f-stop during a shot changes the depth of field and is usually noticeable. Changing the exposure with the shutter angle is cleaner.

Camera Speed

Camera speed refers to how fast the film is moving through the camera and being exposed. Under normal circumstances, the camera speed for American filmmaking is 24 frames per second (fps). In Europe, the camera speed is 25fps. (This annoying difference comes from the fact that in Europe the standard was set to be a multiple of the normal frequency of the electricity—50 cycles per second. Electricity moves at 60 cycles per second here, but our standard frame rate doesn't take that into account.)

Camera speed can change, of course, and does every time a crew shoots slow-motion footage. Slow-motion footage is actually shot at a higher camera speed than normal footage, so when it is played back at the regular speed, the subject will appear to move in slow motion. Because the film is moving faster through the camera on the set, the frame rate is faster, which means less light is reaching each frame. Quick: if you want more light on the film, do you set the f-stop higher or lower?

If you said higher, then all this is making sense. More light needed equals higher f-stop. If you are shooting slow-motion footage, therefore, you need a higher f-stop. (Smaller number, remember?)

But what if you want to change speeds while you are filming? It actually happens more often than you think. In *Forrest Gump*, our hero is running away from his tormentors when a miracle occurs. Because of his love for a young girl, he gains the strength to throw off his leg braces and run faster and farther than ever before. Director Robert Zemeckis and DP Don Burgess depicted this event by slowly changing the shot of Forrest running from normal speed to slow motion. As the camera tracked along beside Michael Conner Humphreys (the actor playing Forrest as a boy), the camera crew slowly changed the frame speed from 24fps to higher and higher speeds, producing footage that, when played back, showed the boy moving slower and slower, becoming more and more heroic. Of course, this means that the exposure had to slowly change, as well, which meant slowly changing the shutter angle on the fly, all while careening down a country road trying to keep a sprinting actor in frame. Now you know why some cameras are computerized.

Color Temperature

Because of film's closer point of view and generally realistic bent, 95 percent of the time, the lighting is designed to look "real." Rarely does film lighting draw attention to itself through color, unlike theatrical lighting, which often uses much more intense shades. (The most glaring exception is when film actually depicts a scene in a theater, as in *Moulin Rouge* or *All That Jazz*.) In fact, film lighting people sometimes refer to theatrical color filters as "party gels," which tells you a little about how film people view theatrical lighting.

Put more simply, film lighting is usually "white" light—at least, it tries to look white. White light comes in a lot of different shades, though, from the orange glow of a bedside lamp to the crisp bluish tint from a cloudless, northern sky.

Film is very finicky about color. Put a "white" incandescent bulb next to a beam of sunlight, and the bulb will look yellow on film. Add a filter to make the bulb look whiter, and the sunlight may turn blue. Next to either of these sources, a fluorescent fixture may look positively green.

The fact is, white comes in a lot of colors, and, while your eye is very good at quickly adjusting to these changes, the camera, whether film or video, is not. In order to produce realistic color on film, we must decide what color we want "white" to be and adapt accordingly.

When we talk about what color white is, we are talking about **color temperature**. Color temperature is a standardized scale that assigns a number to the various shades of white from warm to cool.

These numbers come from a highly regulated experiment in which a specific piece of metal, known as a "black body," is heated up while an observer records what color it is at each temperature. As anyone who has ever played with a hot poker can tell you, the first color that metal turns when heated is red, followed by orange, then yellow, and, finally, blue.

The color temperature scale assigns numbers to these different shades that correspond to temperatures on the Kelvin scale.[10] Warm, yellowish light, such as the light from a household incandescent lamp, is around 2,900 degrees Kelvin. Consequently, we would say that this type of light fixture has a color temperature of 2,900 degrees. A tungsten bulb, like the ones in most movie lights, is around 3,200 degrees, while midday summer sunlight is about 5,600 degrees.

The DP must know the color temperature of the light source in order to create realistic color on film. There is such a thing as a color temperature meter, but most of the time, the DP depends on her knowledge of different light sources. Most light sources fall into three different groups: incandescent, tungsten, and daylight.

So how do we set up our equipment to shoot under these three different color temperatures of light?

For video, we let the camera do the work. Professional and prosumer video cameras have a setting called **white balance**. Once the lighting is ready to go, a crew person stands on the set with a piece of white card. (I've done it more than once with a white T-shirt.) The camera zooms in on the card so the screen is completely filled with white. The DP then pushes the "white balance" button, and the camera automatically calibrates itself to the version of white that is on the card. From that point on, or at least until you reset it, it assumes that color is white and adjusts all the other colors it sees accordingly.

If you take the camera into another lighting situation—if, for example, you move from an indoor set out into the sunshine—you

---

[10] Scientists often use the Kelvin temperature scale because it starts at absolute zero (around –459 degrees Fahrenheit) and uses the same steps as the Celsius scale. Water freezes at 273 degrees Kelvin and boils at 373 degrees Kelvin. (You will never, ever need to know this on a set.)

must set the white balance again, but this is a quick process if you carry the white card along (or have a friend in a white T-shirt). If you don't reset the white balance, the outdoor sunlight will appear too blue. Many video cameras have presets for various kinds of light, but it is always best to set the white balance precisely, if you have the time.

Film cameras aren't capable of this little trick. Instead, the DP must choose a film stock that fits the particular light source she is working with. Film stock is "balanced" for incandescent light, tungsten light, or daylight, so once you know what kind of light you've got, you know what kind of film to buy.

If you are now asking yourself, "But what if you have more than one kind of light on the set?" then this is all making sense to you. Well done.

Yes, what *do* you do when you are shooting in a room with tungsten lights, but there is sunlight coming through the window? And what about that incandescent lamp on the bedside table?

The answer is: choose and correct. You choose one light source as your primary source, get the appropriate film for that light, and correct the other sources to match it. **Correcting** a light source means putting a color filter in front of it that changes the color temperature to match the primary light source. These filters are known as **CT filters**, for color temperature. They come in three colors: blue, orange, and magenta. Leaving magenta aside for a moment, let's focus on the other two. Blue and orange filters, known as CTB and CTO, respectively, move light sources up (blue) and down (orange) the color temperature spectrum. Here's an example:

Because most of the lighting in the example above is tungsten, let's assume that the DP has chosen tungsten-balanced film. Sunlight has a higher color temperature than tungsten, so we will need to correct it down with a CTO filter. CTO and CTB filters come in various shades. The darkest ones are known as "full," as in, "Get me a full CTO." The rest of the shades are referred to in fractions, such as 3/4, 1/2, and 1/4, as in, "Put a quarter CTB over that light." The smaller the fraction, the less color correction takes place. By the way, color filters are generally attached to lights with clothespins, only no one calls them clothespins. Those two little sticks of wood with the little metal spring are known as **C-47s** and every gaffer will tell you a different reason why.

This is not a time for guesswork, so the DP consults a color chart. The chart tells him that, in order to convert 5,600 degrees daylight to 3,600 degrees tungstenlight, he must put a 3/4 CTO filter over the sunlight. It's a little tough to put a color filter over the whole sun, but in this case we are fortunate, as we can just stretch the filter over the window. If the actual glass of the window is visible in the shot, the gaffer will cut pieces of the 3/4 CTO filter to fit in each frame of the window. Thus, the sunlight is converted to match the interior tungsten lights, and everyone is happy.

If the shot were outside, the DP would most likely pick a daylight-balanced film and put CTB filters over the tungsten lights to correct them upwards. Note that this is one reason why people like the **HMI** lights that we will discuss in the next chapter. HMIs are daylight-balanced lights and, when used outside, require no color filter.

Now, about that magenta filter. This is how a DP solves a particularly sticky lighting problem—fluorescent lights. These fixtures actually look greenish when filmed with tungsten or daylight-balanced film. There is no such thing as fluorescent-balanced film, so the gaffer must correct the fluorescent with the magenta filter, usually by forming it into tubes and sliding them over the bulbs. It is an imperfect solution, as the color spectrum from a fluorescent light is a frightening thing to behold, but it can get you through a jam. The real solution is to use the daylight- or tungsten-balanced Kino-Flo fluorescent fixtures that we will discuss in the next chapter.

MEASURING LIGHT LEVELS

Now that we have set our camera speed and shutter angle, decided on an f-stop to light for, chosen a film speed, determined how much depth of field we need, and selected a lens, we need to know how much light is actually on the set right now. In order to gather this all-important piece of information, we need a *light meter*.

If you have ever taken pictures, you are probably familiar with what a light meter does. It measures the available light, then tells you what settings to use on your camera. In some consumer cameras, it doesn't bother you with this information; it just goes ahead and sets the camera for you.

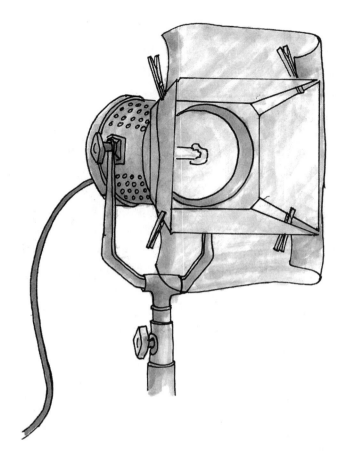

Filters are attached with C-47s.

In order to get an accurate reading, the DP must tell the light meter what film speed, shutter angle, and camera speed she is using. Then, based on that information, the light meter will come up with the proper f-stop. If the DP has a particular f-stop she wants to use, the gaffer just keeps adding light to the set until the light meter comes up with that f-stop.

There are two types of light meters in common usage: the *incident meter* and the *spot meter.*

The Incident Meter

Most of the time, the DP will use a meter that tells him the general level of light on the set. An incident meter measures the average amount of light that is falling on the face of a flat disk. As is, it only measures light coming from the front, but with the addition of a *hemispherical light collector,* which is a fancy name for something that looks like half of a ping-pong ball, the meter will collect light from above, below, and the sides. By holding this meter up in front of an actor's face, the DP can measure how much light is hitting the actor. The meter will read out an f-stop number which, when applied to the camera, will guarantee a proper exposure.

The DP usually wants to know more than just how much light is hitting the actor from the front. He may want to know how much light is coming from the side alone, or from the back. In this case, he may cup his hand over the light meter to shield it from one or more lights. The meter will give him an f-stop reading on those lights alone. He probably won't set the lens to that number—it just tells him how much brighter or dimmer those lights are than the front lights. This is important information when determining **contrast ratio** (something we will get to in a moment).

The Spot Meter

Whereas the incident meter tells the DP the overall light level, the **spot meter** tells her how much light is coming from one specific area. The spot meter has a viewfinder like a camera. The DP points the meter at a specific thing on the set and uses the viewfinder like a gun sight. The meter reads out how much light is reflecting off that thing. She may want to assure herself that there really is enough light on an actor's face. She may want to check a bright object in the frame to see if it needs to be toned down. She may want to check if an object in shadow will be visible at all. The spot meter can sight on a very narrow area, so a DP can get very specific information about how much light is reflected off a specific object or person.

One key difference between the incident and spot meters is that the incident meter is pointed at the lights—that is, it almost always is reading how much light is *hitting* a subject. The spot meter, on the other hand, generally reads how much light is *reflecting off* the subject.

A GENERAL APPROACH TO FILM AND VIDEO LIGHTING

Now that we have figured out the story we want to tell with the lights, made some basic practical decisions, and figured out how to use a meter, we can actually begin to light the set.

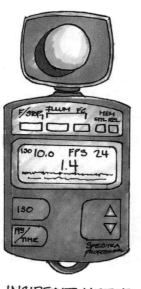

INCIDENT METER

SPOT METER

Light meters

Film and video lighting can be broken down into four principal areas:

1. *Key*

2. *Fill*

3. *Set lighting*

4. *Accents*

Key

The **key light** is the answer to the question, "Where is the light coming from?" Gaffers talk about what light is "keying" a scene. If the scene is a soccer game outdoors on a sunny day, the sun is keying the scene. A romantic scene on a bearskin rug might be keyed by the light from the fireplace. The key light might be candles, overhead fluorescent lights, a table lamp, or any other lighting source that is apparently providing the light for the scene.

I say "apparently" because, in almost all of these situations, the gaffer would add additional lights to amplify and support the key light. In many cases, the actual light source that is apparently keying the scene might never be seen—only suggested. Of course, when using the sun as a key light, you generally don't have to add additional key lights, but with sources like table lamps, candles, and fireplaces, you generally have to help them out.

The key light is the strongest light source on the set. The side of the actor's face that is closest to the key light will be brighter than the other side, and his facial features (nose, lips, eyebrows) will cast shadows because of it. For nighttime looks, the key is almost always behind the actor, leaving his face in shadow and suggesting that the scene is dark. For daytime looks, the key tends to be in front of the actor.

Fill

The key light is usually coming strongly from one direction. This provides a powerful source of illumination, but, as I just mentioned, it can also provide hard, dark shadows. **Fill light** does just what the name suggests—it fills in the shadows and evens out the overall light. Whereas the key light comes from a strong, concentrated source (like a single lightbulb), the fill light comes from a soft, distributed source, like a light that is being bounced off a wide, pebbled reflector. This distributed source means that light beams are coming from lots of directions at once, allowing the light to curl smoothly around the features of the face.

Contrast Ratio

The relationship of key to fill is described with the **contrast ratio**. This is the ratio of the key and fill light together to the fill light alone. If the contrast ratio is high, then the key is much stronger than the fill, producing deep, dramatic shadows. Look at dark, emotional films, like *The Godfather*, for examples of high contrast lighting. If the contrast ratio is low, then the lighting is said to be "flatter," which isn't nearly as bad as it sounds. For incredibly flat lighting, take a look at the evening news. It used to be that you could get a really great lesson in contrast ratio by watching a whole series of late-night TV shows. The ten o'clock news had bright, flat lighting, for an upbeat and no-nonsense look. At 11:00 P.M., *The Tonight Show* took over, with its slightly higher contrast ratio, giving more of an "entertainment" look. At midnight, the old *Late Night with David Letterman* came on, with deep shadows all over the set and a more dramatic, "nightclub" lighting style. After his show came the

Key and fill light.

dramatically lit *Late Late Show*, with a contrast ratio so high you could almost hear the smoky jazz music in the background.

Interestingly, when Letterman left *Late Night* at NBC and moved to an earlier time slot at CBS, his lighting got brighter and the contrast ratio came down. So there you go.

Set Lighting

So far, we've mostly been talking about lighting the actor. But what about the set? Often, the key and fill light will provide the bulk of the set lighting, but additional lighting is sometimes necessary. The DP may add **practicals**, working prop light sources, to the set. In a few remarkable scenes, practicals have actually been used as key lights, as in the party scene in *Eyes Wide Shut*, where hundreds of thousands of Christmas tree lights, strung on every wall, provide the bulk of the illumination. In general, however, practicals are merely dressing. Note that most practicals, in their natural state, will be low color temperature incandescents and, thus, must be corrected upwards to match tungsten light sources. A common solution is to replace the incandescent bulbs with tungsten-balanced *photo floods*, which offer a similar quality of light at a higher color temperature (and a significantly higher price, too, so don't forget them when you leave!).

Backdrops, *cycs*, and **translights** may be lit with specially designed units called **far cycs** or **border lights**. A cyc is a cloth or plaster backdrop often used to imitate sky. A translight is a large, translucent photograph that is usually lit from behind.

The key to lighting a set is to give it enough light to look natural without overwhelming the actors in front of it. In general, unless you want to see the actors in silhouette for effect, the set should be much dimmer (at least a full f-stop) than the actors.

Accents

Sometimes, a DP may choose to pick out a particular object with a special, a single lighting instrument that is focused on an important prop or area. In *Wait Until Dark*, poor little blind girl Audrey Hepburn lives in a Greenwich Village apartment and is threatened by murderous heroin smugglers. The phone becomes her link to the outside world and, she thinks, her savior. As the film progresses and the importance of the phone grows, it begins to appear in a pool of light, almost like a shrine. Considering the light sources in her basement apartment, the pool of light doesn't really make sense after a while, but at that point, we really don't care. We just don't want to see Audrey get whacked.

My favorite special of all time is in *Suspicion*, when Cary Grant is carrying the glass of milk, possibly filled with poison, up the steps to the innocent Joan Fontaine. What you can't see is the tiny, battery-operated light that Grant is carrying behind the glass, which is making the suspicious milk light up like a glow stick. Don't drink it, Joan!

Another common accent light is used for close-ups, especially glamorous ones. This is the **eye light**, a small fresnel placed right beside the camera. In a close-up shot, look for that glint of light in the actor's eyes.

That little star of light is carefully placed there by a kindly DP, all to make the actor look a little more sincere.

Remember when I asked you, at the beginning of this chapter, to look around the room and notice the light? Do it again now. How has it changed? Is it darker? Have the colors changed? Is there more or less light? Is it harder or more diffuse? Where have the shadows gone?

As a film and TV person, whatever path you choose in the business, it will always serve you well to be sensitive to the light. Remember, it is your business and your art. Film is light.

Chapter 5:

THE FILM CAMERA: THE EIGHT-HUNDRED-POUND GORILLA

The camera determines everything; it is the final arbiter, the revealer of all things, the oracle of Delphi, and Merlin's crystal ball. Everything that is done on the set is done for the benefit of the camera.

In the Italian Renaissance theater, the nobleman footing the bill for the show got a special seat right in the center of the house, where he sat while the entire show was played directly to him. All of the scenery was designed to look good from that one spot. Everyone else in the audience was a bystander with bad sight lines, virtually ignored by the designers and actors.

That's pretty much how people feel about the camera. It is the final definition of reality: If the camera didn't see it, it didn't happen. Likewise, the camera determines what is important and what is not: out of frame, out of mind. Like the old joke about what you feed an eight-hundred-pound gorilla, the camera gets whatever it wants, baby, whatever it wants.

The modern film camera is a highly precise piece of machinery, hand-built by an ever-decreasing group of old-world craftsmen. Film cameras come in lots of different varieties, based on the job that you want them to do, but, structurally, they are all basically built the same way.

With the screaming pace of modern technology threatening to blow our doors off, it is comforting to know that some things have changed very little. After you spend the day working on your brand-new computer, storing your schedule on an impossibly small personal organizer, making a call with cell-phone technology that was unheard of when you were a child, and using the World Wide Web that was invented in your own lifetime, it is comforting to go to the movies and watch a technology that was invented in 1896. That's right—the modern motion-picture camera has not substantially changed since the boys at Thomas Edison's studio shot their first student film before the turn of the twentieth century. Edison and an engineer named William Dickson had the idea to take George Eastman's newly invented celluloid and move it past a lens, one frame at a time, in 1889. As each frame came to rest, a metal shutter would swing open to let in light from a lens. The film is exposed, slam goes the **shutter**, off goes the exposed frame of film, and a new one takes its place. When the shooting is done, you develop the film and print it onto another piece of celluloid as a positive image. Then, you run it through a projector, which is built to do the same action as the camera did. This time, though, the film is held up in front of a lamp, which shines light through the film and projects it onto a screen. The shutter keeps opening and closing, just like in the camera, producing a series of images on the screen. By 1896, they had added the precursor to the modern pressure plate, which held the film in place while the shutter opened, creating a close ancestor to the modern camera.

A modern projector shows you this series of images at a rate of twenty-four frames per second. The impression of the image stays on your retina for a fraction of a second after the shutter cuts it off, only to be blown away by the appearance of the next image, one twenty-fourth of a second later. Because your brain persists in seeing the first image after it's gone, the two images appear to be connected. This phenomenon is known as **persistence of vision,** and it is the basis of film technology. Your helpful brain assumes that the two images represent two parts of a continuous motion and marries them together into a moving image. That is how a series of photographs becomes one continuous shot of Butch Cassidy and the Sundance Kid jumping off a cliff to escape the lawmen. That's how they did it in 1896. That's how they do it today. There is, perhaps, no other technology in our culture that has remained so determinedly unchanged.

Which is not to say that there haven't been a few improvements along the way. Film equipment today might be described as very high-tech machinery in service to a very low-tech process.

One thing that has changed is the speed of the film. Early cameras were hand-cranked at whatever speed the cameraman felt like going, usually between ten and fifteen frames per second. That's why people are always walking so fast in old films when they are projected on modern projectors.

THE FILM CAMERA PACKAGE

A camera kit consists of everything that a camera needs to do its job, and that's a lot of pieces. Don't expect to pick up the camera in your two-seater sports car. It is not unusual for an entire truck to be devoted solely to camera equipment, and even a small, independent film can rent a camera package that will completely fill the largest SUV.

A camera package consists of the following pieces:

- *Magazines*
- *The Camera Body*
- *Lenses*
- *Filters*
- *Viewfinders*
- *Video Assists*

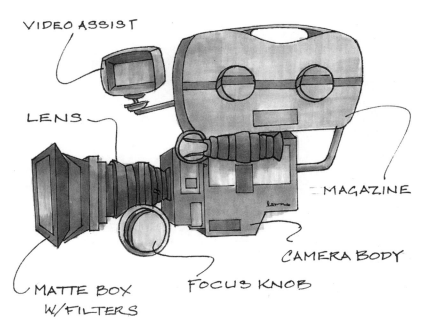

The film camera.

Come with me now as I escort you on a fantastic journey through the intricate workings of a film camera. We'll follow one little frame of film—we'll call her Frieda—as she is exposed to the light and becomes another tiny piece of someone's cinematic masterpiece.

The Magazine

Frieda and her friends are wound, very tightly, on a fresh roll of film that is sent from the manufacturer in a lightproof foil wrapper. On the set, one of the camera assistants puts that roll of film in a ***changing bag***, a lightproof bag with a pair of lightproof cuffs in which you stick your hands. The bag is big enough to allow the assistant to put the reel of film and the empty film magazine inside it, after which she zips up the light-proof zipper. Reaching through the cuffs, the assistant opens the maga-zine by feel, opens the foil bag of film, loads the reel of film onto a rotating post in the magazine, threads the end out the side of the mag, makes a loop, threads it back into the other side of the magazine, and attaches it to an empty reel on a second post. When she is done, she seals up the magazine again, leaving a loop of film outside. It's actually a bit of a trick to do, so don't talk to the assistant while she is doing it.

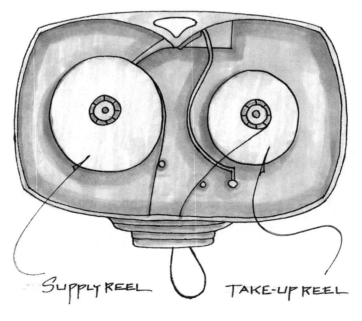

The magazine.

There are a number of ways to mess it up and, unfortunately, a lot of those ways don't show up until the film is processed. For example, if the assistant accidentally pushes the center of the reel in too far and the layers of film rub against one another (this is called "coning the reel"), it can produce scratches that will only show up when the entire production staff sees their precious hard work ruined in the dailies. Good camera assistants (known as "ACs") tend to be very calm, unflappable people, and now you know why. All of your work is in their hands, and if there is one little slip—oops, there went the scene.

In any case, let's assume that all went well with Frieda and her friends in the loading process, and they are all safely nestled in the magazine, ready to go. The magazine is slid into place on top of the camera and the AC opens the camera body. She pulls the loop of film down through the works, threading it over and around and through the inner workings of the camera body. This part of the process is done in the light, because only the first few feet of film are exposed, and they are thrown away, anyway. The magazine has two reels in it, one for the film before it is exposed (the *supply reel*) and one for after (the *take-up reel*). If you are old enough to remember seeing actual films in the classroom (or home movies, for that matter), you may remember the two reels sticking up above the projector. That's exactly what the inside of a magazine looks like—just sealed inside a lightproof box.

Magazines come in various sizes, depending on how much film they are designed to hold. 35mm film generally comes from the factory in 400-foot or 1,000-foot reels (about four minutes and ten minutes long, respectively). Other formats come in various lengths.

Obviously, the magazine must be light-tight, and good camera assistants will go to extraordinary lengths to make it that way. If a little light does leak in, it creates *fogging* on the film, which is just what it sounds like—a white, foggy area on the edge of the film. Uh-oh, time to reshoot.

Magazines come in three basic varieties, depending on how the supply and take-up reel are oriented to each other. A *side-by-side magazine* has the two reels sitting in two compartments, one behind the other, looking for all the world like Mickey Mouse ears. A *displacement magazine* (the most common) is oval shaped and has the two reels closer together. As the film spools onto the take-up reel, it fills the space created by the shrinking supply reel. This design saves space.

Some cameras use an *axial magazine,* where the two reels sit next to each other in separate compartments, like two hamburger buns on their sides. Some people think this style of magazine is noisier because the film has to turn several corners on its journey from one side of the magazine to the other. Others prefer it because it is easier to load. In the displacement magazine, the camera assistant has to thread both the supply reel and the take-up reel inside the changing bag. The design of the axial magazine allows the take-up reel to be threaded in the light of day.

The important thing to note is that each brand of camera has a magazine that is peculiar to it. They are not interchangeable.

Most assistants will run a line of tape around the seams of a magazine, just to be sure that the light can't get in. Many of them also color-code that tape—one color for unexposed film, one for exposed—to ensure that film will not be double-exposed. Are you getting the feeling that ACs are pretty careful people? ACs are really, really anal about taking care of film, and aren't you glad about that? Everything, everything, EVERYTHING that happens on a set comes down to that tiny, fragile strip of silver-covered, light-sensitive mylar wound up tight in that magazine. If that doesn't give you chills, you must have a heart of iron. You would probably make a good AC.

The Camera Body

So, the loading is done, the magazine is in place, and we are ready to go. When the call comes to roll the camera, the assistant pushes the "Run" button on the camera, and the motor in the camera body, powered by the battery attached to it, comes to life. The motor powers a series of wheels that advance the film. The film travels around these wheels at a constant speed (about ninety feet a minute, or a little over one mile an hour) until it reaches the area just above the pressure plate, where the thoughtful assistant has left a little loop. That little loop is very important, because for the next few inches, the film is going to be traveling in short, sharp jerks. The loop absorbs the jerking motion of the film and keeps it from being torn. As the film approaches the pressure plate, it is grabbed by two *pull-down hooks,* like tiny grappling hooks, that yank the film into place onto a series of *register pins*. Those pins hold the film precisely in place as the *pressure plate* slams down and locks it in place. At the precise moment that the plate lands, the shutter slides out of the way and allows the light from the lens to fall on poor light-sensitive Frieda for a fraction of a second. Frieda's little bits of silver react to the light, rearrange themselves, and store that tiny moment in time. Then, just as Frieda was getting comfortable, the plate moves away, the registration pins recede, and the hooks snatch up the film and toss it off the plate to make room for the next frame, the next exposure, the next frozen moment in time, which it slams down within a thousandth of an inch of the last one. And this happens twenty-four times every second, over and over again.

Frieda, fresh from her time on the pressure plate, goes through a second loop, which, like the first one, helps her to transition from a stop-start motion to a smooth one-mile-an-hour ride back up into the magazine. Once she reaches the take-up reel, she lies down against her friends, safe and happy and ready to be processed.

When I first showed this mechanism to my illustrator, Kis, she nodded and said, "Okay, it's a sewing machine," and she couldn't be more right. A sewing machine uses a claw to grab the fabric and pull it into place. Then, a metal plate (they call it the "foot") traps the fabric against the top of the machine while a needle stabs it and makes a stitch. Then the plate lets go, the claw grabs the fabric, and the whole process starts over again. All of these pieces—the claw, the plate, and the needle—are tied together in a single mechanism, just like the claw, plate, and shutter in the camera.

Unlike sewing machines, however, movie cameras are precision instruments on the level of electron microscopes, and they are hardly mass-produced. Any slippage in the mechanism, whether it puts a few frames out of alignment, tears a few sprocket holes or, horror of horrors, scratches the delicate film stock, and it is reshoot, reshoot, reshoot.

Film cameras are hand-built in very small quantities by very talented technicians. Not surprisingly, they don't come cheap, either. A high-budget movie could easily carry a camera package worth a million dollars. Now you know why production insurance is a growth industry in Hollywood.

The Lens

There are two categories of lenses: *prime lenses*, which have a fixed *focal length*, and *zoom lenses*, which can smoothly change from one focal length to another.

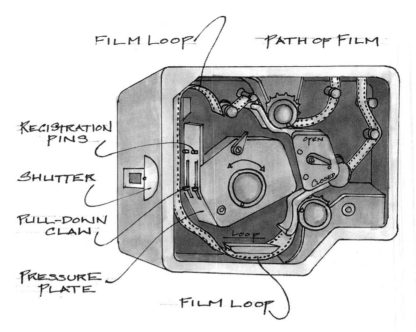

FILM LOOP!   PATH OF FILM

REGISTRATION PINS

SHUTTER

PULL-DOWN CLAW

PRESSURE PLATE

OPEN

CLOSED

LOOP

FILM LOOP

The path of the film.

Okay, so what does focal length mean?

The longer the focal length, the narrower the shot. Think about it this way: If you hold a short tube, say—an empty toilet paper roll—up to your eye, your vision will be restricted to what you can see through the end of the tube. Your "shot" is more narrow than without the tube. If you look down a longer tube, however, like the tube your new Britney Spears poster came in,[11] your shot will be even narrower. Longer focal length (longer tube) means a narrower shot. Of course, whatever the width of the shot, the image will still fill the entire screen; the longer focal length lens just gives you a closer look at it.

As a general rule, a 50mm lens renders people and objects about the same size as your eye does. Smaller numbers will take in more width, while larger focal lengths focus in on smaller areas. Very short lenses—say, anything less than 25mm—are called *wide-angle lenses*. These lenses tend to produce a bit of a "fish-eye" effect, making things in the center of the frame appear larger than those on the side. Straight

---

[11] It's just an example—you don't have to like Britney Spears. (Your secret is safe with me.)

lines will appear to bow outward in the center of the frame. Longer lenses—those longer than 50mm—are known as **telephoto lenses**.

A zoom lens can change its focal length. For example, a 25–150 zoom lens can be set anywhere from 25mm to 150mm. Zoom lenses are considered to produce a somewhat lower-quality image than prime lenses, although this issue is hotly contested. In the 1960s and 1970s, the zoom was used for effect during the shot, carrying the audience suddenly forward or back with a twirl of the lens. Nowadays, this effect is considered dated, and an editor will cut directly to a wider or narrower shot. Still, zoom lenses are more convenient because you don't have to carry as many lenses. The focal length can also be changed more quickly, because you don't have to remove and replace the lens. Also, a zoom lens lets you set the focal length between sizes, whereas with prime lenses, you are stuck with whatever focal length you've got.

Speed. Besides focal length, lenses are classified by their speed. This is a bit of a misnomer, because the lens isn't actually moving. In the context of a camera lens, "speed" refers to how much light the lens can transmit to the film. A "fast" lens has an iris that can open wider, allowing more light to hit the film. A "slow" lens won't open up as wide, forcing you to use faster film or more lighting to get the exposure.[12] Faster lenses can be set to lower f-stops. Any lens with an f-stop below f/2 is considered fast.

Anamorphic Lenses. An anamorphic lens is not round. It has more of an elliptical shape, which means that the light is more concentrated on the horizontal axis than on the vertical axis. In practice, the image that passes through an anamorphic lens gets "squeezed" on the horizontal axis, but not on the vertical one. This means that the film can record an image that is wider than the frame of film. Remember how we talked about aspect ratios in the formats chapter? A normal frame of film has an aspect ratio of about 4:3. An anamorphic image can take in an image that is wider than that and squeeze it down to 4:3. Then, when the film is played back through the projector, an identical

---

[12] Remember that "higher" f-stops actually have smaller numerical values. F/2 is higher than f/4.

anamorphic lens is used to stretch the film back out again. The end result is an image that is wider than 4:3, yet uses a standard frame of film. Pretty sneaky.

THE MATTE BOX

At the end of the lens sits a big square box. The matte box is named for the metal plates (known as **hard mattes**) that are mounted on the front of it, forming a black window that the lens looks through. Each hard matte has its own aspect ratio. If you want to shoot in 1.66:1, you choose the matte with that size hole in it. The camera kit contains a matte for each aspect ratio, so you can choose the one that matches your final output. The matte masks off anything that will not be seen in the final image. It also helps keep light flares off the lens.

Besides mattes, the matte box can also hold **filters**. There are any number of things that a DP might want to do to the incoming light, so filters come in a wide variety. **Neutral density filters** cut down on the overall light level without changing the color balance or depth of field. **Diffusion** filters lend softness to faces, especially faces that aren't as young as they used to be. For a glamour shot, the DP may put a piece of clear glass in the matte box and smear Vaseline around the edges to create a soft-edged look. **Polarizing filters** cut down on glare. **Star filters** and **nets** break up highlights, like candles, into glistening stars. In some cases, the DP might want to alter the color temperature of the light. She may want to tone down the sky but not the ground by using a filter that is darker at the top than at the bottom—a **graduated** or **grad filter**. If a film crew is shooting day-for-night, those filters are placed in the matte box.

By the way, there are two kinds of matte boxes, the **snap-on** (used for smaller cameras) and the **swing-away** (standard on most 35mm cameras).

DAY-FOR-NIGHT

Let's say you are shooting a stagecoach chase at night. The chase goes across a wide landscape, up and down hills, in and out of valleys, all the while following the brave sheriff as he tries to fight off a hoard of bandits.

That's a lot of space to light, and lighting costs a lot of money. The solution? Use the best light ever created: the sun. Every DP has her own recipe for **day-for-night**, a collection of filters that drops the light intensity and shifts the color into the blue end of the spectrum. Usually, it is a combination of blue and neutral density filters. The scene is shot under normal daylight but, when the film is exposed, the combination of the blue filter and the underexposure makes the scene look like it took place at midnight under a full moon.

The Viewfinder

When the camera isn't rolling, the shutter is closed. The light coming through the lens, therefore, lands on the shutter. The shutter has a little mirror on it, however, that sends the light up into the viewfinder where the camera operator can see it. That way, the crew can frame up the shot by looking through the same lens that the film is looking through. Once the camera is rolling, the shutter and its mirror start to spin, causing the image in the viewfinder to flicker. Watch the monitor sometime when the camera is rolling; you will see the strobing image caused by the mirror rotating.

The light from the mirror lands on a piece of glass known as the **ground glass**. It is this piece of glass that you are looking at when you look through the viewfinder. The ground glass is perfectly placed to be the same distance from the lens as the film, so the image will be in focus in both places. The ground glass has lines etched on it, showing the outline of the frame. Most cameras have interchangeable ground glasses so you can install the one that has the same aspect ratio as your matte. On the really nice cameras, those markings glow in the dark. Ooooh.

The ground glass is buried inside the camera body, so the viewfinder has a series of mirrors that bring the image of the ground glass out where you can see it. If the camera is on a tripod, the AC will add an extension to the viewfinder, bringing it to the back of the camera, where it is more easily used. If the camera is handheld, that extension is removed so the operator can nestle his head right up against the camera.

If you happen to be looking through the viewfinder when the camera is rolling, make sure that you keep your eye tightly pressed against the **eye cup**, that rubber fitting that cuddles up against your eye socket. If you pull away, you may allow light to seep back down the viewfinder and land on the film, causing fogging. Uh-oh. Reshoot.

The Video Assist

Used to be, the only person who got to see what the camera was seeing was the camera operator. Everyone else had to wait for the dailies. No longer. In modern cameras, the viewfinder contains a place to attach a tiny video camera that looks down at the ground glass and transmits that image to a monitor. This has become an essential aid in the modern film business. There is a danger inherent in it, however: Because the image is split off from the viewfinder, the quality is suspect and colors tend to look a little weird. Besides, it's video, not film. If you are looking over the DP's shoulder, don't judge the quality of the cinematography by what you see on the monitor. Video assists should only be used to check composition and watch the performance of the actors. For this reason, many directors like to work with a black-and-white monitor, so they don't get distracted by the strange colors.

By the way, did you know that the video assist was invented by Jerry Lewis? Yup, *that* Jerry Lewis.

Chapter 6:

THE CELLULOID CANVAS: THE FILM

Obviously, we have to fill the camera up with something. So what about the film?

Choosing a film stock is one of the most critical decisions that the DP will make. Each type of film has its own peculiarities, its own personality. Each one responds to light in a different way, with more or less contrast, density, color, graininess, and a host of other variables. There are different film stocks for each use and each taste.

Generally, a film or TV show will pick a stock and stick to it throughout the shoot to maintain continuity. On occasion, a DP will mix up film stocks for effect, as Janusz Kaminski did in the opening sequence of *Saving Private Ryan*, where he mixed up different film stocks, lenses, and shutter angles to give it a more patchwork feel, as if it were shot by a hodgepodge of different combat photographers. This is the exception, however. Much as lighting designers or painters develop favorite colors over their careers, so do DPs develop relationships with particular film stocks.

Of course, before filming begins, the DP will run a series of film tests to make sure that the stock lives up to his expectations. These tests are shared with the director, who also has input into which stock should be used for the film.

Choosing a film stock ultimately requires asking eight questions:

1. **What format are we releasing in?** What size film do you want? In most cases, we shoot on 35mm if we are releasing on 35mm, but this isn't always true. Low-budget companies may shoot on 16mm and blow it up to 35mm, accepting the resulting loss of quality as the price of low-budget filming. Some companies who are preparing for the new HDTV format are shooting Super 16 because it matches the HDTV aspect ratio.

2. **Do we want to shoot negative or reversal film?** If this is a "one-off" project and we only want a single copy of the film, we may choose to shoot **reversal film**, which is a "positive" image and can be projected right out of the lab, like slides. Otherwise, we may shoot **negative film**, which must be printed to look right. Regardless of the number of prints, some DPs prefer reversal for its high contrast and brilliant blues. Others feel that it is harder to expose properly. The issue is hotly contested.

3. **Color or Black-and-White?** Of course, most of the films and television that we see are in color, but black-and-white film offers a dramatic alternative. Black-and-white may or may not be cheaper to use, depending on how much you have to pay to process it.

4. **What type of light source do we have?** Films are color-balanced for various kinds of light sources, from incandescent light to tungsten light to daylight, so we need to pick a film stock that is appropriate to our lighting sources. We also must pick a film that is appropriate for the *amount* of light we have. The **exposure index** tells us how sensitive the film is to light. The higher the number, the less light we need to shoot. Of course, the trade-off comes in increased graininess. Films also have an **exposure latitude**, which tells us how wide a range of light levels it can take. A wide exposure latitude means it can see detail in brightly lit objects as well as those in shadow. A narrow latitude is less forgiving.

5. **Will we be using filters?** While we are figuring out the exposure needs, we must keep in mind the filters we are planning on using. Filtering cuts down on the available light, which might make a more sensitive film necessary.

6. **Where will we be processing the film?** Not all labs can handle all kinds of film. If you are shooting in the boonies, it helps to find out what kinds of facilities are available and what types of film they accept. Using a more common stock means more labs will be able to handle it.

7. **How much money do we have?** Faster films (with higher ASA numbers) require less lighting, but will look grainier. A lower ASA

means a finer grain, a smoother image, and more money for lighting.

8. **What do we want the film to look like?** The ultimate question, and the one that is hardest to answer. A good DP will be familiar with dozens of film stocks and what kind of an effect they create. Before shooting starts, however, it is essential that tests be run to see what kind of canvas you will be painting on. Every film stock is different.

Up until now, we have been talking about *camera film*—that is, the film that goes in the camera on the set. All of the above factors must be taken into account in choosing this film. Once you get to the lab, however, you are in the realm of *laboratory films*, which are used to create the intermediate steps, such as "interpositives" and "internegatives." Once your film is ready to be printed, yet another type of film is used: *print film*.

Industry people refer to each film stock by a four-number code, rather than by the manufacturer's name. So, for example, someone might ask you if you want to shoot on "5274" rather than "Kodak Vision 200T Color Negative Film." It's quicker, I suppose, although nontechnical people might appreciate knowing that you are talking about a color negative film with an ASA of 200. One hint about Kodak film: If the first number is a "5," the film is 35mm. If it is a "7," it is 16mm. (I didn't say it made sense.)

STORING FILM

Film breaks down over time, causing a decrease in sensitivity, changes in contrast, and increased fogging. The biggest killers are high heat and high humidity, which is why people tend to keep film in the refrigerator. According to Kodak, *raw stock* should be stored at a temperature of 55° F (13° C) if you are going to use it in the next six months. If you want to keep it longer than that, it should be stored at 0° to −10° F (−18° to −23° C). When you are getting ready to use the film, take it out of the fridge and let it warm up to room temperature before you try to open the can. This prevents condensation and keeps the film from shifting around as it warms up and expands.

If you happen to be traveling with raw or unprocessed film stock, *do not* let the airlines X-ray it. Some X-ray machines will fog unprocessed film. Label the packages clearly as unprocessed film and be prepared for a more intense screening process.

Once the film has been exposed, it becomes even more sensitive, so get it processed right away.

Chapter 7

VIDEO CAMERAS: THE FASTEST CHANGE IN THE INDUSTRY

Video is the fastest changing area of show business for one reason: The average American watches over three hours of television every day. This kind of viewership fills the video industry with the need for constant innovation. As a matter of fact, this very chapter is in danger of being out of date from the day I write it. Still, there are a great many common factors in most video cameras, so a basic discussion has a shot at remaining relevant.

Video cameras are divided into three groups: consumer, prosumer, and professional. Consumer cameras are great for vacations and parties. Prosumer cameras are used by tech-savvy consumers, semi-pro videographers, and professionals on a budget. Professional gear serves TV stations and production companies.

Modern video cameras capture the image with a small piece of silicon called a "Charge Coupled Device," or **CCD**. The CCD has been manufactured with thousands of tiny, light-sensitive areas, called photosites. Each one of these areas forms a part of the image—a "picture element," or *pixel*. Video formats are laid out in a grid that is unique to that format. Most cameras have grids that are a few hundred pixels on each side (e.g., 300 × 500 or 640 × 780), creating thousands of pixels. Each photosite responds to light by sending out a stream of electrons— just like a solar cell. In fact, you can think of a CCD as a tiny array of microscopic solar cells. In a "single-chip" camera, each CCD has three sets of pixels, covered by red, green, or blue filters.[13] This means that

---

[13] Trivia time: There are actually more green filters than red or blue. That's because the human eye is less sensitive to green than the other colors. A CCD chip actually has as many green pixels as red and blue pixels combined.

less information will be gathered about the image, as each section of the grid work is only able to sense one color. In the more expensive "three-chip" cameras, there is actually a CCD for each color, thereby filling in the image more completely.

One of the reasons why video has a lower resolution than film is that the CCD sensors are smaller than a piece of film stock. A typical frame of 35mm film measures 24mm × 36mm. A typical CCD sensor measures just over 4mm × 6mm, giving it less than three percent of the surface area. Less surface area means less information about the image, which means lower resolution.

The electrons sent out by the photosites are compiled and interpreted by an onboard computer, which stores the image on magnetic tape.

So, now that you know what's going on inside that camera, let's pick one out. In choosing a camera, there are a few basic questions to consider:

CAMERA OR CAMCORDER

If you are shooting with a single camera, you will want to choose a camera that also contains a videotape recorder: a *camcorder*. Camcorders are available in every format, from lowly VHS through Beta and DigiBeta to exotic high-end formats like D-9. These cameras can be powered by an extension cord plugged into the wall, but for most applications, they will run off batteries.

For a multicamera shoot, whether in a permanent studio or a mobile event, you want a nonrecording camera. In a TV studio, the individual cameras don't record what they shoot. The cameras feed their video signal to a *switcher*, run by a technician. That technician, under the direction of the director, picks what shot will be displayed from moment to moment. A three-camera shoot is standard for smaller shoots like newscasts and soap operas. For large-scale events, there may be more. The 2000 Super Bowl had thirty-four cameras (plugged into the central console with 83,000 feet of cable), not counting the cameras in the pre- and post-show sets or the thirty cameras that recorded the "Eyevision" 3-D images.

FORMAT

Naturally, every video format has its own style of camcorder. If you are in a studio setup, you can use any kind of camera, and the format choice boils down to what kind of videotape recorder you want to record the footage on. These days, the consumer video market has settled (for the moment) on Digital Video shot on miniDV cassettes. The prosumer market has also gone digital, using miniDV or DVCam cassettes. Professional cameramen are mostly shooting BetaSP. The choice of format is primarily a financial one, with better formats costing more money, but it also depends on where you want to edit. If you are planning to upload the footage into your Mac, miniDV will be easier to deal with. If, however, you are taking your footage into a professional edit suite, they will be much happier if it shows up on BetaSP, because they will have the right deck to play your footage into their computer.

CHIPS

As I said above, cameras and camcorders come in single-chip and three-chip versions. Single chip cameras have to do a lot of digital guessing to fill in the image, so three-chip cameras will give a sharper image (while costing more).

LENS

The major difference between a cheap camera and an expensive one is the lens. More expensive is better. Every time we go to Sears, my dad points out that you can buy a lawn mower for any number of hundreds you want: $100, $200, $300, and so on, right up to $3,000 or more. Spend more money, get more features and better quality.

Video camcorders work approximately the same way. An inexpensive consumer camcorder can be had for $300 and every hundred dollars above that. The major difference between these cameras is the lenses. More money gets you a sharper lens (with a better zoom). This is really true in any kind of photography or videography. More money gets you better glass, better optics, and more finely machined parts. Of course, there are other factors that determine price: special features, better controls, and so forth, but the lens is the key.

Zoom

Unlike film cameras, all video cameras have zoom lenses. Zooming changes the lens from a wide-angle lens to a telephoto and back again. Lenses are rated by how much they zoom. The amount of zoom is expressed in a ratio: a 12:1 zoom has a wide image that covers twelve times as much area as the close-up. A 16:1 zoom lens has an even greater difference between the large and small image. In general, a larger ratio is better because it gives you more flexibility. You can pull out further or push in further. High quality cameras will have a variable zoom speed, usually controlled by how hard or soft you hit the zoom button. Cheaper cameras will only zoom at one speed and will jar to a halt when you stop zooming. Pricier ones glide to a stop.

White Balance

As we discussed in the lighting chapter, all light has a basic color temperature—a fundamental warmth or coolness, depending on the light source. Interior lights are warmer (meaning more orange) than sunlight (which is more blue). Many cameras let you set the color temperature by allowing you to define what is "white." Cheaper cameras will guess for you, mostly causing your interior scenes to look more yellow than your backyard ones. Pricier cameras will allow you to set the white balance yourself, generally by pointing the camera at something white and pushing the "white balance" button. At that point, the camera knows what "white" is and adjusts accordingly.

Focus

Most camcorders have a setting that allows the camera to *autofocus*— that is, to determine the point of focus for itself. This setting works quite well in some situations, not as well in others. The camera focuses itself by searching for solid lines in the image and then rotating the focus wheel until that line gets as sharp as possible. Consequently, an image that is full of fuzzy lines will drive the camera insane. It also will latch on to closer objects at the expense of those further away. That's why you lose your focus on the soccer game when Uncle Ed steps in front of the camera.

Autofocus also eats up batteries, with the constant movement of the motor on the focus wheel. For these two reasons, it is sometimes better to turn the darn thing off. Good cameras will have an "instant focus" button that you can push to engage the autofocus for a few seconds. Once your image is sharp, you can let go of the button and save your batteries.

Iris and Shutter

The video camera controls how much light hits the tape the same way that a film camera does, by adjusting the size of an iris in the lens. This is another area the camera can handle automatically. By constantly sensing the amount of light coming through the lens, the camera adjusts the iris to keep the light at a proper level. This is a good control to leave on, because small changes in lighting level are difficult for the eye to see and respond to quickly. Most consumer-level cameras won't let you change it, even if you want to.

A video image is refreshed sixty times a second, no matter what. This doesn't mean, however, that you can't control the shutter speed. In typical usage, the shutter speed is 1/60 of a second; basically, the shutter closes for only a tiny fraction of a second. If you want to let in less light, however, you can set that shutter speed higher. It will still open every 1/60 of a second; it just won't stay open the whole 1/60 of a second. For example, if you set the shutter speed to 1/120, the shutter will open for 1/120 of a second sixty times per second, leaving the CCDs in the dark the rest of the time. DPs use faster shutter speeds to eliminate blur from moving images and sharpen the image. This can be good or bad, depending on what you are shooting. A sharper image without any blur can be a little disorienting to watch. Blur helps your eye to string the frames of video together. Most of the time, nonstandard shutter speeds are used as a special effect.

AUDIO

Digital camcorders record audio at a quality level comparable to a CD. Consumer (and some prosumer) camcorders have built-in microphones.

Better-quality cameras have a miniplug (like the one on your Walkman headphones) or XLR plug (like the one on your professional microphone) for a separate microphone. These separate microphones generally come in four varieties: *omni*, *lavalier*, *stereo*, or *shotgun*.

Omni mics are found on lower-level consumer cameras. Omni means that they pick up in every direction, including behind the camera. This is great for vacation videos, where you want to shoot and narrate at the same time (also good for protestors videotaping police brutality!), but not so good for pro video, where you don't want to record the cameraman grunting under the weight of the camera.

Lavalier mics are the pencil eraser–sized mics you see on the lapels of newspeople. News crews, reality shows, and upscale wedding videos will tend to use wireless lavs, meaning that the lav mic is connected to a radio transmitter beltpack. That beltpack transmits to a receiver attached to the cameraman (sometimes on top of the camera itself). The receiver, in turn, is plugged into the audio input.

Prosumer cameras will come equipped with a stereo mic attached to the camera. Because it is stereo, it actually records left and right signals, which, when played back, do give a tolerably decent impression of what your ears would have heard, had they been there.

Shotgun mics are designed to pick up sound from far away, without picking up sound to the sides. They are used for **ENG**[14] and sports, among other things. They are not built into cameras—they are mounted separately and plugged into that auxiliary input.

IMAGE STABILIZATION

It is quite a trick to hold a camera steady. It is still the mark of a practiced and professional videographer. However, the little gnomes who design electronic circuitry have given us some help over the years, by designing electronic *image stabilizers* into video cameras. The image stabilizer works by comparing each frame of video with the previous one. If the new one is slightly shifted to one side, indicating that the camera was jiggled a little, the computer corrects the image and shoves

---

[14] Electronic News Gathering: what mobile news crews do.

it back where it was supposed to be. Actually, it's a much more complicated process than that description implies, but let's just leave it at this: A good image stabilizer will smooth out the motion of the camera, making you look like the professional photographer you (or I) may never be.

OUTPUTS

Once you get the image into the camera, you will most likely want to get it out again. When choosing a camera, make sure you get one that has the outputs that you need.

The most basic outputs are RCA plugs for video and audio. RCA plugs are like the ones on the back of your tape deck or CD player. There should be a yellow one for video and a red or white one (both, if your camera is stereo) for audio.

In addition to these, your camera may have an output called *S-video*. This is a slightly higher quality output that can be used if you have a VCR or television that has an S-video plug. Video information is divided into two pieces: chroma (what color it is) and luminance (how bright it is). In a standard video signal, known as *composite video*, these two pieces of information are combined and shoved down the same line, causing some loss in definition. In S-video, the chroma and luminance are separated out and sent on different wires, helping to maintain their quality. While we're on the subject, *component video*, known as RGB video, separates the red, blue, and green signals out onto separate wires. This is what computer monitors use, and that's why you can't view your computer output on a TV screen (or vice versa) without an adaptor.

Professional cameras will have a different type of connector for the video signal than the one on consumer and prosumer cameras. The *BNC connector* is the professional standard for audio and video connections. It is a round, locking plug that makes a solid connection between components.

If you are going to send your video into a computer, you might consider getting a camera with a *Firewire* port. Firewire is a standard invented by Apple Computer as a way to move digital video from cameras to computers. It is the method of choice for digital video in consumer and prosumer equipment.

Chapter 8

SUPPORTING THE CAMERA: TRIPODS, DOLLIES, AND CAMERA MOUNTS

Shooting film and video with a handheld camera did wonders for *The Blair Witch Project,* but it also sent a lot of filmgoers to the rest rooms to clear out their stomachs. Generally, the crew will want to use something else to hold up the camera.

TRIPODS

Ever since people stopped painting on the walls of caves and started needing a place to put the canvas, the **tripod** has been a part of the creative process. Tripods, or **sticks**, as they are called on the set, provide a flexible, level, sturdy place to set your expensive camera.

Let's break the tripod down into its component parts.

The Head

This is the part that actually latches on to the camera. There are three different species—the friction, fluid, and geared heads.

Friction heads are the cheapest and least smooth. Because the head stays in place by friction, you have to push it a little harder to get it to move (to overcome the "stiction"—that is, the tendency for two pieces of metal to want to stick together). This little shove creates a jiggle in the image and, as such, makes the friction head useful only for quick, insensitive movements or a shot that doesn't move at all (known as a "lock-off"). An example of the latter is a time-lapse shot where it is not only desirable, but essential, that the camera not move at all.

Fluid heads are the most common head for film and TV cameras. The two moving surfaces are separated by a thin layer of silicone liquid

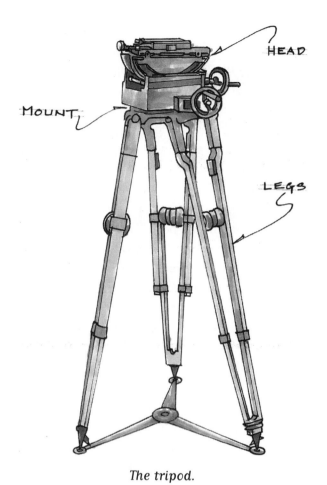

MOUNT

HEAD

LEGS

The tripod.

that overcomes the stiction and allows them to move freely. If you want to know what I'm talking about, spread a small amount of cooking oil on a countertop (ask Mom first), and place a glass on top of it. Push it gently from side to side, and you can approximate what a fluid-head tripod feels like.

Large studio cameras are generally too bulky and heavy to control with a fluid head, so they use the ***geared head***. This head has two large wheels that control the side-to-side movement and the up-and-down movement. The operator moves the camera by spinning these two wheels. It's a bit like patting your head and rubbing your stomach, but the experienced operators can stick a pencil on the top of the lens and write your name on a card using the geared head. They're probably flirting with you if they do, though, so watch it.

Head Mounting

The mounting plate that attaches the head to the legs comes in two varieties—the *Arriflex mount*, used for lightweight cameras, and the *Mitchell mount*, used for everything else. You can recognize the Arriflex by the bowl-shaped mount at the top with the knob sticking out the bottom. The camera is leveled by loosening that bolt and rocking the camera around in that bowl until it is level. Most high-quality tripods have a bubble level built in so you don't have to guess.

The Mitchell mount is much more solid and can handle a lot more weight. A geared head will always sit on a Mitchell mount.

One other exotic mount that bears mentioning is the *gimbal mount*, familiar to anyone who has ever been in a galley on a ship. This is a mount that stays static while the tripod moves around it. If you have ever been in a galley on a small boat, you may have seen stoves with gimbals. They do the same thing for stoves that they do for cameras—keep them level on a surface that is pitching from side to side.

Legs

Originally, the legs were made of hardwood (some of the old ones are beautiful collector's items), but today, stainless steel, aluminum, and titanium have taken over. Tripod legs are in two or three sections to allow you to adjust the height or level the tripod on uneven ground. The bottom of the leg has a spike to dig into the ground plus a little foot that allows the leg to be attached to spreaders (see below).

Tripods come in various heights, each of which has its own special name, but standardization has not yet come to this area. Thus, you will hear crews calling for short, baby, medium, standard, sawed-off, and any number of other sizes of tripods.

If a tripod with *no* legs is needed, the crew will bring out a *hi-hat*—essentially, a tripod head mounted to a flat plate. This might be used if the shot is close to floor level or, paradoxically, if the shot is very high and the camera is going to be mounted on a lighting stand.

If the shot is actually *on* the floor, a *lowboy* is used. A lowboy is a very low hi-hat, the functional equivalent of having no tripod at all.

Spreaders

Funny thing, but some people object to the pointed feet of a tripod digging into their hardwood floors. When shooting indoors, the crew will add a three-pronged *spreader* to the tripod to tie the legs together and protect the floor. The arms of the spreader can be shortened or lengthened to adjust the height of the tripod.

DOLLIES

A *dolly* is a camera platform on wheels, sometimes mounted on a track, that allows the camera to be moved smoothly during the shot. While budget filmmakers are famous for using a wheelchair, professional dollies and the track they ride on are precision machines, carefully built to remove jitters, shakes, and bumps from the movement of the camera. After the camera, the dolly is probably the most expensive item on the set and should be treated with respect.

Whereas the tripod used to be the standard camera platform and the dolly was brought in on special occasions, nowadays it seems those roles are reversed. If there is enough room on the set, the crew will mount the camera on a dolly even if the shot is static. It is easier to adjust the position of the camera between setups if it is on wheels.

Dollies fall into two animalistic categories: crab and spyder.[15] The *crab dolly* is so named because, in addition to driving forward and backward, it can drive sideways like a crab. If anyone ever lets you drive the dolly, look for a control that switches the dolly between regular driving mode, where one set of wheels stays straight while the other set turns, and crab mode, where all the wheels turn in the same direction at once, allowing the dolly to move in any direction while keeping the camera pointed the same way. The other control you should know on the dolly is the height adjustment. It is a circular knob that controls the hydraulic lift arm. Clockwise is down. Counterclockwise is up. Remember lefty-loosy, righty-tighty? Once you've got that one down, you're set. Just remember, tighten *down*, and loosen *up*.

Just to make life confusing, the *spyder dolly* can also move like a crab, but it has another trick as well. The legs on a spyder dolly can be twisted into a number of different configurations, depending on whether you want the dolly to be very narrow (to fit through a doorway), very wide (to be very stable), or in strange shapes to fit in corners or move over uneven ground.

---

[15] This is not a typo.

A dolly mounted on track.

In general, most crews will call for a crab dolly, with its greater stability. If you are scouting a location for a shoot, make sure you measure the width of any doorway through which a dolly must pass. It is not a good idea to turn a dolly on its side, as you might end up with a floor full of hydraulic fluid.

Dollies are extremely heavy, for good reason. This weight is what gives the dolly its stability. It does mean, however, that allowance must be made to move the darn thing on and off the set and the track. It takes four burly people to pick it up and put it on the tracks. Don't plan on moving one up a flight of stairs. Find a location with an elevator. Use a lift gate to get it off the truck. If you are loading out late at night, take special care that tired technicians don't try to rush moving the dolly. Dropping a dolly is bad. Dropping a dolly on a human is a trip to the emergency room.

Laying dolly track is a bit of an art. Any bump or low spot in the track means a ruined shot, so the key grip will run a level along the track, before the dolly goes on, looking for uneven spots. The track should come with a crate full of wooden wedges that are used to level the track. When the grip finds a low spot, he shoves a wedge under that part of the track to level it up. I said it was art, not high tech. Crews will often carry a spray bottle of Pledge or silicon spray to make the track slippery as well.

CRANES AND JIBS

Sometimes a director needs to get the camera up in the air. He may need to look at a scene from above, peer into a second-story window, or follow a flying superhero. There are a number of devices that do this while keeping the camera attached to the ground (as opposed to putting it in a helicopter). All of these devices fall roughly into two categories: *cranes* and *jibs*. In general, a crane is something that takes the camera up in the air along with the operator, while a jib arm picks up the camera but leaves the operator on the ground. Cranes have existed for years, while jib arms are more recent, brought to life with the adoption of video assists that allow an operator to look through the camera via a remote monitor. Both jib arms and cranes are human powered. Electric and hydraulic systems simply cannot produce the smooth starts and stops required by a camera. Even the smallest bump at the beginning or

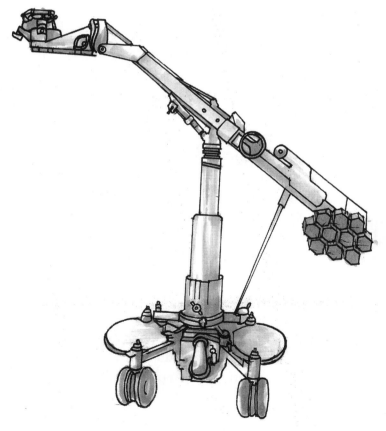

A crane.

end of the movement will ruin the shot, so this is one of those blessed places where human capability still outstrips technology.

Both cranes and jibs are counterweighted, so they must be loaded and unloaded carefully. If a large crane comes down to the ground and one person jumps off without first having the counterweight on the other end adjusted, the effect is not unlike a slingshot. The other person (and the expensive camera) can get flung up in the air like David's rock on the way to Goliath's head.

FLOATING CAMERA SYSTEMS

There are five inventions that have defined the film industry and radically changed how films are designed and shot: the film camera itself (1896), sound for film (late 1920s), widescreen film and projectors (early 1950s), blue-screen compositing (late 1960s), and, in the early 1970s, the floating camera system.

The first floating camera system to become popular was the Steadicam, built by Cinema Products, and because of its firstest-with-the-mostest status, it has become a "kleenex" word—that is, a brand name used as an all-encompassing term for a product, to the dismay of other manufacturers. There are other floating-camera systems—the Panavision Panaglide, for example—but you will generally hear any floating camera system referred to as a Steadicam.

Invented by Garrett Brown (who won an Oscar for it), the Steadicam addressed a bumpy problem in filmmaking. Sometimes, a director wants to follow an actor into places where a dolly (and its associated track) cannot go. He may want to climb stairs, turn tight corners, or run along the dirt paths of Central Park, as John Schlesinger did in *Marathon Man*, the first full-length feature film to put the Steadicam through its paces.

The Steadicam makes use of two innovative concepts. First of all, it changes how the camera is attached to the operator. Handheld cameras were generally perched on the operator's shoulders so he could keep his head next to the camera body and look through the viewfinder. Problem is, your shoulders bounce up and down as you walk (let alone run), so the camera bounces up and down, as well. Brown attached the camera to his hips (which tend to remain level

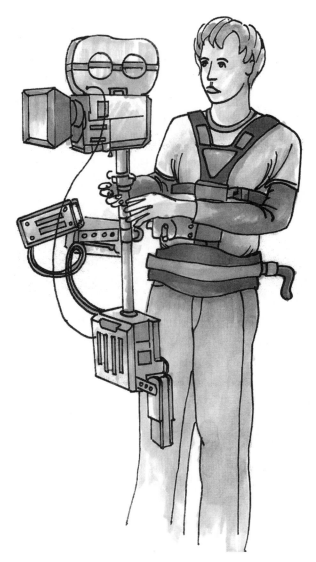

A floating camera system (Steadicam).

as you walk) via a brilliant, shock-absorbing arm. He attached the viewfinder to a video screen mounted on the arm so he could see the shot as well as where he was walking.

The second innovation was something every martial artist can understand. If you want to increase stability, lower the center of gravity. Try this experiment: Get a full glass of water and set it on your outstretched palm. Now, run through the house. Now, get a paper towel and clean up the mess. It's tough, isn't it? Yet this is exactly what we do when we try to move quickly with the camera perched on our shoulders. Keeping the weight up high makes it hard to stabilize. Now, refill the glass and try it again, this time holding the glass by the rim, thereby putting the weight of the glass below your hand. Easier, right? The Steadicam trades on this concept by hanging weight off the bottom of the camera, thereby lowering the center of gravity and making the camera more stable.

For low-to-the-ground shots, the rig can be inverted, with the camera hanging down and the weight on top. The high-speed flying motorcycle chase in *Return of the Jedi* was shot this way, walking through the redwoods of northern California with an inverted floating camera.

Remember, though, the Panaglide and the Steadicam are not cameras—they are ways of supporting cameras. Think of them as tripods for handheld shots. Properly balanced, they can support any video, 16mm, or 35mm camera.

A floating camera shot requires a trained operator—you can't go down to the camera store and rent one. Steadicam operators own their own (rather pricey) rigs, so you generally hire the man and the equipment as a package deal.[16] Operating a Steadicam is physically demanding, as well. Like rock 'n' roll drummers, Steadicam operators tend to get pretty muscular practicing their craft. Plan on building some time into the schedule for the operator to rest between shots. Also, build in some time for the operator to set up his rig. Every camera is different, and the Steadicam must be carefully balanced whenever a new camera is put on it.

CAMERAS ON VEHICLES

When it is time to go mobile, Hollywood has a fleet of vehicles and numerous camera mounts to take the camera along. An *insert* car is the optimum choice when you want to film a car through the front windshield. This is a specially designed vehicle that can carry not only the camera mounted on the outside, but additional lighting, as well. The insert car (it is more like a pickup truck, actually) has speed-rail bars attached all

---

[16] Steadicam does make smaller versions that you can rent or buy. These are for consumer and prosumer video cameras.

around it, with small platforms where the crew can sit. It is used to lead or follow the *picture car*, the vehicle that will actually appear in the shot. Insert cars often carry a generator for the additional lighting, and the really nice ones even have a steering wheel on both sides, depending on where the driver needs to be to get the best view. The best setup is for the insert car to tow the picture car, so the actor doesn't have to think about driving. Otherwise, a lot of his brain space is devoted to keeping the car in exactly the right spot. It is better to let the crew person in the insert car do the driving and let the actor do the acting.

If you don't have access to an insert car, you can attach tracking platforms to another vehicle. The best setup is a frame of tubes that provide a safety rail as well as a place to attach the camera. Beware, however, that this can be a recipe for disaster if there is not good communication between the driver and the cameraman. One low bridge and that, ladies and gentlemen, is that.

Cameras can also be attached to the outside of the picture car, using *limpet mounts*: powerful suction cups with a camera mount attached. These can usually be installed with no alteration or damage to the car.

These kinds of mounts are used for the "over-the-shoulder" shots when two people are having a conversation in a car. The camera is attached to the outside of the door and focused across the car at the actor on the other side. You play the scene with the camera attached to one door, then move it to the other side and play the scene again. Edit the two shots together, and presto! You've shot a conversation in a car.

When *The Streets of San Francisco* was filming in its namesake city, the crew would use limpet mounts to attach a camera to the outside of the police car. Karl Malden and Michael Douglas would climb in, the camera would be started, the actors would wave good-bye, and off they would go, driving around the city, playing their scene by themselves until the film ran out. The soundman rode in the trunk.

For helicopter shots, there are three ways to go. One is to mount the camera on a counterweighted arm and shoot through the open door on the side of the helicopter. The heavy arm dampens out the pitching and rolling movement of the helicopter. The second way is to attach the camera to the bottom of the helicopter, pointing forward, essentially making the pilot the camera operator. This works for forward-looking, "point-of-view" shots.

The third way is with specially equipped helicopters that have a glass dome on the bottom that the camera can shoot through. This is the best and, naturally, most expensive option. Some private jets have glass nose cones with a camera mount inside so you can shoot other aircraft air-to-air, *Top Gun*–style.

Chapter 9:

STINGERS AND DOUBLES AND HEADS, OH MY!— LIGHTING EQUIPMENT

Somewhere back in the Stone Age of movie lighting, somebody had a sense of humor. Somebody decided that film work was too backbreaking, too frustrating, and too boring for us to just sit around and suffer. Some joker knew the fundamental truth about life in general and show business in particular: To wit, if you're not having fun, why bother?

I am absolutely convinced of the existence of this person. Why else would film and TV lighting be so chock-full of goofy terms that could only have come from a giddy, late-night gigglefest perpetrated by some joke-cracking minister of mirth?

Where else do you find a light called a "betweenie?" How about a lighting effect called a "Cuculoris?" (That's "cookie", for short.) Why else would we plug "stingers" into "putt-putts" while the rest of the world plugs extension cords into generators?

I don't know who he was; all I know is he created a wealth of goofy names that persevere despite the onrush of acronym-laden technology and degree-carrying engineers. And I love him for it.

Some people say that the plethora of strange names for movie equipment is a way of keeping new people at a distance, like having a secret code, and there may be truth in that. But I choose to believe that moviemaking can and should be fun, so heat up that stinger, strike the heads, and let's look at lighting equipment.

Lights are nothing without electricity, so let's look at some basic electrical concepts, first. Then, we'll look at the power commute from the power station to your lights. Finally, we'll talk about the lights themselves, the stands that hold them up, and the grip equipment that keeps everything under control.

POWER

What is electricity?

Okay, an analogy: When I lived in Seattle, we used to go down to the fish market where all the tourists hang out and buy fresh fish. The shops had these long tanks full of fish and, whenever somebody wanted one, the sales guy would reach in with his bare hands, yank one out, and toss it over the heads of some surprised tourists right into the hands of another guy by the cash register, who would wrap it and sell it, singing in Sicilian the whole time. It was pretty impressive, but even more impressive when you consider that this is how electricity works. Imagine a long tank full of fish. I mean, really full. Imagine a tank so full that you could not put one more fish into it. Absolutely jammed. Now, imagine the sales guy down at one end reaches in and pulls one fish out. With one fish removed, there is room for another fish. Now, imagine there is a fisherman who pulls up to the other end of the tank with his catch of the day. He sees that there is room for one more fish in the tank, so he dumps a fresh one in. However, he does not stop there. He keeps trying to force more fish into the tank. No matter how hard he pushes, though, he will not be able to get another fish into the tank until the sales guy down at the other end pulls one out. The fisherman keeps trying, though, and every time the sales guy pulls a fish out, the fisherman succeeds in getting a new one in. Sometimes, the fisherman pushes so hard that, when the sales guy reaches into the tank, he comes up with not one fish but two, or three. In fact, if the fisherman pushes really, really hard, the sales guy might be overwhelmed by fish when he reaches into the tank.

This is electricity.

Confused? Of course! Okay, the fish are electrons, and they are swimming around inside the fish tank, which is a cable. The fisherman is the source of the electricity, which means that he is the power company. The sales guy is the *load*—the thing that is using the electricity. He could be a stereo, a toaster, a clothes dryer, or a light on your set. It does not matter. A load is a load. The load (the sales guy) is pulling electrons out of the cable. He is using electricity. (The guy at the cash register singing in Sicilian does not figure into this analogy. I only put him in for local color.)

This analogy breaks down in one place. Power requires a round-trip ticket—a circuit. There must be a complete path from the power source to the load and back again to make a circuit, and there must not be any breaks along the way. If the circuit is broken at any point, no power will flow, no matter how hard the fisherman pushes or the sales guy pulls. The simplest way to break a circuit is something we do every day—turning light switches off. Turning a switch off creates a physical break in the circuit and interrupts the flow of power. I could improve the analogy, I guess, by having the sales guy throw the fish back into the ocean for the fisherman to catch and bring back to the market, but let's not split hairs.

There are three terms we use to describe how the fish move through the tank, or how the electrons move through the cable. The *wattage* is how many fish (electrons) the sales guy (load) can pull out at a time, and it is a function of how big he is. All loads, whether they are lights or toasters, are rated in watts. A small load cannot pull out as many electrons as a big load. A 200-watt lamp cannot pull as many fish as a 500-watt lamp.

The *voltage* is how hard the fisherman (power company) is trying to push fish into the tank. Voltage describes how much pressure is being put on the electrons in the cable, and in turn, on the load. More volts mean more pressure. If the voltage is too high and the load is not strong enough to deal with it, it may be overwhelmed, as the sales guy could be overwhelmed by the fisherman pushing too hard. When this happens, the load may burn out. Any lamp will burn out sooner or later, but higher voltage shortens its working life. If the voltage goes really high, the load will burn out instantly.

Every load is designed to work with a particular voltage. In the United States, the power company is pushing around 115 fish—uh, volts—so lamps sold for use in this country are designed accordingly. In Europe, the power company is pushing around 220 volts, so the lamps must be built to handle more power. This is also why you have to take a voltage adapter with you when you travel with appliances that are made for use in the United States. The adapter sits between the power company and your hair dryer and takes some of the pressure off.

The third term describes how quickly the fish are moving through the tank. This is *amperage*. The cable (the tank) is rated by how many amps it can handle at one time. If the voltage goes up (the power source is pushing harder), so will the amperage. Likewise, if the wattage goes up (the load is pulling harder), that also forces the amperage up. No matter how far up the wattage goes, the power source will just keep throwing more electrons into the cable as fast as the load pulls them out. This can lead to an over-load situation, where the power company and the load are pushing and pulling so hard that the cable itself is in danger of being damaged. This can result in the cable breaking down, and it is a major cause of fires. That is one reason why we have *circuit breakers*. These devices monitor the flow of power and, if it gets too high, they shut down the system by breaking the circuit. Circuit breakers, like cables, are rated in amps.

These three terms—wattage, voltage, and amperage—are related to one another by a simple formula known as the "West Virginia" law. It says: Wattage equals Voltage times Amperage, or:

$$W = V * A$$

Let's try a few problems. Say you have some 100w lamps plugged into a circuit with a 15a circuit breaker (a common size in most hous-es). How many of the lamps can you plug into the circuit before the fuse blows? Fill in the formula (remember, the power company in the United States provides 115 volts):

$$W = V * A$$
$$W = 115v * 15a$$
$$W = 1,725$$

You can put 1,725 watts into the circuit, so you can plug in seventeen 100w lamps with a few watts to spare. The eighteenth one will trip the fuse.

How about trying it from the other direction? Say you have three 250w lamps and you want to know what size cable you need. First, add up the loads:

$$3 * 250w = 750w$$

Now, solve the formula for amps. (Come on . . . you did it in tenth grade):

$$W = V * A$$
$$W/V = A$$

Fill it in:

$$750w/115v = A$$

Do the math . . .

$$6.5217391304 = A$$

Yeesh! Save me from that kind of number. Of course, you can round off your answer to find you need a 7a cable, but you still have to carry a pocket calculator around to do the long division. (At least, I do.)

Or, you can do the whole problem an easier way.

You still have to use the West Virginia law, but with a slight change. If you are in the United States, just assume the power company is putting out 100 volts. It will make the numbers come out a little high, but that is okay, since it will make us a little more conservative. Look what substituting 100 volts does to the problem above:

$$750w/100v = A$$
$$7.15 = A$$

When you divide by one hundred, all you have to do is move the decimal two places to the left, and you are done. Now your answer says that you need a 7.5a cable, which is a little bigger than before, but we can call the difference a safety margin. So, we now know that, rather than bothering with the formula at all, we can just add up all of our loads and move the decimal place two spaces to the left to get our answer. Try it again. Let's say you have two 500w lamps and you want to know how big a cable you need:

Add up the loads:

$$2 * 500w = 1,000w$$

Now, move the decimal over two places to the left. Your answer is 10a. 1,000w equals 10a.

So, if you know how many watts you have, just move the decimal over two places and you will know how many amps you need. Likewise, if you know how many amps you have, just move the decimal two places to the *right* to find out how many watts you can plug in. You can also just say "hundred" after you say the amperage, i.e., if you have an 18a cable, you can plug in eighteen "hundred" watts.

Of course, like any kind of mathematical formula, this one gets much easier after you work with it for a little while.

Last one: Suppose you are shooting on location and your gaffer tells you that you have 30a available on the generator. Your electricians have lots of 500w instruments. Using the West Virginia rule, figure out how many lights you can plug into that generator. (The answer's at the bottom of the page.)*

Enough math! (Don't worry; it comes easy with a little practice.)

Whether you are shooting on a soundstage or on location, the availability of power is a major issue. Now that I've said that, let's take a quick tour through an average power system.

The power company generates electricity by using some kind of power (oil- or coal-powered engine, wind, falling water, etc.) to turn a very large magnet inside a coil of wires. The movement of this magnet pushes electrons out into the cable. Electrons moving through cable is what electricity is all about. In order to get these electrons to move long distances, the power plant sends them out into the world with a strong, high-voltage push, around 10,000 volts.

Those huge towers out in the countryside carry these high-voltage lines to a neighborhood power station, where they are converted to a lower voltage so they can travel down city streets, either overhead or underground. When they get to the electric pole (or the manhole) outside your house, they go through another transformation, down to the 115 volts that actually enter your house. If you live somewhere where the power lines are still on poles, look for a trash-can–sized container hanging off the electrical pole on your block. This is called a **step-down transformer**, because it steps the voltage down to a level that won't fry your toaster. Think of the whole process as a mighty river running in reverse: the power flows from the plant like a wide, powerful river that is then divided up into smaller tributaries. Finally, it is reduced to a small stream that can safely enter your home. Hooking up your house directly to a high-voltage line would be like trying to run the Mississippi River into your kitchen sink. (I don't recommend it.)

So, now the nice, tame 115 volt (still enough to kill you, remember) flows into your house through two wires, a "hot" line and a "neutral." When

---

* Using the simplified formula: W = 100 volts * 30 amps = 1,500 watts

the electrician opens your circuit-breaker panel, ask her to point out the hot wire coming from the outside. It will probably be black and attached to a large fuse. That large fuse is designed to blow if some huge electrical spike comes through the line, such as when a utility pole gets knocked down by a truck or struck by lightning.

The fuse, in turn, connects to a metal rod, known as a *bus*, that runs down into the circuit breakers. Each of the breakers locks onto the bus. On the other end of the breaker is a wire (again, usually black) that disappears into a conduit and goes out into the house, where it provides power to an outlet or a light fixture. The outlet (or light fixture) provides power to whatever you've got plugged into it (a toaster, a lightbulb), then takes that power back once it has done its job and sends it back to the panel on the white, or neutral, wire. Those neutral wires are collected together on another bus in the circuit-breaker panel. That bus is attached to a wire that heads back out of the house, taking the electrons back from whence they came.

So, this is the power commute: out of the power company at high voltage, through a series of step-down transformers to the hot line in your circuit-breaker panel, through a big fuse and a smaller circuit breaker, through a conduit to a light fixture or outlet, through some kind of load (a lightbulb, a toaster), back to the outlet, onto a neutral wire leading back to the panel, and then, off through a conduit back to the power company.[17]

One of the reasons why soundstage shooting is easier than location shooting is that soundstages have big, fat power lines running into them that are designed to run large numbers of power-sucking movie lights. Having enough power is rarely a problem. In fact, many large movie studios generate their own power for their sets, taking power from the electric company only for their offices.

Shooting on location is another story entirely. Even a small-scale shoot will put a significant drain on an average home or business power supply. A small lighting kit, the sort that might be used for a video

---

[17] Purists will note that the neutral line does not, in fact, go back to the power company—it goes off to a metal post that is driven into the ground somewhere—but I find it most useful to think about power making a complete round-trip to and from the electric company.

interview, can be plugged into the wall, but you must take care not to overload the circuits. The average household circuit is 15 amps (quick, how many watts is that?),[18] so don't plug more than that into any one outlet.

Furthermore, most household and business circuits control more than one outlet, so you can't plug more than 15 amps into all of the outlets combined.

There are two ways to find out how many outlets there are on each circuit. The first is to find the circuit panel and read the labels. If the box has been labeled correctly, it should say things like "din. rm. recep.," which means that breaker controls all of the receptacle (outlets) in the dining room. All of the outlets in that room are controlled by a single 15-amp breaker. In other words, it will not matter if you plug your three lights into one outlet or plug one light into each of three outlets. All of the power in the dining room will pass through one breaker and, if you plug in more than 15 amps, that breaker will trip. By now, you have done the math problem I gave you above (or read the footnote), so you know that you can plug in 1,725 watts (1,500 if you did the simplified 100-volt version). Ergo, if you plug in two 1,000-watt lights into the dining room outlets, the determined little circuit breaker is going to show you who's boss. Click. Darkness. Before you get annoyed, however, remember: That little circuit breaker is trying to save you from yourself and cut off the power before the overload melts a wire and starts a fire.

It ain't rocket science—2,000 watts is more than 1,725. You will need to use smaller lights or, if you really need all 2,000 watts, find a second circuit somewhere else to plug into.

The second way to gather information about the circuits is to just plug the two 1,000-watt lights in and see what happens. If the breaker trips, you can't do that. This caveman electrician method does work, but I don't recommend it unless you have no other information. For one thing, it opens up some dangerous territory. If the breaker doesn't work properly, you might create a dangerous overload.

---

[18] Remembering the West Virginia law, where Watts = Volts x Amps, multiply 115 volts by 15 amps and you will get 1,725 watts. If you use the simplified 100-volt equation, the answer is 1,500 watts.

Most of the time, when you are working with household circuits, the process involves a little bit of both modern and caveman techniques. I have never seen a circuit panel that was 100 percent correctly labeled, but they usually give you enough information to keep you from tripping too many breakers. Repeatedly tripping a breaker can weaken it over time, but tripping it once or twice is no big deal. The good news is, if a breaker finally gives up the ghost and fails altogether, it almost always fails in the "off" position, which means no power and no melting wires.

If you do trip a breaker, take a deep breath. Relax. It's just a breaker. Make sure that your lights are turned off, go to the panel, find the offending breaker (the switch will be in a different position from all the others), turn it all the way off, then turn it on again. Split the lights up into different outlets and try it again. Sometimes, you will have to plug in and turn on lights one at a time, looking for the one that breaks the camel's back. If your overload is slight—that is, if the amount of juice you are pulling from the wall isn't very much over 15 amps—the breaker might not trip right away. It may take a minute for it to heat up enough to go off.

If you plug in a single light and the breaker trips immediately, your problem is not an overload; it is a short circuit—that is, a light with bad wiring. Give that light to a trained electrician and press on forward with another one. Relax, you're in show business.

For larger setups (like lighting a whole room or several rooms), the electrician may need to open up the circuit panel and tie into the **mains**, the large power cables that come directly from the power company. This is dangerous territory, so I will print the following in all caps: DO NOT OPEN A CIRCUIT PANEL YOURSELF. Get a qualified electrician to do this work (known as a **tie-in**) for you. There is more than enough power in there to kill you stone dead. If you are going to tie into the mains, however, and you have a helpful electrician to do the job, it can be instructive to look over her shoulder and ask a few questions before she starts. DO NOT talk to the electrician while she is making the tie-in. In fact, no one should talk to the electrician while she is moving high-voltage cables around. Film crews are (quite rightly) strict about this. No one wants to see an ambulance arriving on set because someone distracted the electrician during tie-in. Some crews will station another person alongside the electrician. Along with keeping the onlookers away, that person sometimes holds a broomstick or a long board. If the electrician does happen to slip and touch the wrong wire, the surge of power flowing through her body will "freeze" her and prevent her pulling away. In this (highly unusual) situation, the helper can use the nonconducting wooden board to pry the poor soul loose and, perhaps, save her life.

So, if your power needs are small—i.e., no individual lights over 15 amps and no more circuits than you have available in your home or office—then you can plug into the existing circuits and be okay.

If your needs are larger (and they often are), you must either tie into the mains or bring in another power source, a generator. Remember, you are not just powering the lights. You might also need power for the camera, the monitor, the dolly, makeup lights, hot plates and coffeepots for catering, and who knows what else. Power requirements can get really big really fast, and I have rarely been on a set where people were saying, "Jeez, we've got *way* more power than we need."

An average household power panel can provide around 200 amps, which is just fine for a small film or video shoot. A small business may have a little more. Power is not cheap, though, so remember to budget money to reimburse the home or business owner for the power that you use.

Sometimes, 200 amps may not be enough. Or, the mains may be unreliable or unavailable. Some homeowners may not want you mucking around with their power. Or, you may be shooting outside with no power panel available.

For these reasons and countless more, many films carry **generators**. A generator is a miniature power plant. It uses some kind of power (usually gas or diesel fuel) to power a motor that turns a magnet in a coil of wires, just like the big boys. Generators come in lots of different sizes, from small **putt-putts** that fit in your trunk to huge ones that sit on the backs of semis, but they all work the same way. Add fuel on one side and power comes out the other. Generators are rated in amps, so add up your wattages and use the $W=VA$ law to find out what you need. Make sure you have extra gas. Also, generators make noise (as a general rule, the smaller the generator, the noisier it is), so make sure you have a place for them that is far enough away from the action not to intrude on the sound recording.

There are so-called silent generators that can put out an astonishing amount of power with only a muted humming sound, but be prepared to open your checkbook and say, "Ack!"

Whether you tie into the mains or bring a generator, you will still need to convert those big, fat 200 amps into something that you can use for individual lights (not to mention that coffeepot). Enter the distribution box, known to sparkies worldwide as a *distro box*. The distro box has several large receptacles on one end. This is where the beefy cables running from the mains or the generator go. On the top or sides of the distro box are bunches of outlets of different sizes, from 60-amp Bates plugs (see below) to 15-amp household-style Edison plugs. The electricians will place the distro box as close to the set as they can, so the cables running to the lights are as short as possible. Smaller distro boxes are known as *lunchboxes*.

Please note that, like tying into the mains, setting up a distro box requires knowledge and experience. It is not a job for a nonelectrician.

THE LIGHTS

Because film and TV lighting is an art that is both varied and precise, there is a vast array of lights to fill every purpose, from lighting a football field to putting a sparkle in the eye of a leading lady. Gaffers refer to the lights themselves as *heads*, by the way, as in, "Get the stands out of the truck and put the heads on them."

Fresnels

When a DP is looking for a "hard" light to use as a key light, more often than not, she will reach for a *fresnel* (pronounced "fur-NELL").

The original fresnel was invented by a Frenchman named Augustin Fresnel, who was actually trying to solve an entirely different problem—how to keep ships from running aground.

Fresnel was trying to come up with a lens that could be used in lighthouses. The arc light had just been invented, and the coastal authorities wanted to use them to make lighthouses more visible. Arc lights create light by pumping electricity into a carbon rod and then

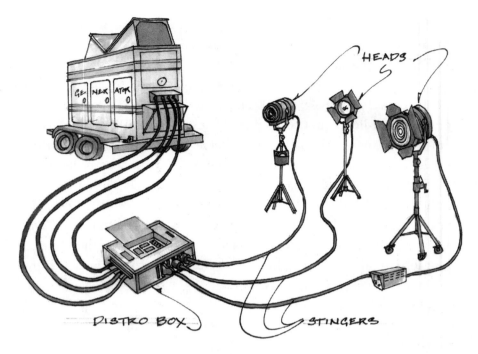

Power distribution on the set.

forcing it to jump across a narrow gap to another carbon rod.[19] The lamp was very bright, but it threw that brilliance in every direction, allowing the light to dissipate quickly in thick fog. What was needed was a lens that could gather the light into a powerful beam that could cut through the fog and reach the ships at sea. Of course, this beam had to be pretty big, so the lens had to be large, as well. To further complicate the problem, the arc lamp burns very hot, and thick glass has a tendency to shatter when heated. The thicker the glass, the more heat it retains. The more heat, the greater the chance that a disastrous crack will appear.

Fresnel solved the problem once he realized that it wasn't the width of the glass that focused the light—it was the curved surface of the lens. When light crossed this curved surface, it was deflected toward the center of the lens, creating a tight beam of light. As long as the surface of the lens was properly curved, it didn't matter how thick the glass was. Fresnel cut away the bulk of the glass in a series of stair

---

[19] Early arc lights used a block of lime as a reflector; hence, the term "limelight."

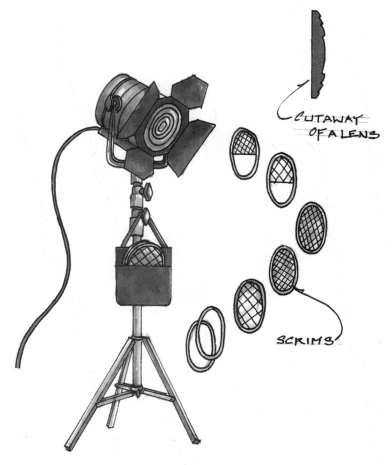

CUTAWAY OF A LENS

SCRIMS

The fresnel with scrims.

steps, leaving a curved surface but losing all that costly, heat-retaining glass.

It worked wonders for the lighthouses, and soon became a standard lens for theatrical (and, later, movie) lights.

The company that defined the fresnel in Hollywood was called Mole-Richardson. Even today, the distinctive copper-colored Mole fixtures still dominate Hollywood sets. Mole-Richardson built a fresnel for every size and purpose, from the 200-watt "Tiny" you could hold in your palm to the 10,000-watt "Teners" that turn night into day.

In the middle are a cartoon character list of heads that someone had great fun naming. From small to large, they are Tiny, Mini, Midget, Betweenie, Tweenie, Baby-Baby, Baby, Baby Junior, Junior, Baby Senior,

Senior, and the aforementioned Tener. Never let it be said that electricians don't have a sense of whimsy. Listening to some muscle mountain of a gaffer talk about his favorite "baby-baby" makes me smile.

When pointed directly at an actor, a fresnel is generally a key light, as it is highly directional and creates a hard shadow. It can also be a fill light, however, if it is bounced off a foam board, a white piece of fabric, or a wall.

Fresnels can be focused, after a fashion. The lamp sits on a little tray that slides in and out of a shiny reflector. Moving the lamp closer to the reflector concentrates the light into a tighter beam. This is known as *spotting*. Moving the lamp further away from the reflector (closer to the lens) is known as *flooding*, as it makes the beam larger.

Fresnels are also used with a set of **barn doors**—two or four metal plates that can be swung in front of the lens, cutting unwanted light off of . . . whatever you don't want light on. The barn doors come separately from the light itself, but on rental units they are often chained to the light, partly for safety (in case they fall out when the light is hung overhead) and partly for the same reason your mother clipped your mittens to your overcoat—to keep track of 'em.

A film and TV fresnel (as opposed to a theatrical one) will also come with a set of **scrims**. Movie lights are rarely put on dimmers (dimming a light changes its color temperature), so electricians use mesh screens in front of the light to reduce the intensity. A scrim is a metal frame filled with mesh screen and designed to slip into a tray in front of the lens. Scrims come in **single** and **double** versions, where the single one is a lighter weave that takes away less light. There are also **half singles** and **half doubles**—scrims with a screen that only covers half the frame. Half scrims are used when a gaffer only wants to reduce the light on half of the beam. Scrims are color-coded. The singles have a green metal frame; the doubles are red.

Open-Face Lights

What happens when you take the fresnel lens off the fresnel? You get an **open-face light**.

Not having a lens to gather the light, the open-face instrument throws light around more indiscriminately. The barn doors become even more important with this light, and some types of open-face lights have them built into the instrument, so you don't need the little mitten chain.

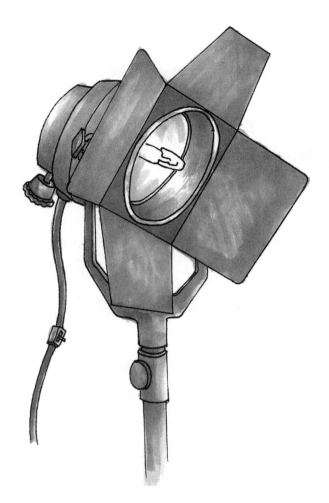

An open-face light.

(Please note that the term "mitten chain" is an invention of this author and is not an official Hollywood tech term. Yet.) Open-face lights can be hazardous because they put out a lot of heat. Be careful not to put meltable or flammable things too close to the front.

Open-face lights come in a lot of shapes and sizes, loosely grouped into four types: prime fixtures, broads and nook lights, cyc lights, and lighting kits.

Prime Fixtures. The prime light has a movable reflector, allowing you to focus the instrument much as you would a fresnel. They usually have barn doors built in, as well, so you have a little control over where the light goes, even though there isn't a lens.

Two popular prime fixtures are the mysteriously named 2,000-watt "Blonde" and 1,000-watt "Redhead." These lights are often bounced off a bead board or griffolyn to create soft light.

Broads and Nook Lights. A *broad light* is a lamp inside a metal box, and that's about it. It creates a powerful, hard-edged light that is good for those jobs where you need a lot of bright light and you don't need to do anything fancy with it. They are used for things like backdrops and work lights.

Nook lights are the same deal, only smaller, making them a good choice for sticking in a little, um, nook where you need some light. Think refrigerators, medicine cabinets, and under dashboards.

Bouncing light off a griffolyn.

Cyc Lights. **Cyc lights** are named after the big piece of fabric they are designed to light. The **cyclorama** is a large, unpainted piece of fabric that provides a neutral backdrop or a fake sky behind a set.[20] This large, flat expanse of fabric is a special lighting challenge, as it must be lit smoothly and evenly, all the way across without dead spots in the center.

Various kinds of cyc lights have been developed over the years, including the multicell **border light** (basically just a string of lightbulbs) to the slightly higher tech **far cyc**, which has special parabolic reflectors designed to throw light across a wide space. Cyc lights are often hung in sets, one at the top of the cyc (the **cyc heads**) and one at the bottom (the **cyc foots** or **groundrow**).

Lighting Kits. One lighting company has made its name in the business by designing self-contained lighting kits specially designed for the use of fast-moving video crews. The Lowell company makes a variety of kits called, not surprisingly, **Lowell kits**. These kits are the staples of ENG and other video applications where you need to set up quickly in a remote location with house power. A Lowell kit consists of a small number of lights complete with stands, reflectors, diffusion, and all the accessories you need, all neatly packed into a case that fits in your trunk. It is designed to be a complete lighting solution for small video setups like interviews and very low-budget narrative video, like the ones where people undress.

The wattages of the lights in a Lowell kit are such that they can be plugged into one or two household circuits. Set up one light as a key, a second as fill, sprinkle a few more around to light the room, and boom, you're on.

Portable Battery Lights

When shooting handheld video, the cameraman will often use a small, battery-powered lighting instrument. The most popular is the **sun gun**,

---

[20] In case anyone ever asks you on a test, there is such a thing as a "hard cyc," a large, smooth backdrop that is built out of a solid material, like plaster, and permanently installed. Many TV studios have a hard cyc on one wall for a quick and easy setup. If you want to be unpopular, lean against the cyc and leave a trail of greasy fingerprints. Oh, you're in trouble now.

a small HMI light that provides daylight-balanced light at various wattages from 100 to 300 watts. With an orange color correction, the sun gun can match indoor tungsten or incandescent light, as well. A piece of diffusion over the light takes some of the edge off, if you don't mind losing a little of the punch.

The sun gun is useful for remote locations where power is unavailable, or for fast-moving crews trying to follow a moving subject. Rarely used for feature work, these battery-powered lights are the prize possessions of documentary and news cameramen. They are light, portable, and can be handheld by an assistant or mounted atop the camera. The downside is the batteries, which rarely last longer than an hour. For that reason, cameramen will shut them off immediately when not shooting.

Softlites

Strictly speaking, any light can be a soft light if it is bounced off a reflector or run through diffusion, but there is a specific group of lights that takes this name all the time.

A softlite has a lamp buried deep within a metal housing. None of this light hits the actor directly. Instead, it is bounced off a large white reflector that diffuses the beams and makes them wrap more softly around the actor's features. Softlites create a diffuse wash of light that is suitable for fill light or, in certain situations, key light. There was a period in the '80s when many commercials used a softlite coming from one side as a solitary key light for those yuppie "We're-your-bank-and-we-care-about-you" commercials. That mood has apparently passed, and we are now back to using softlites as fill.

HMI Lights

When it comes to film and TV lighting, HMI lights are one of the great inventions of the late twentieth century.

For starters, they put out daylight-balanced light that can be mixed with daylight without color correction. They are much more efficient than tungsten lamps, putting out four times as much light at the same wattage. And, if that weren't enough, they burn much cooler than tungsten lamps, which is good for everyone on the set. The HMI's gift is the ability to turn the energy that a tungsten lamp wastes on heat into useful illumination.

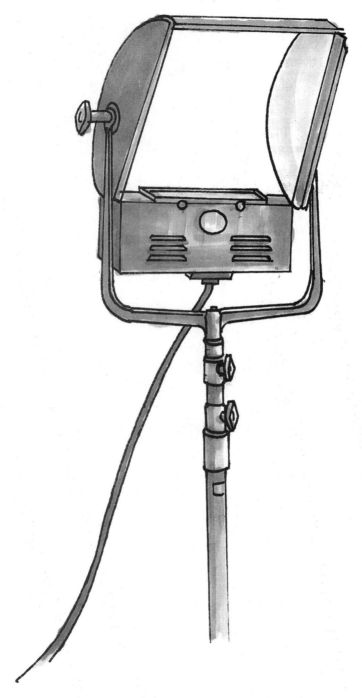

A softlite.

An HMI with ballast.

When you get right down to it, an HMI is similar in concept to those arc lights in Fresnel's lighthouses. In an HMI, electricity is converted into light by making a spark jump across a gap between two electrodes, just like the arc lamp. In the case of the HMI, however, the gap is measured in thousandths of an inch, instead of the tenths of an inch in the arc light. Furthermore, the electrodes in the HMI don't erode like they do in the carbon arc, so the HMI doesn't have to get a new set of electrodes every forty-five minutes like the arc light does.

The HMI does its magic with sophisticated electronics, which leads to the first downside of this unit—namely, the high price tag.

An HMI lamp requires a separate ballast, a heavy metal case of electronics about the size of a bread box (about the weight of a bread box, too, if your bread is made out of lead). The ballast sits on the ground next to the stand holding the HMI and performs the electronic wizardry that helps the lamp do what it does. With all these electronics, there are a lot more things that can go wrong, of course, and when they do, the solution is rarely as simple and cheap as changing a burned-out lightbulb.

The big problem that has dogged HMIs is *flicker*. Although you can't see it with your naked eye, an HMI lamp is actually turning on and off very quickly—120 times a second, to be exact. If the camera is running precisely at a frame speed that is a factor of 120 (like 20, 24, or 30), this isn't a problem because every frame of film gets the same amount of light. But if the camera speed wanders up or down at all, a noticeable flicker will be seen on film.

The first solution was to precisely control the speed of the camera motor using crystal-sync motors and only to use frame rates that were factors of 120. Later, electronic ballasts (as opposed to the magnetic ones that were first developed) appeared that could operate in "flicker-free" mode. They became flicker-free by making the curving sine wave of the HMI power into a square wave, reversing the flow of power instantly, instead of gradually.[21] Unfortunately, the hard corners of the power wave caused the lamps to resonate and emit a high-pitched whistling sound. If this doesn't mean anything to you, don't sweat it. The important thing is, the "flicker-free" mode on a ballast causes the lamp to whistle, an unacceptable notion when you are recording sound, but still useful for silent shots. More recently, ballasts have appeared that can operate silently and still be flicker-free. These ballasts round off the sharp corners of the square waves and get rid of the sound, but they are unable to operate at faster frame rates.

---

[21] Normally, AC (or alternating current) power reverses direction 120 times a second in a steady, back-and-forth motion. Making the power into a square wave means it goes completely in one direction for 1/60 of a second, then instantly changes direction.

Bottom line: When shooting at any frame rate up to about 30 frames per second, you can use a silent, flicker-free electronic ballast and not sweat the precise speed of the camera. Above 30fps, use a crystal sync and factors of 120, or use a standard electronic ballast and wear earplugs.

To use an HMI, you plug the ballast into your power source, then plug the ballast into the light itself (the "head") with a heavy-duty head cable (it comes with the HMI).

Hitting the "on" switch sends a high-voltage jolt of electricity up to the lamp, where it jumps the gap and "strikes" the light. When an HMI first comes on, the lamp is quite dim. It takes a few minutes for the lamp to come to full intensity and also to reach the proper color temperature. Once the unit is on, leave it on. Many HMIs are so-called cold-strike lights. In other words, they will not restrike until the lamp has cooled all the way down. Turning off an HMI between shots is a great way to annoy a film crew, as everyone will have to cool their heels while the HMI cools its head enough to restrike. An hour-long dinner break is usually enough time to cool the head, so the gaffer will shut down the HMIs then. Otherwise, they stay on, whether we are shooting or not.[22]

There are HMI versions of many of the lights that we already described, including fresnels and softlites.

The most common kind of HMI is the HMI fresnel. The smaller units, like the 575-watt version, are often used as interior key or soft light when mixing with daylight coming through windows. The larger units, like the 12,000-watt or 18,000-watt versions, are used for fill light when shooting outside during the day. For nighttime exteriors, these workhorse lights are often mounted on cranes and hoisted high

---

[22] A point of trivia to show how times have changed: Before HMIs, the large-scale fresnels on sets were all carbon arc lights. In these instruments, the arcing electricity actually eats away at the electrodes. In order to keep up, the electrodes would be slowly driven toward one another by a motor, under constant supervision by an electrician. After an hour or so, the electrodes had to be replaced. With all this carbon burning all the time, the lights were shut off, or "saved," between takes. Hence, the Hollywood cry, "Lights! Camera! Action!" The lights would be turned on at the last minute to save the carbons. Today, the call for "Lights!" is unnecessary, as the HMIs are never shut down.

above the action, where they can light up an entire block. That moonlight flooding down on the nighttime chase scene in every good thriller is probably coming from an HMI on a crane overhead. In Los Angeles, you can always tell when someone is shooting a night exterior because the huge HMIs are visible for miles, looking for all the world like brilliant stars that have dropped from the sky and landed in the San Fernando Valley.

Fluorescent Lights

Until recently, the word "fluorescent" was considered another word for "pain in the keester," at least when it came to film and video lighting.

The Kino Flo.

Fluorescents are a pain for a lot of reasons: They only reproduce a narrow part of the color spectrum, they flicker, they can't be dimmed, and their color temperature is positively green. In general, they made people look pale and sickly. Then, along came Frieder Hochheim, Gary Swink, and their company, Kino Flo, Inc., which manufactures film-friendly fluorescent fixtures. Kino Flo units are lightweight, efficient, flicker-free, and, most importantly, color-correct. Life is good again.

But why bother? Why would we want to use fluorescent fixtures when there are so many other options? Aside from the fact that directors sometimes want to shoot in existing locations that already have them, fluorescent lights produce a soft, diffuse light that wraps around an actor's features and fills in shadows.

Like HMIs, Kino Flo fixtures have a separate ballast, but it is much lighter than the cinder block that accompanies HMI lights. The fixture itself is quite light, as well, a fact greatly appreciated by location-weary electricians who have dragged one too many HMIs up onto one too many light stands.

Because of their smooth, shadowless light, Kino Flos are often used to light green-screen backdrops, one of the foundations of modern effect photography.

My personal favorite Kino Flo fixture is the 12-volt car kit that plugs into the cigarette lighter. A lot of those nighttime talkin'-and-drivin' scenes are lit with a couple of these babies taped to the dashboard. Or did you think that light was coming from the radio?

CABLES AND PLUGS

Having a wide variety of lights to choose from is useful, but without a way to plug them in, you have a whole bunch of high-tech sculpture.

On a set, the power cords used to plug in the lights are known as **stingers**. The larger cables running from the generator to the distro boxes are called **cables**. The smaller sizes of wire, such as the wire coming from your bedside lamp, are known as **zip cord**.

Cables, stingers, and zip cord are rated in amps. Just for comparison, your household outlets are 15 amps, as are most industrial extension cords.

Zip cord, stingers, and cables are also rated by gauge, which is the electricians' word for size. Gauge is abbreviated as "AWG," for American Wire Gauge. In a cruel joke on logical people, the larger the gauge, the smaller the wire. Zip cord is 18 or 20 AWG, the orange extension cord in your garage is 14 AWG, and a standard stinger is 10 or 12 AWG. At the big end of the gauge scale, the numbers reverse, so progressively larger sizes of cable are called:

- **4 AWG**
- **2 AWG**
- **1/0** (known as "one-ought")
- **2/0** ("two-ought")
- **3/0** ("three-ought")

. . . and so on.

These larger "ought" sizes are the ones you will see coming straight out of the generator. Their larger size allows them to carry huge amounts of power. One piece of 3/0 cable can carry 350 amps, for example. Compare that to a 12-gauge stinger that is rated for 25 amps, at the most.

Putting too much power through a cable can result in the cable's overheating and melting, which can cause a fire. Set electricians use specific tables and their own experience to balance loads on cables, keeping the loads at a safe level. Of course, every cable and light on the set should be protected by fuses and circuit breakers—safety devices that are designed to shut the circuit down if such an overload occurs.

Plugs are also rated in amps. Obviously, they must match the cable they are attached to. Set lighting uses four main kinds of plugs:

Edison Plugs

These are the plugs you have in your house, except the ones on the set will always, always, always have a ground plug, whereas your household ones may not. Because an Edison plug has two parallel blades and a ground plug, it is sometimes called a **PBG plug**, for "parallel blade ground." Edison plugs are rated up to 15 amps.

Twist-Lok

Twist-Lok is more of a theatrical plug, but you might run into it if you are filming in a space that doubles as a theater. Like the PBG plug, it has three blades, but they are set in a circle, allowing them to rotate and lock the plug into the outlet. Rated up to 20 amps.

Stage Pin

Like the Twist-Lok, the *stage pin* is primarily a theatrical plug, but you might see one sooner or later. It is a flat, rectangular plug, slightly smaller than a pack of cigarettes, with three round pins sticking out in a row on one side. Rated up to 20 amps.

Bates Plugs

The *Bates plug* is an overgrown stage pin plug that is rated to 60 amps. It is a little larger than a pack of cigarettes, with three pins sticking out in a row on one side. It is used for larger instruments like 5K fresnels and large HMIs. A standard distro box will have several Bates plug outlets, as well as several Edison outlets.

Cam-Lok

Up until now, we have been talking about plugs that are put on multi-conductor cables; that is, cables with more than one piece of wire in them. When plugging in very large power sources, electricians prefer bundles of single-conductor wire. This keeps the power from "bleeding" between the cables and overheating. The plugs for these larger cables, therefore, are single cable plugs. The most common is a round plug about the size of an ear of corn. These *cam-lok plugs* are inserted into the outlet and rotated to lock them in. They can handle a huge amount of power. They are almost always color-coded to tell the electrician which is the hot line (or lines), the neutral, and the ground. Depending on the size and style of the cam-lok, it can take up to 600 amps. Whoa.

LIGHTING STANDS

If you are shooting on a soundstage, most of your lights will go on pipes hung overhead. Studio soundstages will usually have permanent, walkable catwalks, known as the *perms*. In most cases, the perms are too high up to hang the lights. They exist as a place to hang temporary, movable catwalks known as *greenbeds*. The lights are hung off poles on the sides of these greenbeds, down closer to the set where they can really do some good.

If you are shooting on location (and, often, when you are on a soundstage as well), the lights will be mounted on individual stands. Different size lights get different size stands. Lighting kits, such as the Lowell kits, come with their own stands. Kino Flo fluorescents can be mounted on C-stands. Everything else goes on a rolling stand.

A light stand has an open hole at the top. A standard film or video light has a pin sticking downward from the light. To mount the light on the stand, drop that pin into the hole and crank the little handle on the side to tighten it.

Just as with the fresnels, Mole-Richardson has created a standard set of stands that are used throughout the industry. They go from the small Baby stand, through the Junior and Senior stands, to the large, crank-up stands that have a crank built in to raise the light higher. If you need to get a light really high (like when you are hanging a large HMI to simulate moonlight), you rent a crane and mount the light on that. Young electricians who are just getting started often pull "crane duty," where they sit in the crane basket next to the light and freeze their buns off all night.

Chapter 10:

APPLES AND CUP BLOCKS AND SHOW CARDS, OH MY!—GRIP EQUIPMENT

Newcomers may be confused by the distinction between grips and electricians. Both of them appear to be involved in setting up lighting equipment, yet you may be rebuffed when asking an electrician to adjust a flag that is shaping a light, or when asking a grip to spot down a fresnel. Yes, both teams work on the lighting, but if it plugs in, or is attached to something that plugs in, it belongs to the electricians. The rest of the stuff belongs to the grips.

THE MIGHTY C-STAND

Perhaps no other piece of film equipment is so ubiquitous, so useful, and so common as the C-stand. Named for the C-shaped legs (okay—to me, they look like an "L," but I am young and have not yet learned the mysterious Ways of the Grip), these stands hang on the doors of production trucks all over this great nation. They are the answer to the question, "How do I make that thing stay in one place?"

A C-stand is composed of three legs (which can be folded together for storage) that hold up a vertical pole. This vertical pole also has three pieces, but they are nested inside one another so they can be extended to various heights. Three toggle bolts tighten these poles (called *risers*) into place. At the top of the tallest riser is the *head*, a circular bracket with holes of various sizes. Different pieces of grip equipment fit into the different holes. The head has a large crank on one side that pinches the pieces together to hold whatever is mounted in it.

The most common thing to go into the head is a metal arm that can reach out to the side. That arm, in turn, has another circular head that can hold equipment. The C-stand, therefore, can be used as a straight stand or, with the arm, as a boom stand to hold equipment out to the side.

Almost everything that grips use can be mounted on a C-stand. The head is designed to be completely flexible, holding a huge variety of equipment at any angle, at any height. "How to Set Up a C-Stand" is number three on my list of things that every film and TV person should know, so let's get to it.

How to Set Up a C-Stand

1. *Choose the proper length of stand for the job:* Most of the time, a standard-length stand will do, but sometimes you might need to

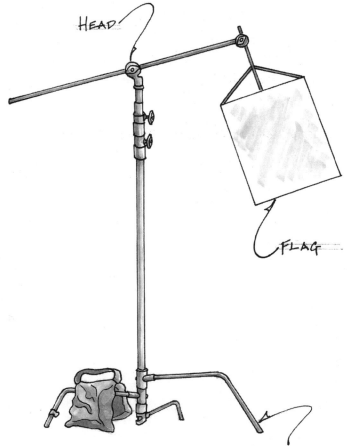

HEAD

FLAG

LONG LEG TOWARD SET

A properly assembled C-stand.

mount something close to the ground, necessitating a **baby stand**, a stand with shorter risers. Taller jobs will require a **combo stand**, a larger version of a C-stand that has wheels. Combo stands are so named because they also do duty as lighting stands.

2. *Unfold the stand:* The three legs should be rotated into the same plane when stored, but once you have gotten the stand where you want it on the set, you will want to rotate the legs until they drop into their working position. Each leg drops into its own little slot, so make sure that all the legs are where they are supposed to be before you continue.

3. *Put the stand where you want it:* Keep in mind that you should place the stand on the "offstage" side of whatever piece of equipment you are mounting, so as to keep the stand out of the shot as much as possible. Also, keep in mind that you should mount the arm of the stand so that putting weight on the arm tightens the head. That's "righty-tighty" to you junior grips out there, so put the weight on the right side of the head as you look at the crank. Finally, note that the three legs are all different lengths. Put the long one on the side where you are putting the weight. This will help stabilize the stand.

4. *Mount the gear:* Attach the flag, finger, silk, monitor, coffee tray, or whatever to the arm. Again, put the weight to the right of the crank.

5. *Set the height of the stand:* You may choose to set the height before you mount the gear if it is very heavy. Whichever order you do it in, always remember to unscrew the top riser first. If you unscrew the bottom one first and then run up the riser, you will find that you have put the other two risers out of reach. Silly you. While people are laughing at you, remember that every single one of them made the same mistake at some point. I make it every six months, just to keep my edge.

6. *Sandbag the stand:* Never walk away from a stand without putting weight on it. Drop at least one sandbag over the leg farthest from the weighted arm. Put enough weight on it so that someone casually bumping into it will not send it over. Remember, sand is cheaper than heads. If you are outside, put enough weight on the stand to withstand the wind. If the C-stand is holding up a large flag or a big piece of fabric, consider driving stakes into the ground and attaching guy wires to the stand.

THINGS TO HANG ON A C-STAND

Now that you know how to set up the stand, what will we put on it? The following are common items that are held up by C-stands. All of these items will store on the grip truck.

Solids

A **solid** is a piece of black fabric designed to cut off light completely. Larger sizes (they commonly come up to twenty feet by twenty feet) are mounted on a frame like a painting. That frame, in turn, is held up by C-stands or combo stands. The smaller sizes are permanently stretched on metal frames and come in lots of different shapes and sizes:

- *Four-by-Four:* Yes, you guessed it. Four feet by four feet.
- *Flags:* A smaller, rectangular piece that is the workhorse of the solids. Used for almost anything.

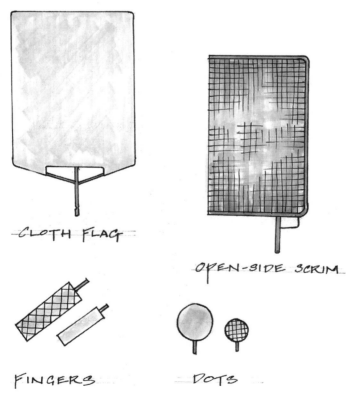

CLOTH FLAG

OPEN-SIDE SCRIM

FINGERS

DOTS

Flags and scrims.

- **Cutters:** very long and slender solids used to cut off a sliver of light.
- **Dots:** Circular solids of various sizes for creating a "hole" in the light.

Solids have a lot of specific uses, and many of those uses have specific names, like:

- **Topper:** a solid that cuts off the top of a beam of light. Used to knock light off scenery but keep it on the actor.
- **Courtesy Flag:** A solid that keeps the merciless sun off the director, the cameraman, or the monitor.
- **Lenser:** A solid used to keep glare from the lights off the camera lens. In some cases, lights can cause a flare on the lens, even if they are out of frame.

Silks

Silks are white fabrics placed in front of a light to diffuse it. They come in many different thicknesses and weaves. The thicker the silk, the more diffusion it creates.

Silks can also be mounted on a three-sided metal frame, leaving the fabric hanging loose on the fourth side. This **open-ended silk** is useful if you want to diffuse part of the beam without leaving the shadow of the frame.

Scrims

Like the metal scrims that electricians place in front of lighting instruments, the grips' fabric scrims are used to decrease the intensity of the light. Like the metal versions, they come in two thicknesses—single and double. They even have the same color scheme—green frame for single, red frame for double. Unlike the metal ones (but like silks), they also come in open-ended versions.

Beadboard

Beadboard, known to many by the trade name Styrofoam, is a white, opaque, semirigid foam board that is excellent for bouncing light. The surface is pebbled, creating an attractive, diffuse light. Take note that beadboard will melt if it is too close to a lamp, so take care to set up the light far enough away to avoid a hazard. This is especially important with open-face lights.

Another version of this is called **foamcore**. This style of board is thinner and flatter, without the pebbling of beadboard. It is available in huge sheets, up to 4' x 8'.

Bounceboard

Also known as a silverboard, this is a hard piece of material with one silver side. It is used to bounce light up into an actor's face. When the two lovers are spooning on the grass in the middle of Central Park, that nice, warm uplight on the actress' face is from a **bounceboard** resting on the grass. Good thing, too. If the light were bouncing off the grass, it would be green.

Griffolyn

A large, white, semitransparent drop used to bounce or diffuse light. Sometimes a **griffolyn** will be stretched over a small outdoor set (like a couple of sportscasters during a pregame show) to diffuse the harsh sunlight. Occasionally, when a DP wants a very soft light source, a griffolyn will be set up in front of a set, then lit brightly. The bounce light from the fabric provides a soft, diffuse light on the set, without any instruments being pointed straight at the actors.

Show Card

A big piece of card stock, like the poster board you used for projects in grade school. Generally white on one side and black on the other, it is used to reflect or absorb light in smaller areas. Often, a **show card** is placed in an actor's lap, to bounce light up into his face. If certain areas are already getting too much bounce light, the black side of the card will be placed over whatever is reflecting the unwanted light.

OTHER GRIP EQUIPMENT

So, you're staging a love scene outside the heroine's door as she kisses her new boyfriend good night. She reaches up to put her arm around his neck, only to grasp at air, because the actor is shorter than she is.

No problem.

Grips carry around a pile of wooden boxes for just such emergencies. Because of their size and shape, they are known as **apple boxes**, and they are used in any situation where anything needs to be a little higher than it is. Solidly built and reinforced, they can be stood on, stacked, and screwed into. They are a bit like those cardboard blocks you had as a kid. Because problems come in many sizes, so do apple boxes. A "full apple" is about eight inches high, but there are also half, quarter, and "pancake" sizes.

The grip truck also contains a host of other problem-solvers, like the following:

- *Cup Blocks:* Wooden cups that are placed under stands to level them or prevent them from rolling away.
- *Wedges and Cribbing:* Pieces of wood used to level dolly track.
- *Sandbags:* The essential safety item. Used to hold down light stands, C-stands, and anything that wants to be somewhere else than where you want it to be. Note that sandbags absorb water, thus becoming like blocks of concrete. Keep them dry if at all possible. If you do get them wet, dry them out before you return them or face the wrath of the rental company.
- *Snot tape:* This disgustingly named substance, like its namesake, is an all-purpose fastener. Used to attach gel to windows and gel frames.
- *Silicone spray:* Used to lubricate dolly tracks.

Grip equipment is stored on a rolling cart known as a ***taco cart***, I suppose because of its resemblance to a rolling food vendor. The term was undoubtedly invented in California. If New Yorkers came up with it, it would be called a "pretzel cart."

The taco cart has a large, flat space running down the middle, where the solids and silks are stored. Be careful when sliding things in and out of this area; it is easy to hook a corner on a piece of fabric, and tear it. The cart also has milk crates on all sides full of mounting hardware, cup blocks, wedges, apple boxes, and so forth. On one end of the cart is a rack for C-stands. On the other end are drawers for expendable items like tape, chalk, and silicone spray.

Chapter 11:

PRODUCTION SOUND: CAPTURING DIALOGUE

In many ways, sound is the redheaded bastard stepchild on the set—the one area that tends to get the table scraps while the lighting and camera crews get first shot at the banquet. It's not that good sound isn't important. On the contrary, high-quality sound is one of the most impressive achievements of modern TV and film production. A great many television shows broadcast in stereo, theatrical film has become a showcase for talented sound engineers, more homes than ever have installed "Surround Sound" audio systems, and, in general, the listening public has become quite sophisticated in its understanding and appreciation of high-fidelity sound.

So why do sound people get less respect on the set? Primarily because many production people view sound as something that can be added, changed, and messed with in postproduction, after the shooting is over. The problem with this statement is that it is true, with a major caveat. Yes, sound effects will be added, external noise can be filtered out, and dialogue can be fixed up or replaced. But the process of putting a sound track together in postproduction can be made much easier by taking the time to record dialogue clearly on the set.

A sound crew on a set has one basic mission: Record the dialogue as faithfully as possible. The more dialogue they record cleanly, the less time (and time equals money) will be spent creating the sound track in postproduction. So do the show a favor and help out the sound crew.

Most sound for film is recorded in a *double-system* format. That is, the sound and picture are recorded simultaneously but separately, then married up again in the editing suite.

Why is sound recorded separately from film? When you pick up your video camera and push "play," the sound is recorded on the same piece of media, in the exact right place, and, on digital video, at a fairly high level of quality. So why bother with an entirely different crew and an entirely different process? Why not just record the sound on the film?

The first answer is that sometimes people do, particularly in documentary film. This "sound-on-film" style of shooting is fast and convenient, but it is much more problematic in postproduction if you want to work magic with the picture or sound track. It is also hard to get good quality sound when recording directly to film, something that documentary filmmakers are more willing to put up with than narrative filmmakers.

The creation of the sound track is a multifaceted process that is separate from the creation of the visuals. Sounds will be chopped up, changed, moved around, combined with other sounds, and stirred up like a tossed salad to create the masterpiece that you hear in the theater. Because those processes are happening separately, you might as well separate them right at the get-go. Besides, with the DP and his crew focusing intently on the visuals, it serves everyone well to have a crew that is equally focused on the sound. Simply put, it brings out the best of both media.

When shooting video, however, the sound is generally recorded right on the master tape, removing the need to marry it up later. Most of the time, people shooting video don't have time to play games with the sound track, and the advantages of automatically having the sound in the right place outweigh the lack of flexibility. Furthermore, modern digital videotape formats record sound at a very high level of quality—comparable to a compact disc or even better—so video production gets good quality sound even when recording onto the master tape.

Let's take a look at some basic audio concepts and check out the different types of microphones, mic placements, and recording decks. Then, we'll walk through the soundman's process on the set.

SIGNAL LEVEL

When audible sound enters a sound system, it is changed from a physical vibration to an electrical signal by the microphone. While the sound is being shunted around the system, it stays in this electrical form, known as the "signal." Once it reaches the speakers, it is changed back into a physical form by the vibrating speaker cone.

As the signal travels through the sound system, it goes through some changes. Some of the most important changes it goes through are changes in strength, or **signal level**. Signal level refers to the amount of electrical power that is being pumped through the system. A signal may appear in various places in the system at various levels. Let's look at the different levels:

Mic (Pronounced "Mike") Level

When you speak into a microphone, the air pressure from your voice causes a small magnet inside the microphone to move, creating a tiny electrical charge. This electrical energy travels down the microphone cable to the mixer. This is an extremely low-level signal, a sort of electronic whisper. This "mic-level" signal must be boosted by a **preamp** before it is useful to the sound system. That is why you cannot take a microphone, plug it into the tape input on your stereo, and expect it to work. The tape input has no preamp. If there is an input on your stereo marked "mic," that input is equipped with a preamp that boosts the signal up to a higher level. On a mixer, there is generally a switch by each input that allows you to make that input a mic input. Turn it to "mic" if you are plugging in a microphone, and the preamp will boost the signal properly. The mic on the boom will be plugged into the mixer through such a preamp. The preamp will push the signal up to a level that can be recorded on tape, a level known as . . .

Line Level

The signal that gets sent to the tape deck is **line level**. Tape decks, CD players, and electronic musical instruments all record and put out line-level signals, so they do not need to be boosted when they get to the mixer. In fact, line level is the level that all electronic devices use to talk to one another. If you are plugging two electronic devices together, the signal that is traveling down the wire is at line level.

The mixer may adjust the volume up and down, but the signal level that it puts out remains the same. This distinction can be hard to understand, because sound people sometimes use the terms "level" and "volume" interchangeably. Just remember, both **mic level** and line level refer to a range of volumes. A high mic level is still less powerful than a low line level. Think of it this way: A high-school teacher's salary may fluctuate over the years, but it is still in the range of high-school teachers' salaries. The CEO of General Motors has a much higher salary, which may also fluctuate. The range of the teacher's salary, however, will never be anywhere near the CEO's. (Then again, his employees won't sit in his office eating licorice and gossiping about the prom, either. Some things are better than money.) In the same way, mic level, though it may fluctuate, will always be lower than line level.

Speaker Level

Once you are done combining the signals and adjusting their volumes, the resulting signal gets sent to the amplifier. Here, it is pumped up to a level that will actually drive the speakers. This level is way above either line level or mic level, so you definitely don't want to plug the output of an amp into anything other than a speaker. If a line level signal is a CEO's salary, *speaker level* is like the budget of the Pentagon—during a Republican administration.

MICROPHONE TYPES

On the set, the microphone only has one job: to pick up as much of the dialogue as possible, as cleanly as possible. To that end, the sound mixer may use various kinds of microphones to pick up the action:

Omnidirectional

Every mic has a *pickup pattern*, a chart that shows where the mic is more sensitive to sound. "Omni" means all, and "direction" means direction, so this mic will pick up sound coming from every direction. Therefore, the pickup pattern is a perfect circle, showing that the mic is equally sensitive in every direction. In many cases, this is problematic on a set, because you generally want to pick up sound from just one direction—wherever the actor is. There are a few situations, however, where omnidirectional mics are useful.

Lavalier Mics

Those little pencil-eraser mics that news commentators clip to their lapels are called *lavalier* (or simply *lav*) microphones. They are mostly omnidirectional, because you never can tell if that thing is going to be pointed directly at the commentator's mouth.

Boundary-Layer Mics

Boundary-layer mics trade off an audio phenomenon that you can witness firsthand. When a microphone is placed next to a hard surface, like a wall, it will not only pick up the sound that hits it directly, but also the sound that is bouncing off the wall. If the mic is not right next to the wall, the reflected sound will arrive later and become an echo that muddies up the sound you want. If, however, you put the mic right up against the wall, the two sounds arrive so close together that they amplify each other, producing a more powerful signal. You can experience the boundary effect by putting your head against the wall and listening. Notice how sounds around the room are amplified? Notice how much more high-pitched sound you can hear? Notice how people are staring at you?

The Crown audio company came out with a mic called the **PZM** mic (that's "pressure zone modulation," and aren't you glad you asked?) that did an amazing job of capturing this effect. Crown's reward was for sound technicians everywhere to refer to any boundary-layer mic as a PZM (the so-called kleenex phenomenon). Note that PZM is a brand, however, and there are now other mics in this category that are excellent, as well.

Boundary-layer mics are placed on the walls, floor, ceiling, or against large pieces of scenery. It's also a good way to mic a piano; just tape it to the inside of the lid.

Cardioid and Hypercardioid Mics

On a *cardioid mic*, the pickup pattern is heart-shaped, with the thin point of the heart at the mic itself. The pattern spreads out in two ventricle-shaped areas to the front of the mic. Any sound in that area will be picked up by the mic. Cardioids tend to reject sound behind the mic, which is good, because that's where all the crew people are shuffling their feet, wondering out loud what's for lunch.

Hypercardioid mics have a similar pattern, but the two ventricles are much more concentrated, forming a stretch-out heart shape that picks up from a narrower area in front of the mic. This is a popular pickup pattern for a boom mic hanging over an actor's head.

Shotgun Mics

The pickup pattern on a *shotgun mic* is very narrow, meaning it only picks up sound from directly in front of the mic. Like their namesakes, these mics are long and narrow and tend to reject sound coming from any direction except right in front. Some shotgun mics will pick up sound dozens of feet away without hearing a sound just a foot or two to the side. Some boom mics are shotguns, particularly when they have to be a fair ways above the actor's head, as on a TV talk show.

Parabolic Mics

Parabolic mics are not named for the mic—they are named for the reflector. These are those round, clear plastic dishes that you see being carried around on the sidelines of football games. The ones that look like a big salad bowl with a mic suspended in the center. Parabolic reflectors collect sound coming straight from the front and focus it to the microphone mounted in the center of the dish. Parabolic mics are even more directional than shotgun mics. Think of a searchlight beam. That beam is coming from a parabolic reflector with a light source mounted right about where that mic is mounted. Imagine that search-light beam coming out of your parabolic mic, and it gives you some idea of the pickup pattern. A sound technician standing on the side-lines of a football game can use that mic to pick up a quarterback call-ing signals from half a field away. They are also used in nature shows, to pick up birdcalls and stuff.

LOW IMPEDANCE VERSUS HIGH IMPEDANCE

Impedance is a fairly mysterious audio phenomenon that even some professional sound engineers do not understand. They do understand its importance, however. Put simply, impedance is the amount of resis-tance an electrical circuit puts up to an incoming signal.

Why is impedance significant? Three words: Noise, Noise, and Noise.

A microphone is like a toddler crawling around stuffing sound into its mouth. One of the unsavory things it will wrap its chubby little fists around is electrical noise. Lots of things create electrical noise on a set: extension cords, lighting equipment, fluorescent lights, even wall sock-ets. Video monitors are particularly notorious, as are refrigerators. Where there is electricity, there is electrical noise. This noise isn't audi-ble to us, but it can be deafening to a microphone circuit. Remember, everything the microphone sends to the sound system is going to be amplified, first by the preamp, then by the amplifier. Silent electrical noise will become clearly audible by the time it gets through the amplifier.

Here is a little secret, however. Electrical noise does not create sound pressure, so it is not really the microphone that picks it up. It's the cable. A mic cable operates like a big radio antenna, sweeping up any kind of electrical impulse it can get its hands on. Actually, it is not *like* an antenna, it *is* an antenna (the radio antenna on your car is just a cable), so do not be surprised when passing police cars start broadcasting into your soundstage.

Audio engineers shut out noise by using **balanced lines**. A balanced line is a microphone cable that sends the signal out on two wires at once, one running from the mixer to the mic and one running from the mic to the mixer. Any noise that the cable picks up gets sent in both directions at once, effectively canceling it out. An **unbalanced line** sends all the noise in a single direction: towards the mixer. Result: The noise enters the sound system.

The catch is, you have to use a low-impedance microphone to use a balanced line. Better-quality mics are always low impedance, and it's easy to tell the difference. Look at the plug coming out of the end. A low-impedance mic will have a three-pin **XLR plug** coming out of it. This kind of plug is required for a balanced line, because a balanced line has three wires: one running in each direction, plus a ground wire.

A high-impedance mic will have a **phono** (or **quarter-inch**) plug. This kind of plug only has two wires; ergo, it is unbalanced.

Without the balancing effect, the cables will tend to pick up extraneous noise.

Bottom line:

Low impedance = balanced line = XLR plug = better.
High impedance = unbalanced line = 1/4" plug = cheaper.

Don't understand it? You are not alone. Electricity boggles a lot of people's minds, including mine. Here's the REAL bottom line:

All mics should run on balanced, low-impedance lines using cables with XLR plugs.

And don't try to beat the rule by putting an adapter somewhere in the stretch of cable between the mic and the mixer. Any piece of unbalanced line will cause you trouble. Maybe not today, maybe not tomorrow . . .

All this impedance- and balanced-line nonsense only applies to microphone lines. Tape decks, CD players, keyboards, and many other kinds of sound equipment can be happily plugged in with quarter-inch plugs on unbalanced lines. Because this equipment operates at line level (not mic level), it tends to wipe out the noise. Of course, high-dollar sound studios run every signal on a balanced line. Just to be sure.

MICROPHONE PLACEMENT

Having chosen a microphone, the sound technician must now find a proper placement for his mic on the set.

Overhead Mics

The number-one best place to put a microphone is right over the actor's head, hanging down from a *boom* or a *fish pole*. A boom is a long rod attached to a rolling stand. The operator moves the mic with a set of cranks to get it in the right place. A fishpole is just what it sounds like: a handheld rod about the length of a fishing pole held over the actors by a boom man just off-screen. This is the instrument of choice for a fast-moving film crew, while a boom will be used in a studio with a smooth floor that won't hang up the wheels.

Placing the mic directly overhead gives the best sound quality and quantity. Because the microphone can be pointed directly downward, it will tend to reject sounds that don't come from directly underneath—a good thing when you are shooting somewhere with lots of ambient noise, like traffic, planes, or other people. An actor's head is usually placed towards the top of the frame, so an overhead mic can get closer to the face than one placed underneath. A mic beneath the actor will tend to pick up an unnatural amount of bass sounds, as well, because the performer's body acts as a sounding board for low-frequency sound. Furthermore, a mic underneath will pick up the rustling of the actor's clothing as well as her footsteps. An overhead placement captures a more natural sound, while avoiding all these pitfalls. All things being equal, it is the way to go.

Not everyone is happy about placing the mic overhead, though, because of the potential for **boom shadows**, dark lines that can fall on the actor's face if the boom swings under a light source.

Overhead mic placements might not be possible in a wide- or low-angle shot, where the boom would be visible. In this case, another option must be found.

Planted Mics

Mics may be planted on the set in some cases. This is an imperfect solution, as the mic will tend to pick up the low-frequency sounds mentioned above. Also, if the mic is buried inside scenery or behind greenery, the sound may be muffled. The best mics to use in this situation are the boundary-layer mics, placed flush against a wall, ceiling, or tabletop. Of course, putting the mic on a tabletop where an actor sets something down would be a poor choice, unless you like the "clunk" you hear when that beer stein hits the table.

One of the more interesting effects of a planted mic is used for baseball. ESPN plants mics inside each base, to capture the impact of the base runner's foot.

Body Mics

If there is no better option, the actors may be fitted with body mics and wireless transmitters. A body mic can be placed just under an actor's chin, but it will suffer the low-frequency gain discussed earlier. Putting the mics on or inside clothing can lead to the sounds of the clothing being recorded along with the dialogue. If the camera is far enough away, mics can be placed over the ear or at the hairline, producing high-fidelity sound at a strong level. If body mics are in use, actors must remain aware of them, since a quick hug can produce a deafening "thunk." If the soundman is running for the door with his hands over his ears after that last love scene, you'll know why.

Wireless body mics are quite common in sitcoms, where live audiences preclude the use of booms, close-ups are rare, and time pressure is intense.

Wireless transmitters can also cause a slew of problems, due to interference from set radios and passing police cars. Modern "frequency-agile" mics can be switched around to different frequencies to find one that is clear for use. On movie lots, the sound department must carefully track which sets are using which frequencies, so the kids from *Friends* don't end up being recorded for *NYPD Blue*.

Recording Decks

Now that we've made some sound, we have to have a place to put it. Enter the recording deck. There are a number of different issues here, including:

Analog versus Digital Recording

Analog recording was the accepted technique for recording sound until the very end of the twentieth century. The analog process records the sound to tape as a continuously changing electrical signal. This signal is fed into a magnetic head that is pressed against a flexible tape that has been impregnated with carbon fibers. As the strength of the magnet fluctuates, the carbon fibers are turned to line up with the magnet. The stronger the signal (the louder the sound), the more carbon fibers are reoriented. When played back over a head that is sensitive to magnetism, the orientation of the carbon fibers is interpreted and the sound is reproduced. That's why setting a magnet down on an audiotape is a really bad idea.

Digital recording depends on something called **sampling**. When an audio signal enters a digital system, that system measures the level of the sound for an instant and assigns that level a number. The number is the sample. Then, the system listens for another instant, measures the sound again, and assigns another sample. This string of samples is stored on tape, just like you store a spreadsheet on your computer. When played back, the system reads the numbers and produces that level of sound. What makes this sampling process work is the fact that digital systems can do it very quickly, at least forty-four thousand times a second. Two sampling rates are in common use—44.1 kilohertz (meaning 44,100 times per second) and 48 kilohertz (48,000 times per second).

Also growing in popularity is 96 kilohertz, although some people consider it overkill.

Besides the sampling rate, digital recording comes in different **bit rates**. This describes how accurate the sample is. More is better. The standard is 16 bit, but 18 and 20 bit are coming along soon.

The important thing about digital recording versus analog is that it is less susceptible to noise. Because the samples are just numbers, they cannot be distorted like the constantly changing electrical signal used in analog recording.

To this day, some audiophiles will swear that analog recording is warmer, richer, and more realistic than the digital form. Whether or not you agree, the fact is, with its higher fidelity and ease of use, digital recording has won the battle of the formats, hands down.

Point of trivia: Analog, tape-based recording was actually invented by the Germans during World War II in order to broadcast Hitler's speeches. The first tape-based recording decks were copied from the Germans by U.S. Army officers and brought to Hollywood after the war.

Nagra Tape Decks

The venerable **Nagra** reel-to-reel tape deck deserves a seat in the film and TV hall of fame, especially now that its career as the reigning champ of analog audio recording is winding down.

The Nagra was designed specifically to record production sound, and it has been a ubiquitous presence on sets around the world for decades. The original Nagra was an open-reel, analog tape deck that recorded on quarter-inch tape. "Open-reel" means that the tape spooled from one reel to the other out in the open, as opposed to inside a casing, like a cassette. Later on, Nagra appeared with time code, removing the need to have the marker slate clapped before every shot. (People still do it, just to be sure.)

Analog tape decks have had their day, however, and film and TV production has moved into the digital age, at least in the area of sound recording. Nagra analog machines have, for the most part, been swept aside by . . .

DAT

DAT (or R-DAT—it is the same thing) has become the medium of choice for production sound recording. The sound is recorded digitally;

plus, professional quality DAT machines have time code built right in. Both open-reel and closed-cassette DATs exist. The Nagra company has, in fact, begun to put out digital versions of its venerable deck. The ubiquitous Nagra name, however, has been joined by many other manufacturers, like Sony and Panasonic.

DAT machines come in stereo (two-channel) versions, as well as multichannel models like the ADAT or Tascam DA-88. The multichannel digital decks are used in more complex setups where the engineer needs to record multiple tracks simultaneously, like on a complicated film shoot or sitcom. These formats are also used to pass sounds around in postproduction.

THE RECORDING PROCESS

We already know from the "Who Does What" chapter who the sound crew is—a sound mixer and a boom operator, at the very least—so let's walk through their process on the set.

In normal shooting circumstances, the soundman's setup is fairly simple, so he will wait until the lighting guys are done before even stepping on the set. Once he has arrived, he will find an out-of-the-way spot relatively close to the set and set up his mixer. Then he will begin to scope out mic placements in the scene. If life is good for him, he will get to use the optimum placement—an overhead boom. If life is complicated that day, he will have to put together a solution involving planted or body microphones. In any case, once shooting starts, he pays close attention to the shot and take numbers, making sure they get recorded on the audiotape. If the camera assistant calls it out when clapping the slate, great. Otherwise, the sound mixer will record them onto the tape himself, using a mic at his position.

Before the first shot, the mixer takes the slate and hooks it up to his tape deck to *jam sync*. This involves syncing up the time code in the slate with the time code in the tape deck. Once the two are running in sync, they can be disconnected with the reasonable certainty that they will stay that way. A good mixer will grab the slate once or twice more during the day to jam sync again, just to make sure.

At the beginning or end of scenes, it is good practice to wait a few seconds before saying "Action" or "Cut." This leaves time for the operator

The boom operator.

to get a little **room tone**, the sound of the space where you are filming. This is useful stuff for the sound editor when she tries to piece together the dialogue track. Editors use room tone to provide a bed for the dialogue or to fill empty spaces where noises must be cut out.

As the shots progress, the mixer and the boom operator must communicate closely. The boom operator wears a headset so he can hear what he is recording. The mixer can use the mic at his mixer to give instructions to the boom operator over those headphones. The operator, in turn, can talk into the recording mic if he wants to reach the mixer. Of course, they must be completely professional if the tape is running.

Speaking of professional, Hollywood sound people have a strict unwritten code about not revealing what they have heard through their mics between takes, so don't ever ask a soundman to break that confidence. Many a Hollywood soundman has taken celebrity secrets to the grave.

It is not unusual, at the end of a shot (or the end of the day), for a sound mixer to request **wild lines**. These are lines that are recorded without rolling the camera. They are insurance for the mixer—just in case a line is lost during a scene, he will have a replacement on tape. The mixer may also ask for a few moments of quiet to record more room tone. The longer the chunk of room tone he can get, the happier the editor will be. Getting room tone at the end of a shoot is hard sometimes—

the rest of the crew can smell the end of the day, and they are anxious to start loading out. Making them sit silently is like making a six-year-old have breakfast before opening presents on Christmas Day.

AUDIO PLAYBACK

Occasionally, a production sound mixer will be asked to make noise, instead of just recording it. The most common situation is playing back prerecorded music for a music video or dance number. In this case, the sound mixer will bring a time-code DAT machine to the set, along with an amp and speakers. By jam syncing the slate to the DAT, the mixer can ensure that each chunk of film shot will be time-coded to that exact place in the music. This makes life easier in the editing suite, because the editor can call up all the pieces of film that were shot during a particular line of music. He can then quickly switch between them, creating a montage without having to go through the painstaking process of matching each movement of the singer's lips to the words in the song.

Chapter 12:

CONTINUITY, COVERAGE, AND CHAOS: LIFE ON THE SET

The first people to arrive on the morning of the shoot are usually the electricians. For one thing, almost anything that anybody has to do on a set requires power, and the "sparkies" are in charge of providing that. They will run power to the makeup trailer for makeup lights, to catering for coffee, and to the camera crew to charge their batteries.

The second group of people to show up is usually crafts services: the snack people. They have an essential job, and they don't take it lightly. They must provide coffee. Stat.

You think I'm kidding.

The set is run by the first assistant director, known as the 1st AD (or just the AD). The AD's job is as thankless as a galley slave master. He is in charge of keeping the production on track, the day on schedule, and the shenanigans to a minimum. That voice you hear making announcements on the set is theirs. They constantly ask, "How long until you're ready?" They are paid to be impatient. (Question: How many ADs does it take to change a lightbulb? Answer: "I asked for that light to be fixed an hour ago!") A good 1st AD doesn't spend the whole day yelling, however. Professional film people understand that someone has to be the whip-cracker, but the good 1st ADs are both firm and friendly.

ADs are always letting people know what is "up." I don't mean what is up as in "wazzzzzuup?" There is always one process that is currently the central focus of the crew. The AD will let everyone know what that is by yelling, "Rehearsal is up!" or, "Lighting is up!" or, when we are actually shooting, "Picture is up!"

Shortly after the lighting crew, the camera and sound crews will show up and begin to stake out space on the set. Camera needs enough room to store all the pieces of the camera package (and the bulky cases it all comes in), as well as a table to put the camera on to clean it, load film, and change lenses. The sound crew needs a small, out-of-the-way corner to set up their mixer.

The actors are called in well before the shooting starts because they must do an all-important rehearsal with the director. Under the watchful eye of the director and the DP, the actors rehearse the scene that will be shot later. The director is planning the angles, composition, and camera movements he will use, while the DP is mentally arranging the lighting to create the proper effect. The real camera is not used at this point; it is still out in the camera area being cleaned and set up. Instead, the director looks through a *director's viewfinder*, which is a fancy name for a viewfinder with a place to attach a lens. Using the viewfinder, the director can look through the lens that will be attached to the camera without having to lug around the whole camera. This helps him see what the camera will see. The viewfinder can be fitted with all the same lenses as the actual camera, but it is small enough to fit in the palm of your hand.

The director, with the help of the 1st AD and the UPM, has already created a shot list showing which shots will be filmed that day. This list is the supreme reference that everyone will use to plan the day. The film's progress is measured (among other ways) in feet of film shot. A full-length feature film will shoot around 250,000 to 300,000 feet of film in all, more or less, depending on the budget and the style of the director. A professional crew will shoot around six thousand feet a day. Do the math, and you will discover why forty-five days is considered a normal shooting schedule.[23]

If a film has complicated action sequences, the production may hire a *storyboard artist*, who prepare a set of drawings that graphically show the placement and movement of the camera. Sadly, many productions act penny-wise and pound-foolish by cutting the storyboard artist out of the

---

[23] There are exceptions, because of mishaps or directorial style. Kevin Costner's *Waterworld* shot in 220 days due to a series of disasters, including the entire set sinking to the ocean floor. Director Stanley Kubrick shot over four hundred days on *Eyes Wide Shut* because, well, he was Stanley Kubrick.

Examples of storyboards (based on work by Josh Hayes of Storyboards, Inc.).

budget, leaving the director to communicate his vision through explanation, wild gestures, and script-margin doodles.

The director walks around the actors and the set, peering through the eyepiece and trying different angles. He talks with the DP about the style of shot he is after, and they agree on a lens. As they talk and gesture, the 1st AC walks behind them, marking the floor with tape, showing the locations of camera moves and actors. If you are an actor, make sure that the AC marks where you stand. Cameras rarely film the floor, so feel free to give yourself whatever help you need. Of course, one of the major skills that all film and TV actors must learn is the ability to "feel" your mark—that is, to feel where you are on the set, so when the camera is rolling, you don't have to look down to know you are standing on your mark. When you are rehearsing, take note of your position relative to the furniture. The corner of a table or the end of a drapery may give you a visual reference to find your mark. If you are really having trouble, have a grip put a sandbag on your mark so you can feel it with your foot. Then, don't trip over it.

After the actors have run the scene to the director's satisfaction (full-out acting is rarely necessary; doing the right movements will suffice), they are sent off to makeup. Immediately, the lighting and grip crews attack the set, putting up the lighting and grip equipment under the direction of the gaffer and key grip, both of whom are following the DP's instructions. The grips must also set up the dolly and track if one is in use. Once that is done, the camera crew members slide up with their expensive toys and begin to find their place. As the lighting is taking shape, the crew will call for *stand-ins*, actors or PAs who must sit quietly where the stars will sit, giving the crew a live body so they can focus the lights and practice the camera moves. On a low-budget film, the stand-in is an unlucky PA who may or (more likely) may not resemble the actor at all. On high-dollar shows, a stand-in is hired specifically because he resembles the star in question, particularly in height, weight, and hair color. The stand-in is given an identical costume and a really dull job. (Sit there and let us light you.) Most major stars have one person who works as their stand-in on a regular basis, at least when the movie is shooting in L.A. or New York.

While the set is being lit, the actors are getting their makeup and rehearsing the scene. The director may leave the set and work with them, or he may choose to leave them alone.

Back at the set, the lights are coming on, the camera is up and running, and the sound crew is testing its system. It is a time of furious activity at the beginning, but, after a while, the main chunks of lighting are in, and the "tweaking period" begins.

Film is a highly precise art, best practiced by people with an eye for detail. Once the basic chunks of light are in, the DP and the gaffer will begin to endlessly shift things around, trying to eliminate (or create) tiny shadows, produce interesting patterns, and generally pursue perfection. At this point, most of the crew is standing around, waiting for the call to action. Long periods of discussion and small changes will suddenly come to a head with a shouted request and a body on the move. Maybe the shot needs more light, maybe the color is wrong, maybe the sun came up a little higher than we thought. In any case, changes are in order, and no one wants to be the one that everyone is waiting for. The lens is too short, so an assistant sprints for a longer one. A flare is hitting the lens, so a grip leaps into action with a flag. We need a slash of light on that wall, so an electrician is sent running for another redhead. It's a game of hot potato, essentially. When the AD walks up and says, "What are we waiting for?" you just don't want it to be you. This rhythm of inaction and sudden, explosive action will continue until the setup is complete. This is perhaps the most boring time of day for the actors, who wait, doomed to inactivity, while the bees buzz around the set. Sometimes, it seems like the lighting setup cannot possibly take any longer, and, then, it does.

When the lighting is almost done, the actors are called to the set, accompanied by a makeup person or two who will keep them looking fabulous under the hot lights. There always seems to be a frantic period that happens just as the actors get to the set. There always seem to be a host of last-minute details right before the moment of calm.

GETTING THE SHOT

So, the time has come. The set has been lit, the camera moves have been rehearsed, the actors know their lines, exorbitant salaries have been paid or crazed volunteers recruited, the sun is at the perfect level, the mood is expectant, and it is Time to Make a Movie. Here's how it goes:

Amidst the controlled chaos brought on by up to seven different crews (camera, lighting, grip, sound, wardrobe, makeup, and special effects), all trying to do their thing, the AD is yelling things like, "Is camera ready? Is costume ready? Is the rain ready?" Finally, as the moment nears, things begin to calm down a little bit. Grips, electricians, wardrobe, and makeup people all stand aside while camera and sound people move in. The actors, fresh from makeup and running lines in the trailer, thread their way through a forest of C-stands looking for their mark. "Rehearsal is up," calls the AD, sometimes followed by, "Settle, please!"—a request for quiet. When things have mostly calmed down, the actors will run another rehearsal. If there are camera moves involved, the camera crew and dolly grip will rehearse them, as well.[24] Once everyone is clear, the AD may yell, "Last looks!" This is the cue for all the art directors, props people, greensmen, and so forth to take one last look at the set (and the monitor) to make sure that every little thing is in place. Then, it's time for:

"Picture is up!"

When picture is up, we're actually going to roll film. From this point forward, there should be a predictable, reassuring series of commands from the AD and the director. This rhythm helps people deal with the stress and focus on the goal: create a few minutes (or seconds) of usable film.

"Quiet, please!" from the AD. At this point, if there are PAs on radios outside the set or soundstage, they will be notified that the scene is about to begin. They should call out to everyone in earshot: "We're rolling!" If you haven't already done so, TURN OFF YOUR CELL PHONE AND YOUR PAGER.

"Roll sound!" from the AD.

Sound is always rolled before the film for one simple reason: It's cheaper. Thirty-five millimeter film runs at ninety feet per minute and costs anywhere from fifty cents to two bucks a foot, including the processing. I usually tell people that if the camera is rolling, you are spending a hundred bucks a minute. Audiotape is dirt cheap compared to that. Therefore, sound rolls first.

When the sound rolls, you might see a flashing red light, called a *wigwag*, come on. It looks like a rotating police beacon, but it is connected to the soundman's tape deck. Whenever that deck is rolling, that light will flash, telling everyone to shut up, stand still, and for God's sake, don't yank open the soundstage door and yell that lunch is ready. When the wigwag comes on, whatever you are doing, just sit tight until it goes off.

---

[24] There is a school of thought in high-budget filmmaking that you should always film the rehearsal, on the theory that, who knows, they might nail it the first time. If you can afford to commit the film, this approach takes advantage of the freshness that the actors bring to the scene when they first come onto the set. If you are shooting just two or three takes, you risk wasting that film on a rehearsal that isn't good enough for the film.

The marker slate.

In older times, it took a few seconds for tape decks and cameras to get up to speed, so when the machine was ready to record, the sound mixer would yell, "Sound speed!" The tradition has hung on into the digital age, even though modern decks come up to speed instantly. Some mixers will yell, "Rolling!"

"Roll camera!" from the AD.

Now the real money is being spent, so we move quickly.

"Speed!" from the camera operator.

"Marker!" Now the AD is asking the person with the ***marker slate*** to step in front of the camera and "mark" the film. The marker slate, or ***clapper***, is that black slate with the hinged bar on the top that you see in every Hollywood gift shop. On it is written the name of the film, the number of the shot, and various other information that will be useful to know in the editing suite, like which roll of audiotape we are currently recording on. Scene numbers come from the script. Every time the crew creates a new shot of the scene, it is given a new letter. For example, the first shot of scene 14 (usually the master) is called scene 14A. If the crew moves on to a different shot of the same scene—say, a two-shot—that would be 14B. As long as you are shooting the same piece of script, the scene number does not change, only the letter. Every time you do another take of the same shot, you get a new take number. The clapper (the term also refers to the person who does this job) steps in front of the camera and says the number of the shot and the take out loud. This marks the audiotape, as well. So, for example:

"Scene fourteen C, take three!" He then slaps down the little bar on the slate, providing a visual and audio cue that can be used to synchronize the film and tape later. He steps away and there is a moment of silence before the director says the magic word:

"Action!"

A PATHETICALLY INCOMPLETE LIST OF WHAT CAN GO WRONG WITH A SHOT

- The actor forgot his line
- The actor broke character or laughed
- The actor missed his mark or stepped into a shadow
- A motorcycle drove past
- A plane flew over
- An air conditioner turned on
- The costume was hanging funny
- The costume was worn differently (more/fewer buttons open, tie untied/tied) from the master shot
- The actor handled a prop (cigarette, watch, priceless gems) differently than in the master shot
- The boom got into the shot
- A light got into the shot
- Someone walked through the background
- The explosion didn't go off
- The rain didn't turn on
- There was a police siren in the distance
- The car didn't start
- The camera jiggled

- The dolly grip missed his mark
- The focus was wrong
- The film ran out
- A cloud passed over the sun
- There was a hair in the gate

This list isn't even starting to be comprehensive. Hundreds, perhaps thousands, of things can go wrong. And I'm not just talking about the gross errors listed above. As a shot develops, people start watching things unfold on the monitor, and the suggestions start to flow. "How about if he turns the other way?" "Can we get the light off that tree?" "Can she sit up straighter in the chair?" "The spaghetti looks funny. Can we add meatballs?" A good director knows when to let these suggestions happen and when to shut his ears and keep moving. The fact is, the tiniest, most insignificant shot can be ditzed with until Judgment Day, and it will probably be better. The question for a director or a producer is: How much better and how long will that take? One of the greatest skills of any director is knowing when to say, "Next setup."

Directors like Steven Spielberg and Woody Allen, both of whom are known for bringing in pictures on time and on budget, know when to cut their losses. Sure, the shot through the bottom of the glass as the alcoholic takes it from his lips would be extra-super-cool, but when it isn't coming together and the clock is ticking, it's time to move on.

The action continues until the director yells, "Cut!" If we are going to do it again, he will nod at the AD and the call will go up, "Back to one!" meaning that everyone should reset everything to the opening position, 'cause we doin' it again.

By the way, every now and then the clapper won't get the slate in front of the camera before the scene starts. This happens a lot when shooting unpredictable things, like children and animals. Sometimes, you have to just dive right in, because the thing you want to shoot is already happening. Or, the camera is still rolling from the previous take and the director doesn't want to break up the flow by interrupting the action with a slate. Whatever the reason, the clapper will solve the situation by putting the slate at the end of the scene, but holding it upside down. This is known as a *tail slate*.

"CHECK THE GATE"

Did you notice the last item in that list above, the one about the hair in the gate? If you didn't know what that meant (and you should), read on.

As we talked about in chapter 5, the film passes through a winding, twisting path on the way to where it actually gets exposed. When the critical moment comes, the film is slammed home between two pieces of metal and locked in place for 1/24 of a second. The shutter opens, and the light coming from the carefully lit blockbuster scene floods through the gate and exposes the film. The two pieces of metal fly apart and the film is dragged off to the take-up reel like a bad comedian getting the hook. Those pieces of metal are called the *gate*, and they can be trouble. Because the film flies by the gate just a fraction of an inch away, any dust or hair or gacky thing that is riding on it can get deposited on the gate, where it can produce a beautiful dust or hair or gacky-shaped shadow on the film. *Checking the gate* before the shot is good, but it doesn't tell you if anything arrived during the shot. Hence, the last thing the camera assistant will do after a shot is open the camera body and check to see if there is anything in the gate. If not, we're done, move on. If yes, then we have to clean it out and do the shot again. If the camera assistant is good, there will very rarely be anything in the gate. If the AC is lagging and not following the rules of camera cleanliness, it's gonna be a long day.

"Checking the gate" is a bit of housekeeping that the camera assistant does continually throughout the shoot. Generally, it's done after each setup. That's why you hear, "Cut! Print! Check the gate!" when the crew is done at one location. Oh, and Jim Carrey says it in *Dr. Seuss' How the Grinch Stole Christmas* when he is directing his dog, Max. So, now you know the inside joke.

SHOOTING RATIO

A film crew's efficiency can be partly determined by the *shooting ratio*. This ratio shows how much film you shot versus how much you will actually use in the film. If you are making a 120-minute movie and you shot 1,200 feet of film, your ratio is ten to one. Multiple takes drive up the shooting ratio, as does "dead time" at the beginnings and ends of shots. A lower shooting ratio is not necessarily better. More than anything else, the shooting ratio is directly related to the budget. Microbudget films, which rarely do more than one take of a scene, may shoot three to one (or less, God forbid). Low-budget films, where every foot of film counts but scenes are shot from multiple angles, may shoot five or even ten to one. Big-budget Hollywood pictures shoot twenty to one or more. It is a question of economics. If you are paying Tom Cruise $20 million, then it doesn't make sense to scrimp on film. You've got one chance with your star and you want to make it count. If, however, you've got a volunteer crew and you sold your car to make the film, you want to shoot more economically.[25]

COVERAGE

On the other hand, no director wants to shortchange himself in the editing suite. In classic 1950s-studio-style filmmaking, the rule for shooting a two-person scene was, shoot the scene five times: once from the front, including all the action (the master shot), then once over each actor's shoulder, then once in close-up on each actor. The editor would have five options at any point in the scene, depending on whether he wanted to show the whole scene, focus on one actor or the other, or move in tight to reveal emotion or inner thoughts. Getting *coverage* means to cover all the angles of a scene in order to give the editor enough options in putting it together.

Of course, rules are made to be broken (but only by those who understand them). Many people consider *Citizen Kane* to be one of the greatest movies ever made because it violates these rules with abandon. The camera is placed in all sorts of uncommon places, and standard shots, like the "over-the-shoulder" shot, are barely used. Even for the budding Orson Welleses of the world, however, the concept of coverage still holds—cover all the lines and action in the script from several different angles so your editor doesn't lose hair, sleep, or stomach lining over your film.

---

[25] The record, according to the *Guinness Book of World Records*, is the chariot race scene in the 1925 version of *Ben-Hur*, where editor Lloyd Nosler cut down 200,000 feet of film (about 2,222 minutes) into 750 feet (about eight minutes), a shooting ratio of 267:1.

CONTINUITY

When the chase scene through John Malkovich's subconscious happens in *Being John Malkovich*, Catherine Keener and Cameron Diaz fly through room after room, inside and outside, screaming and yelling, clawing and kicking and (in Cameron Diaz's case) firing a revolver wildly. All of these scenes were shot at different times, on different sets, days or weeks apart. In order for the sequence to flow smoothly, someone had to keep track of the actresses' hairstyles, clothing, smudges or bruises, and countless other details so they looked the same going into a door as they did coming out the other side. Did Cameron have the gun in her left hand or her right? Was Catherine's blouse torn yet? And on and on.

And it isn't just clothing. If you want to cut from a wide shot of an actor peeling an orange to a close-up of the same actor, the orange must be in approximately the same state of unpeeling. It won't do to have a half-peeled orange in the wide shot only to have an unpeeled one in the close-up. And yet, this is a tricky thing because those shots were not made back to back. They may be hours apart.[26]

And how about smoking? Cigarettes don't just stop burning when the camera turns off. If a character is smoking, he must smoke that cigarette the same way, at the same speed, in every take. Otherwise, the cigarette is likely to suddenly grow in the middle of the scene, "unsmoking" itself and becoming longer. It's enough to make you quit. Smoking, I mean.

Keeping all these details straight is known as maintaining **continuity**, and it is principally the job of the script supervisor. Their scripts are covered with notes about the state of people's dress, which hand they used to grab the cigarette, and what line they were saying when they opened the window.

Of course, nobody's perfect, and things get missed. These are known as **continuity errors**, and they fuel some of Hollywood's best trivia games. Producing a full-length feature film with no continuity errors is a Herculean task, and most films have at least one slip somewhere. Film fans have put up Web sites listing these tiny slipups (*Star Wars* has,

---

[26] This actually happens in *Out of Africa*, when Robert Redford is peeling oranges while talking to Meryl Streep.

literally, dozens), and those people who have not yet found direction in their lives spend hours combing DVDs looking for evidence of errors. In the movie *Casablanca*, for example:

- One of the knights in Rick's chess game momentarily disappears.
- While chatting with the inspector outside the Café Americain, Rick lights his cigarette twice.
- When Rick steps out of the pouring Paris rain and onto the train, his coat is bone-dry.

Oops.

Well, what can you do? A few tiny slips are inevitable, regardless of the valiant efforts of script supervisors and others. How else do you keep the film buffs happy between Oscar seasons?

The best thing an actor can do is keep track of her own continuity. Try to remember which hand you used to pick up the book, how much wine was in your glass, and whether you spoke first and then sat down, or vice versa. Actors have a lot to think about on a set, but maintaining your own continuity is important and will help the crew love you. You don't have to mind every little detail—you are there to act and you do have help—but the more you can pay attention to these things, the more you can contribute to the process.

Continuity errors are occasionally used to dramatic effect. Watch the scene in *A Clockwork Orange* in which Malcolm McDowell is slowly drugged while eating spaghetti. In each shot, the level of spaghetti rises and falls, regardless of how much McDowell eats. At one point, it even sprouts a meatball. Kubrick deliberately changed the spaghetti in various shots to increase the sense of distorted reality.

Well, that's the story, anyway. And they're sticking to it.

ACTING TIPS

Besides helping to maintain your continuity, there are a few other things you can do as an actor to help the crew love you:

- **Hit your mark**. When the scene is being set up, the camera assistant and 2nd AD will place marks on the floor, showing the camera crew where to move and the actors where to stand. Learn how to land directly on these marks without looking down. If you miss, the focus and framing of the shot may be wrong, forcing the crew to do another take, especially if a long lens (with shallow depth of field) is in use.

- **Stay steady in close-ups.** If you are being shot in a close-up, the slightest movement left or right might throw you out of the frame. Moving forward or back may destroy the focus. Learn how to be still and to emote with your voice and face. In long shots, you can use your body. Of course, this means you have to be aware of how big the shot is.

- **Don't step on the other actor.** No, I don't mean his feet. I mean his lines. When the dialogue is edited, the sound people will want to put your voice on a different track than your scene partner's voice. That way, they can tweak the voices independently of one another. For example, your voice may be too soft and need to be turned up, while his may not. For that matter, the editors may decide you said the line better in the previous take, so they may want to import that line into this scene. Therefore, when playing a scene, try to let the other actor stop speaking completely before you speak. If you are supposed to interrupt, that can be created in the editing room. Half an instant is all that is required. You don't have to leave a hole to drive a truck through. The exception to this rule is a two-shot where both actors' mouths are visible. If this is the case, play the scene, including interruptions, as it should finally appear.

- **Find your eye line.** The *eye line* is an imaginary line that starts at your eyes and extends out to whatever you are supposed to be looking at. In many cases, the thing you are supposed to be looking at isn't really there, so make sure you ask the director where he wants your eye line to be. If you are supposed to be talking to a child, for example, then your eye line will be pointing down. Once your shot is cut together with the rest of the shots in the scene, it is essential that the eye lines match. If you are doing effect shots and you are supposed to be sharing the frame with a computer-generated creature, the crew should mount an object (a tennis ball is traditional) wherever that creature's eyes are going to be. Finally, if someone is sitting in your eye line and distracting you, it is perfectly okay for you to ask them to "Please clear my eye line."

- **Learn your lines.** Everyone forgets a line now and then, but a film crew never forgets an actor who arrives on the set each day with a professional attitude and memorized pages.

Chapter 13:

TELECINE AND "THE DAILIES"

Like any photographer, the first thing a DP has to do is get the film developed. During the production of a film, it is important for the director to see the product of his crew's labors as soon as possible. It takes a lot of effort and money to get a cast and crew together, so the director wants to know right away if a scene was shot successfully— that is, if "we got it."

At the end of the day, the reels of exposed film are sent to the lab.[27] This is a time of great stress for a DP, as the film he has lovingly and carefully exposed to the light is snatched away from him, then plunged into a succession of toxic chemical solutions that can bring out the finest nuances of light and shadow or brutally destroy the fruits of his labor. It is no wonder that DPs foster deep relationships with labs, sometimes sending film stock thousands of miles to have it processed by a reputable firm. Of course, any professional lab in Los Angeles could kiss its livelihood good-bye by ruining just one reel of a major production (people talk), but the chances of losing irreplaceable footage to a lab mistake increases when you work out of town. Even without creating a disaster, though, a lab can wreak havoc in lots of small ways, from mistaken exposures to swapping reels to scratching the film stock.

The film is developed overnight and transferred to video the next day. After another day of shooting, the director, producer, DP, and anyone else who has enough juice to be in the room gather to screen the previous day's footage. Because they are viewed every day during

---

[27] Sometimes, a crew won't even wait until the end of the day. When *The Godfather* was shooting in New York, the crew was periodically threatened by the local Mafia bosses, who didn't like the unflattering portrayal of gangsters. As each reel was shot, the crew would yank it from the camera and immediately sprint it off the set.

the shoot, these pieces of raw footage are known as the **dailies** or the **rushes**.[28]

Dailies may be shown in one of two ways: either on film or video. Showing them on film is more expensive, not only because the film has to actually be printed, but also because a screening room and a pro-jectionist must be hired. Video dailies are cheaper to produce and can be sent all over the world. Many directors and DPs, however, object strongly to video dailies, because they do not give a clear indication of what was actually shot. Colors will be faded, contrast will look differ-ent, and details that can be seen on film may not be seen on video. For this reason, all established DPs will require film dailies and will state this in their contracts.

One famous story from the original **Star Trek** series shows the challenging relationship between the DP and the lab. One particular episode featured a green-skinned girl doing a sensuous dance for Captain Kirk. When the dailies came back, her skin looked healthy and pink, so they shot the scene again with even greener makeup. Still, the film came back with not a hint of green. After they spent several days shooting and reshooting the poor actress with ever-increasing layers of green body paint, the crew figured out that the lab guys were looking at the film and saying, "Wow, that girl's skin looks green!" Thinking they had botched the processing, they corrected the color to make the actress look normal again.

The master film—the one that was shot on the set—can never, ever be replaced. It is a product of thousands of person-hours and, poten-tially, millions of dollars. Even the most hardened cinematographer can feel a knot in his stomach when handing over raw, undeveloped stock to an unknown lab. It takes nerves of steel to develop film. There are just too damn many things that can go wrong. And once they're wrong, they stay wrong. These days, high-budget films shooting in exotic

---

[28] Until recently, the dailies were actually viewed on film, requiring that a positive print be made from the negative that was exposed on the set. The economically motivated switch to video dailies is a pain for filmmakers, who can no longer see the real colors and texture of the film print, but it is a financial reality we are stuck with for now.

locations will often bring an entire lab with them to the set, both to insure quality and to allow the director to see the results right away.

Cinematography is a black art, for sure. A DP must trust his camera package, his light meter, his instincts, his assistants, and the lab to do what he expects of them. In video, the tape can be rewound after the shot and everybody can have a look. In film, you don't get to see what you have done until the set is closed down and the actors have gone home, and it is mind-bogglingly difficult to set it all up again.

Once the film successfully emerges from the lab (and it is a rare piece of film that doesn't), it enters the mysterious realm of *telecine*, the home of another black artist, the *colorist*.

TELECINE

Most of the film that is shot in this country never sees the inside of a movie theater. That's because most of it is destined for television. Commercials, music videos, made-for-TV movies, and television dramas are shot on film. A few sitcoms are shot on video, as are daytime soaps, sports, news, game shows, porn, and the current money tree, "reality TV," but a huge portion of television content is still shot on film. The greater resolution and smoother picture that film creates are still state of the art, even in multicamera live shoots like *Friends*. (Interestingly, these shoots are still called "tapings," to distinguish them from films that are shot with one camera and no live audience.)

All this film stock is converted into video as soon as it is processed. That way, the originals can be locked up in a climate-controlled vault, guarded by a seven-headed dog, and not be damaged. Most of this original footage will never again be used. Only the film destined to become feature films will ever see the light of a projector again.

The process of converting film into video is called *telecine*.

A telecine (*tel'-eh-sin-ee*) machine is an enormous and complicated machine that looks like a big film projector with its lens pointed into a box. The film is projected through a video lens hooked up to an electronic chip (several of them, actually) not unlike the chips in your video camera. Those chips convert the light coming through the film into a video signal and lay it down onto videotape. As that process is happening, the colorist is controlling a bank of dials that determine how much of each color should actually get through onto the tape. A good colorist can shade footage to make it more comic, more frightening, or later in the day. He can pick out certain colors and change them. He can add shadows or take them away. The colorist (usually working side by side with the DP) can alter the entire look of a project (turning a green-skinned girl pink again, for example). He is a good guy to be nice to.

There are several levels of color correction that the colorist can perform:

- **Lab Transfer:** The quick and dirty transfer. The colorist will use a standard color-correction chart, plugging in common values and working very quickly. This is used only when time and money are at an absolute minimum, like when you are producing dailies. It's fast, efficient, and cheap, but of lower quality.
- **Best Light Transfer:** The middle of the road. Each scene will be attended to individually, but not compared to the rest of the film. Still not high quality enough for a professional release but often done when the footage is just being sent to an editor or a vault. Generally, a "best light" correction will be done early in the production process when everyone knows we will be back to do a better job later. Also known as a *one light transfer*.
- **Scene-by-Scene:** The best level of color correction. The colorist will stop at each scene and come up with the best possible look, using all his tricks. Plus, he will compare each scene to other scenes in the film, ensuring that things look good when seen in sequence. This level of correction is applied when the film is ready to be distributed. It is the most time-consuming and, no surprise, the most expensive.

At the center of the telecine system is the *da Vinci color corrector*. It comes in several levels of quality, along with several predictable levels of price. The higher-level units offer the ability to focus on particular portions of the frame (even moving portions), adding or subtracting colors in isolated areas. By the way, if you ever wondered how old black-and-white films are colorized, this is how.

There are a number of technical details and challenges involved with telecine. One of the most basic is frame rate. You may recall that most film is shot at twenty-four frames per second. Video, however, plays at thirty frames per second. Each frame of video is drawn with two *fields*; that is, two passes of the electron gun that actually puts the image on the screen. So, we have, in one corner, twenty-four frames of film and, in the other corner, thirty frames and sixty fields.

In order to create harmony between these two media, a telecine machine does a bit of magic: it pauses every now and then and creates two duplicate fields from one frame of film. It adds this extra field to every other frame of video, creating a pattern of AAA, BB, CCC, DD, etc. Because of the three-two rhythm of frames, this process is known as *three/two pulldown*, and it is what allows twenty-four-frame film to become thirty-frame video.

As the film footage is converted to video, it is also married up to the audio. You may recall how the audio was recorded (either on the analog Nagra machine or the digital DAT) separately from the film. Remember that marker slate the camera assistant held up in front of the camera lens before every shot? Well, in the old days (and today, in ultra-low-budget filmmaking), that slapping sound caused by the clapper being brought down onto the slate was used to synchronize film and tape. The editor would find that short, sharp sound on the tape and physically line it up with the frame of film where the clapper hit the slate. The magnetic tape was then run in sync with the film, on a separate reel, so that the director and editor could watch the footage. These giant machines are called *flatbeds* or *Moviolas*, and you will still see them here and there in film schools and third-world countries.

TIME CODE: THE CONDUCTOR OF THE MEDIA ORCHESTRA

Imagine an orchestra sitting down to practice a symphony. Each section—violins, horns, percussion—knows what it is supposed to play, but no one has appeared to give the entire group the proper timing—that is, when to start and how fast to play. This is very much the situation with modern media production. Each section—audio, camera, editing, special effects—has its own chunk of the movie ready to go, but they all need a unifying element in order to play together. Orchestras have conductors. Film and TV have *time code*.

In the early years of film production, there were really only two elements that needed to be synchronized: the sound and the film that were recorded and shot on the set. The sound of Clark Gable talking had to be synchronized with the movements of his mouth. Enter the *marker slate.* At the beginning of each take, a camera assistant would hold up a small, black board in front of the camera lens. That board listed the name of the movie, the director, and the cameraman, as well as the number of the scene and the take. That slate became a label for each physical piece of film. With an editing room full of footage, all the editor had to do to identify a piece of film was look at the first few frames and read the slate right off the film. The slate also had a small wooden board attached to it, hinged on one end. After calling out the scene and take number, the assistant would slap that little board down onto the top of the slate, thereby "marking" the scene. Later, in the editing room, the editor would line up the smacking sound on the audiotape with the frame of film where the marker hit the slate. Then, by running the tape and the film together, the picture would be synchronized with the sound.

Like most good solutions, it was low-tech and it worked. There were problems with it—it could be a little inexact and the tape or the film might "drift," or run a little slow or fast over time—but the marker slate existed for decades, becoming part of the mythological image of moviemaking.

Life got more complicated, though, with the advent of video and the growth of special effects and complex audio tracks. A more flexible and exact timing standard was needed. Enter the Society of Motion Picture and Television Engineers, a group of frighteningly brilliant pocket-protector engineers, who set out to invent a timing standard that the entire industry could live by. In 1967, with a remarkable lack of proprietary fuss, they gave birth to SMPTE (pronounced "SIMP-tee") time code, a digital timing standard that allowed filmmakers to lock together audio, film, video, computers, and all sorts of other things in perfect synchronization. *SMPTE time code* is an eight-number code, consisting of hours, minutes, seconds, and frames, written like this: 00:00:00;00. Note the semicolon before the last number. Thus, the time-code number 01:34:24;17 would be read as "one hour, thirty-four minutes, twenty-four seconds, seventeen frames."

Time code can be printed on audiotape as an audible signal, videotape as a digital code, and even (much later) on the film itself.[29] Adding time code to videotape is called **striping it**.

In practice, time code works like this:

The soundman on a film set has a recording deck, usually a Nagra reel-to-reel or a DAT tape, that spits out time code continuously. The marker slate is plugged into the audio deck and synchronized with it, just like that moment in all good spy films where the conspirators "synchronize their watches." The display on the slate shows the same numbers as the tape deck. Even when the slate is unplugged from the audio deck, it still continues to run at the same speed. Therefore, no matter where the slate goes on the set, you can still see the time-code numbers that are being recorded on the tape. Where the slate goes, of course, is in front of the camera, where the running time-code numbers are filmed at the beginning of each take. Then, in the editing room, the editor simply stops the film at any frame where he can read the time code, runs the audio deck up to that time-code number, and then lets the film and tape run together, perfectly in sync.

Time code still continues to be used in the editing process, even after the film and sound are synchronized in the telecine suite. The tape that the film and audio are transferred onto has its own time code, separate from the time code that is recorded on the set. That time code is used throughout the editing

---

[29] The Aaton camera company created Aaton time code, which is actually printed on the film stock itself, like little bar codes. This is extremely useful when shooting a live event (like a concert) with several film cameras. By setting all those cameras to the same clock, you can use the time code numbers to bring together two raw pieces of film that were shot at the exact same instant—very helpful when you want to cut from one angle on the lead singer to another.

process to keep track of which cuts are being used in which order.

Time code is also used to synchronize special effects, computers, musical sound tracks, and many other things in television, film, and even live performance. Theme parks use time code to coordinate sound tracks with lighting and animated effects.

SMPTE did a wonderful job of creating a universal standard, but, nevertheless, time code evolved into different species for different uses. The most common are 24fps, 30fps, and 30 (drop frame). All of that nonsense refers to the number of "frames per second." Film runs at twenty-four frames per second and, therefore, gets 24fps time code. Video runs at thirty frames per second; hence, the 30fps time code. Just to be difficult, though, video actually runs a little more slowly than thirty frames per second: more like 29.97fps. Hence, a new form of time code was created that drops a frame about every thirty-three seconds to allow the tape to catch up, sort of like a reverse leap year. This is really only an issue in longer programs, but you might run into it. It doesn't really matter which variety of time code you use, as long as everyone on the project has the same. Otherwise, you run the risk of things drifting out of sync over time.

On many modern film sets, however, the slates are electronic and have a digital readout on the front. Those numbers that are running on the slate are called *time code* (see the sidebar above), and they are the glue that holds the audio and the film together. In order to synchronize the film and the tape, the colorist looks at a frame of film where he can see the time code running on the slate. Then, he calls up that precise place on the tape and pushes "record." The picture from the film and the audio from the tape both flow magically onto the video, perfectly in sync with each other.

You may ask, if the synchronization is done with the time code and not with the clap of the slate, why bother clapping the slate? Well, there are two reasons. For one, you never know when you might still need that sound; second, tradition dies hard in the film business. I think most people find that the clap of the slate centers everyone and focuses them on the task at hand. Remember, if you are the camera assistant, you should try to clap the slate softly (ACs call it "soft sticks") when you are close to an actor. If you are an actor, you can ask for soft sticks if the slate is distracting you.

Of course, there are many productions still working with a non-electronic marker slate. In these cases, the editors use the slap of the slate to synchronize the footage. There's no tech like low tech.

The final result of a telecine session is a videotape of the raw footage: "the dailies."

Based on the dailies, the director, DP, and producer may decide to shoot more footage of a scene, alter lighting or costumes or, hopefully, move on to new things. If the shoot is in a remote location, it is not unusual to set up a film lab right there, although in these days of Federal Express, it isn't always necessary. A second unit that is shooting remotely without the talent may not see the dailies at all, simply sending the footage off to Los Angeles, making do with phoned-in comments from the producers. "It's too dark, it's too moody, it's too blue," and so forth.

Of course, if a shoot is low budget or not repeatable (like a documentary), then you are stuck with whatever comes up, and you get to make the best of it.

The other product of a telecine session is a *flex file*, a computer-generated file that keeps track of video time code and film *edge numbers*. Film actually has numbers printed on it by the lab—these are the edge numbers. Guess where the lab puts them. On the edge. Okay, that was a gimme. These numbers are also known in some circles as the *keykode* (or, in the case of Aaton cameras, the *AatonCode*, a slightly more sophisticated system). It is *extremely* important that the relationship between the video time code and the film keykode be documented. Otherwise, you will go out and edit that video, then come back to the film stock and have absolutely no idea where to start cutting. The flex file keeps track of which time-code numbers (video) connect to which keykode numbers (film). It also keeps track of audio time code, so we know which piece of audio goes where. The telecine computer creates this file. The colorist puts it on a disc and hands that to the postproduction supervisor or some other responsible person at the end of the telecine session. Once the film is edited on video and the film is ready to be cut, the flex file is delivered to the negative cutter so he can translate the EDL into a list of edge numbers. Once he knows the edge numbers, he knows where to start cutting.

Chapter 14:

EDITING: HOW TO CREATE A REALITY

I once shot a documentary about a company that was using theatrical artists—singers, dancers, directors, etc.—to teach uptight medical researchers how to work in teams. It was a brilliant concept, really: Put a bunch of M.D.s, Ph.D.s, and other multilettered professionals in a hotel conference room and teach them to sing and tap-dance. If they work together as a team, they look brilliant; if not, they look silly. Teaches teamwork and interdependence. Simple, and visually interesting. I got the call to produce a video about it so the upper brass could see why they spent all this money sending the best and the brightest to a hotel in the Poconos.

The documentary that resulted contained a conversation between the head of the division, talking about why he believed in the idea, and a doctor who was deeply skeptical. They went back and forth about it, each airing separate views, until the division head prevailed and the doctor walked away, still skeptical but willing to give it a shot.

Trouble was, this conversation never existed. I taped the division head one afternoon briefing his assistant for the upcoming week. A few days later, I happened to catch a lunch-table conversation where the doctor was expressing his views and getting feedback from the table. I sat down in the editing suite after everyone had gone home and began putting together alternating shots of the two men as though they were talking to one another. I had to rearrange a few things, but it worked. An evening of editing later, the two of them were having a deep meeting of the minds and reaching a level of corporate détente. Was this moral? Well, if I had been a reporter, no. But I wasn't. And the fact that the sequence reflected the debate that was going on around the hotel helped me justify putting it in. I heard later that the doctor was quite pleased that his "conversation" with the director had been caught on tape, because it made a deep impression on him at the time.

This is the magic of editing.

I have been pondering this concept a lot lately as I watch the current crop of "reality" TV shows like *Survivor* and *The Mole*. The producers and editors of these shows boil down hours of footage into a forty-seven-minute show that, hopefully, tells a coherent story about what went on. In my opinion, the "reality" in these shows is thinly stretched. Through careful editing of the footage, including juxtaposing images from different moments (as in my example above), the producers can depict the events in any way they want. Aware that the audience is sucked in by a good story, the editors focus on the most interesting conflict and play it for all it's worth, often subverting or ignoring moments that are unimportant or give away the ending. To the participants on the scene, it may be completely obvious who is going to be voted off that night. Skillful editing, however, can ignore relevant information, bend conversations, or skew the audience viewpoint, even leading television-watchers down a narrative cul-de-sac that leaves them completely deceived about the outcome until it happens.

I'm not suggesting this is a malicious plot to deceive the audience. On the contrary, it is just good storytelling, and it is absolutely what the viewer wants to see. We want to be surprised, sure, but when it's over, we want to look back over the show and say, "Ah, *now* I see where this was going." If we see the ending too soon, we are bored, we change the channel, and the show doesn't get renewed for next season.

Editing creates a reality. And the reality it creates is completely dependent on who is doing the editing. Ultimately, however, the editor is after the same thing as the director, screenwriter, and actor: He wants to tell the story. Filmmakers are fond of saying that a film is written three times: once by the screenwriter, once on the set, and once in the editing suite.

Video and film editing existed as two separate things for many years, the film people editing on flatbed editors like the Moviola, the video people editing on multiple tape decks run by electronic controllers. Recently, however, these two styles of editing have merged into a new world: nonlinear editing.

Let's step back into the past for a moment and see where film editing came from. Then we'll look at the genesis of video editing, and lastly, we'll see how the two things have come together in the modern editing suite.

FILM EDITING

Editing used to be easy. Back around 1910, I mean. The camera was set up in front of a set that was indistinguishable from a stage set. The cameraman cranked up the camera; the actors entered from the "wings" and played the scene as if the camera were an audience member sitting third row center. A movie was made by cutting together these scenes with cards containing narration or the actor's lines.

The distinction between plays and movies wasn't really made until people like D.W. Griffith began monkeying around with something called a *close-up*. Griffith would run the scene the regular way once, then move the camera in closer and shoot the scene again, this time focusing on the actor's face. Then, he would insert the close-up shot into the middle of the scene, so the audience could really see the emotions on the actor's face. Of course, this technique is second nature to us now, but at the time, it was a real shocker. Suddenly, the actor's face would explode onto the screen, filling the entire space and jolting the audience out of its emotional detachment, taking them boldly where no audience had gone before—into the mind of the character. Griffith took the audience from benign observer to involved voyeur. Thus, modern editing was born.

And what a pain in the butt it was. Until fairly recently, film editing could only be done by splicing the actual pieces of film together. The process took place on a machine called a *Moviola*—basically, a table with several reels and a lamp that projected the image on a small screen. Using a heated plate, the editor would melt the pieces of film together, constructing the movie like a pennant at a junior-high-school prom. The room was filled with pieces of film hung on clotheslines. Unused fragments would fall to the floor, creating the film slang "cutting-room floor," the place where unused scenes go to die. If the editor changed his mind, the whole thing had to be cut apart and re-glued into a new sequence. Of course, this editing process was never done with the original film—the editor would create copies called "work prints"—but the whole thing was still a tedious and time-consuming process.

Of course, the audio had to be married up to the film, as well. Audio was printed on **mag film**, strips of magnetic tape with sprocket holes like film. The mag film was strung up alongside the regular film, synchronized through the clapper on the slate, and run alongside the picture in sync. Any time you wanted to make an edit, you had to get out the razor blade, cut the film, cut the mag film, and put the two of them back on the Moviola, hopefully, still in sync.

As with any technical process, over time, a group of talented editors appeared and mastered this process, supporting the visions of countless directors and producers. It was tedious, however, and made it difficult to make changes.

The process did not become any less tedious with the introduction of video.

VIDEO EDITING

There are two basic styles of video editing, one of which is about to become extinct. Still, the dinosaurs hung on for a long time after the meteor hit, so these older systems will persist. Plus, a lot of the editing terminology and concepts that were created for the older system are still used in the newer one. First, the edit-a-saurus:

Linear Editing

Linear editing was the standard for a very long time, so I speak of it with respect, even as we witness its demise. Here's how it works:

You take the tape with your footage on it and put it into a video deck called the **source deck**. You put a second, blank tape into the **master deck** (a.k.a. the **destination deck**). These two decks are both plugged into a device known as an **editing controller**. The controller tells the decks what to do.

You run the source deck up to where you want your first shot to start. You run the blank tape on the master deck up to where you want your program to start. You push a couple of buttons on the controller, telling it to read the location of both tapes. This is called setting the **in point**. Then, you run either of the two decks up to where you want this shot to end. If you want to concentrate on a particular amount of time in the original footage, you mark the end point, known as the *out point*, on the source computer. If you are more concerned with filling up a specific amount of time in the final product, you mark the out point on the master deck. The important thing is that you mark three points. That's why we refer to this process as *three-point editing*. The controller now has everything it needs to make the edit. It knows where to start both tapes rolling together, and it knows how long to go before it stops. The editor hits the "Edit" button, and the controller takes over and automatically backs up both decks a few seconds before the in point. There is a breathless pause, and then it starts both decks rolling in sync. When it gets to the in point, it starts transferring the picture and sound from the source to the master. When it gets to the out point, it stops. Simple as that. Because the two tape decks are running in sync, you don't need to mark the out on both machines. Once the controller sees an out point on either machine, the edit is over.[30]

Once the edit is complete, the editor clears all the edit points out of the controller's memory and starts on the next shot. She continues building up the program this way, shot after shot after shot.

This works great as long as you want to start at the beginning of your program and go straight through to the end, without jumping around. Imagine you have three shots: A, B, and C on a master tape. You decide you want to add shot D between A and B. Unfortunately, because these images are being physically recorded on a tape, you can't just slide them around. You have to go to the end of A, then start recording D, which, of course, wipes out B. Once you are done with D, you have to re-record B after it, then re-record C, which was wiped out by B. And so on, and so on, right to the end of the program. Pain in the butt, is what it is.

The other problem is transitions. What if you want to fade from one shot to the next? With the setup described above, you can't do it. Once you start laying down a shot on the master, it completely wipes out whatever is there. There is no way to fade from a shot that already recorded on the master deck to a shot that is playing on the source deck.

---

[30] You don't have to mark two ins and one out for three-point editing to work. It does just fine with one in point and two out points, as well. Basically, you give the controller any three points and it will figure out the fourth one.

What you have to do is have two source decks, then use the controller (a more elaborate version, naturally) to tell the two decks when to play. The controller can fade between the two source decks while both are running, laying the resulting image down on a master deck.

This whole situation resulted in linear editing being divided into two different processes: **offline editing** and **online editing**. The offline editor would put together an edit of the video without any fancy transitions—known as a **cuts-only edit**. Once the whole thing was done, he would send the **Edit Decision List (EDL)**, a computer-generated list of which shots would be used in what order, over to a more expensive online editor, who would program his multiple-source decks to recreate the whole program with all the transitions. This took some planning, because you had to make sure that your original images were shot on separate tapes, or you risked having to "lose a generation" by copying your original source footage onto a different tape. Losing a generation means copying video onto a different tape, and it always means a loss in quality. Because linear editing involves moving the program from one tape to another, it always means losing at least one generation, if not two.

Nonlinear Editing

Then, in the early '80s, two things happened, two events that will be forever locked in a chicken-and-egg relationship. In 1981, a group of young television executives in New York City launched a risky new channel on a revolutionary technology called "cable television." Cable was just starting to creep into suburban homes like tree roots through a sidewalk, and the new channel provided a much-needed boost in content. This new channel was devoted entirely to broadcasting a new form of short media that revolutionized every form of broadcast media in the world. The new medium was called a "music video," and the new network was MTV. The videos were highly unusual, were tremendously creative and, once they got started, created an entirely new style of editing. The montage flew by like lightning, just barely keeping up with the frantic techno-pop of '80s artists like Devo, Madonna, and Culture Club. MTV popularized an exciting, blazing-fast style of editing, sometimes making the shots so short that the viewer couldn't even register them completely. It was image interruptus, strobe-light pacing, video impressionism, verging on subliminal, and it gripped the American viewer (particularly the young) like nothing ever had before. It didn't take long for that style to infiltrate prime-time television through hyper-cool shows like *Miami Vice* and ad campaigns directed at the same teenage viewers (and their disposable income) MTV had discovered. By the mid-1980s, lightning cutting was the dominant style of television editing. By the end of that decade, it had taken over film, as well.

If music video editing was the chicken, **nonlinear editing** was the egg. As MTV stretched its wings in New York, a fledgling company on the opposite coast was creating something just as revolutionary—the Avid editing system.

The Avid did for video editing what word processors did for typists. Once the footage is digitized, or loaded into the computer, the editor can arrange the shots on a time line, shifting them around at will, quickly creating new sequences and trying out ideas. Changes are accomplished with a flick of a mouse and without disturbing the rest of the program. The Avid gave editors (and the directors leaning over their shoulders) unlimited ability to change, manipulate, and complicate their final product. With the growth of nonlinear editing, editing styles became faster and more complex. The more you could do, the more people did do. Shot lengths dropped from seconds to fractions of seconds as viewers became more sophisticated at following complicated montages. The jury is still out on whether this is a good thing. Some people feel this editing style exhausts the viewer, while others see it as exciting and fresh. As I write this, I am watching the new video, "I Want Love," from Elton John, which, interestingly enough, does not show Elton John. Instead, it follows an actor (Robert Downey, Jr.) as he walks around an empty house, singing the song to himself. The video is highly unique, as it is shot in one continuous take, with no editing whatsoever. In the current context of rapid-fire editing, the single continuous shot is almost as arresting as Griffith's close-ups must have been.

In any case, the symbiotic relationship between nonlinear editing and music-video montage changed the American style of editing forever, and not just on TV. It wasn't long before filmmakers like Francis Ford Coppola were *digitizing* their footage and loading it up on nonlinear systems to edit their films. With the flexibility of nonlinear editing, the filmmaker could manipulate the pieces of the film quickly and easily, trying different approaches and testing ideas. Once the edit is done on the computer, the EDL is sent out to the keeper of the original footage, who cuts it (or "conforms" it) to match the computerized edit.

Avid was not the first nonlinear editing system, but they became the de facto industry standard in the 1990s. They still rule the roost as far as top-quality editing machines are concerned, but a number of companies have rushed in to challenge its superiority, including Lightworks, Media 100, Digital Origin, and Apple Computer. The folks at Apple came out with a program called Final Cut Pro, which currently seems to be the weapon of choice for independent video producers working in digital video.

The final format for any project seeking a theatrical release is still film, but this is destined to change. As of this writing, the debate is raging in Hollywood over digital distribution. If the digerati have their way, films may never again be distributed to theaters on celluloid. Instead, the output from the editing system will be piped via satellite right into the theaters and played on digital projectors. This sea change in technology will require a frightening amount of money, so it may be awhile before those film canisters stop showing up at the multiplex, but the day will come—oh, yes—when the entire production process—from camera to editor to movie screen—will happen inside digital brains and computer networks.

But let's not get ahead of ourselves. For the moment, film editing and video editing have come together in the nonlinear editing suite. Let's look more deeply at how they do it.

THE EDITING PROCESS TODAY

After the footage has been transferred to tape in the telecine process, it is logged by an assistant editor. This person makes a list of every shot and where it starts and ends on the tape. If the script supervisor has done her job, this is merely a process of marking which shots are where. The script super should have kept track of details like what lines are included in each scene, which takes show the best angles, which ones had goofs, and so on. Each clip will be numbered and lettered to indicate the scene, the shot, and the take.

On a large-budget feature, the editor will cull through the shots ahead of the director and begin to assemble a rough cut before the director is even done shooting. On very large-budget features, this process might happen right next to the set, so the director can come in and look at rough cuts and see what shots are still needed. Nothing is more frustrating in the editing process than to discover that you really need just *oooonnnne* more angle on that moment to really make a sequence work. By the time shooting is done, the director can step smoothly into the editing process, which should already be well underway.

On low-budget shows, the editing doesn't start until the shoot is over, and then, it is usually the director himself who is culling through footage looking for shots.

In any case, once a group of shots is assembled, they are digitized into the computer. This is a time-consuming process and must be done in "real time." In other words, if you have four hours of tape, it will take four hours to digitize it.

Digitizing is a fancy word for recording the footage onto the hard drive of the computer. It is really important, however, that someone from the film is sitting there, making sure that shots are properly named and grouped. A feature film can put out a frightening amount of footage, and it is easy to lose time trying to locate that stupid little shot you need ("I KNOW it's in here!") while expensive people are waiting around.

Besides organization, the other key issue when digitizing is disc space. Digitized video takes up a lot of room—hundreds of megabytes per minute, depending on the level of resolution you choose to work with. Higher resolution looks better on the screen but might slow the process down because the computer takes longer to render each frame and process effects. Plus, there is the issue of disc space. Higher resolution video requires more disc space.

When you are getting ready to do a nonlinear edit, the first question out of the editor's mouth will probably be, "How much footage have you got?" She is asking because she must plan on setting aside that much disc space for you. In many cases, you may have to rent a set of drives to hold your footage while you are editing.

Because digitizing is time-consuming, it is often a good idea to get your tapes to the editor a couple of days before you plan on starting your editing. That way, you can jump in as soon as your session starts.

The key to successful editing is preparation. The more you know about what you want the final sequence to look like, the more smoothly your session will go. This is not to say that you shouldn't listen to the advice of your editor. One of the most successful pieces I ever did came from being late to the editing session. The editor had gotten bored and had started throwing clips together, playing with an idea he had. By the time I arrived, he had put together something completely different from my script—and better. I tossed my script in the trash and started working with his idea. While I don't recommend this as a production technique, the point remains. Listen to the pros, and they will help you.

Take a moment before you start to get the lay of the land on the computer screen. Every editing program looks a little different, but the main elements are always there. One window of the screen, usually called the "bin," will contain a listing of the digitized shots, as names alone or with the first frame of the shot. There will be another window, variously called the "preview" or "monitor" window, that shows whatever shot you are currently working with. The third window (called the "program" window, among other things) shows the current program that you have assembled so far. The rest of the screen will be taken up with a "time line" or "sequencer" that shows what is happening over time. There will be one or more tracks, running left to right, for the video and one or more for the audio.

The sequence is created by moving shots, one after another, from the bin to these tracks. Shots can be butted up to the ends of other shots or slipped between them. Once in place, the editor can trim the shots by adjusting the edit points between them. When a new shot is added in the middle, the editor can slide all the shots over to make room or let the new shot wipe out part of the old one. The editor can also add effects, split screens, text, and darn near anything else you can think of.

In addition to the video tracks, the editor also allows you to edit the audio tracks. Although a picture-editing program does not allow you the immense flexibility of a dedicated audio program like **ProTools**, it does allow you to fade volumes and perform other simple manipulations.

Besides video and audio tracks, the sequencer will also carry tracks for visual effects, such as dissolves, wipes, and other kinds of transitions. You can add graphics or text here, as well as all those spinning, bouncing color effects you see on TV. All the elements in all these tracks can be moved forward or backward, combined and mixed, played with for days at a time. The possibilities are endless, so some discipline is essential. This process is known as "nondestructive" editing, because you are not using the actual piece of media, just a representation of it. In other words, you are not physically cutting up tape; you are just telling the computer what order to play the clips in.

It is best to start by creating a "spine" for the scene. If you are dealing with a spoken-word scene, start by assembling a group of shots that get all the dialogue said. Don't worry if it doesn't look perfect. Just get all the words said. If you are doing a commercial with a voice-over, lay the voice down first. If you are doing a music video, start by putting in the song. Get an overall picture of what you are trying to create. Don't get microscopic at first.

Once you have created the spine, watch it a few times, and then dive into the details.

Editing goes through several stages.

Rough Cut

In the **rough cut** stage, you make basic decisions: which scenes to include, and how the piece will be laid out in general. The purpose here is to get a rough idea of how things will fit together. This is also when you find out which shots you didn't get and where you stand as far as **total running time (TRT)**. Are you too long or too short? (Here's a hint: You're always too long.) This cut is often put together by the editor while the director is still on the set or taking a much-needed post-wrap vacation. For that reason, it is sometimes called the **editor's cut**.

Fine Cut

More precise decisions are made in the **fine cut**. The flow is cleaned up. Now is when you get microscopic, focusing on timing and absolute clarity. If you are editing comedy, this is when you work on the split-second timing required to "sell" a joke. This is also when you take a step back and ask yourself, have we told the story as cleanly as possible? More importantly, where is the dead weight? What can we get rid of? One editor friend likes to say, "This is where you kill your darlings," i.e., this is where you force yourself to drop those shots you have always been in love with. If they aren't essential to the story, they gotta go. This cut is the director's baby—it is the way he feels the movie should look. This version is screened by the producers, who, depending on how closely the film matches their expectations, will either contribute minor notes or call for drastic changes. This is where the fur can really start flying between the director and producers. If the director is established (meaning famous), he may have *final cut*, meaning that he must sign off on the final edit before it can be released. In some cases, a director is contractually obligated to produce a film with a certain rating, so he may be compelled to cut out graphic sex or violence in order to insure a more family-friendly rating. In very rare cases, he may have to add a little sex or violence in order to escape the dreaded "G" rating.

While the picture is being cut, it may periodically be screened for invited audiences, to get some feedback.

Picture Lock

Once you decide to stop cutting, your picture is *locked*. At this stage, no more changes can be made.[31] Once the picture is locked, it is sent to the sound editors for sound effects work and to the composer to create the music. Of course, all of these people need to stay alert and flexible, because a picture is "unlocked" and changed more often than anyone wants to admit. Once a picture is locked, the editor will create time-coded video copies for use by the sound editors and the composer.

Online Editing and Conforming

The concept of on- and offline edits still exists in nonlinear editing. Once the EDL is complete on the nonlinear computer, it is sent to an online editor who does a high-quality edit using the original video footage at its full resolution, attaching the final sound track at the same time. If the final output medium is video, then out the door it goes. If the final output is film, then the EDL is sent to a *negative cutter*, a steel-nerved professional who uses the EDL to cut the original

---

[31] Actually, it would be more accurate to say that this is where changes become very expensive. In the world of nonlinear editing, for better or worse, you can always go back and change something. The question is, how much other work, from music and sound effects to negative cutting, will have to be redone because of your change?

(read: completely irreplaceable) film in order to create the final film. This process is called *conforming*, because you are making the original camera negative "conform" to the edited version. The negative cutter works in a dust-free, ultraclean room wearing white gloves.

Prints

Film is divided into thousand-foot reels for the purposes of editing. Even though more of the editing process becomes digital every day, the concept of "reels" lives on, partly because it is still convenient to deal with a film in thousand-foot (or ten-minute) chunks. The average movie is still about ten reels of film. Film is shipped in two-thousand-foot reels, however; so if you work at a movie theater and only five reels show up at your door, don't worry.

When the negative cutter is done, you have a final cut of the film in the form of a negative. The lab will combine this negative with the sound track (which has been printed on negative film, as well) and print them to a *composite answer print*, so called because it is designed to get an "answer" from a client.

Screening this answer print is both exciting and disappointing. As we saw during the telecine process, it is essential and difficult to get the color right when printing from the original negative. The principal function of the answer print is to get the color balance and density of the film right from scene to scene. Density refers to the amount of light in the film. The answer print is always "too something." Too dark, too bright, too green, too . . . something.

Enter the *color timer*. This unknown Hollywood foot soldier has more to do with the final look of your film than you know. His title comes from the old Hollywood practice of controlling how much color was in your film by controlling how long it spent in the developing baths. Nowadays, the timer uses a *Hazeltine color analyzer* to control changes in color balance and density. The Hazeltine reverses the colors on the negative and displays them on a television monitor, allowing the timer to bring the primary colors (red, green, and blue) up or down accordingly.

Once the color balance has been adjusted (as well as dozens of other problems, like scenes out of order and sound tracks out of sync), the lab makes another stab at the answer print. Normally, there will be several stages of answer prints and corrections before everyone is happy.

When everything has been corrected, the lab is ready to start creating release prints. This process is hard on a negative, though, and there's only one to go around, so the lab creates an **interpositive**, a high-quality copy of the negative, but in a positive form. We can now put the precious, irreplaceable negative in the vault and never worry about damaging it again.

Our final goal is to create lots of positive prints that can be sent to theaters everywhere. Unfortunately, you can't make a positive from a positive—you make positives from negatives. So, we make a print from the interpositive, an **internegative**. Now that we have separated ourselves from the original negative, we can start knocking out **release prints**.

At each stage of this process, there are two different ways of making prints, each of which has a specific use.

1. **Contact printing:** In this process, the two pieces of film are physically pressed together to transfer the image from one to the other. Contact printing is faster and cheaper but doesn't allow any

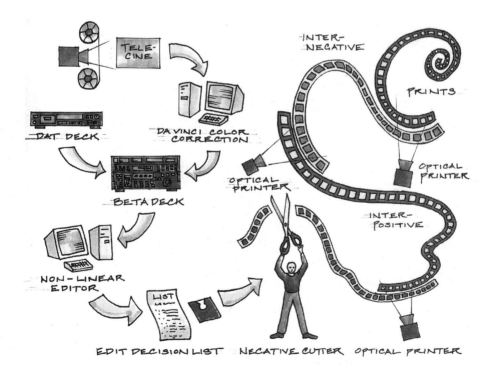

From negative to final print.

changes. This might be used for the internegative-interpositive steps.

2. *Optical printing:* In this process, the original is projected onto the print stock with a projector. This allows the filmmaker to create effects like dissolves, titles, reframing the image, or blowing up the negative (from 16mm to 35mm, for example). Optical printing is slower and more expensive.

When film reels arrive at a modern multiplex, the first thing the projectionist does is splice the five reels together onto a giant platter. Once the film is coiled up on the platter (which is the size of your dining room table), he plucks the beginning of the film out of the center and feeds it into the projector. The film uncoils from the platter, runs through the projector, and coils up on another platter. When the show is done, the projectionist just picks up the beginning of the film out of the center of the second platter, feeds it back into the projector, and coils it up back on the first platter. No rewinding. No fuss. Some multiplexes will stretch one print into two showings by feeding it out of one projector, through a series of pulleys in the projection room, and into another projector. If you see side-by-side theaters showing the same film fifteen minutes apart from one another, that's probably what they are doing.

In older theaters, the projectionist uses two projectors, placed side by side. He leaves the film mounted on two-thousand-foot reels, placing the first one on one projector and the second one on the other projector. When the first reel is approaching the end, observant moviegoers will notice a small, white dot that momentarily appears in the upper right-hand corner of the screen. This is the "motor start cue," and it tells the projectionist to start the motor of the second projector. A second white dot, the "changeover cue," comes a few seconds later, telling the projectionist to switch from one projector to the other. While the second reel is playing, the projectionist rewinds the first reel and loads the third. When the second reel comes to the end, he repeats the changeover process. You can see how this would become unmanageable in a twelve-screen multiplex. You can also see why the projectionist's union has a lot to cry about these days. With platters, a couple of workers can keep an entire multiplex happy.

It's quite a journey for our little film, from original, to interpositive, to internegative, to answer print, and, finally, to release print, but it ensures that the picture looks like we want it to look and that the original negative is carefully protected.

Chapter 15

SCULPTING THE SOUND: POSTPRODUCTION AUDIO

A movie's sound track is divided into three parts, generally referred to as **DME**. That's dialogue (including set dialogue and ADR), music (the sound track, as well as source music), and effects (including sound effects and foley). By the way, when a picture is shipped overseas, the sound editor will usually prepare M and E tracks, containing music and effects but lacking dialogue so it can be dubbed into another language.

Each of these areas is overseen by a specialist: the dialogue editor, the composer (working with the music editor), and the sound-effects editor. All of them are prejudiced towards their respective areas, but none of them has become successful without learning how to blend his work into the other areas. Of course, all of them are guided by the director's vision.

As a sound track flows through a picture, particular areas take precedence from moment to moment. When important dialogue is playing, sound effects are held back. Likewise, music may dominate a moment of emotional impact while the dialogue and sound effects slip to the back row, as when Luke Skywalker, desperate to experience adventure, watches the double sun set over his desert planet in *Star Wars*. In some cases, particularly recently, sound effects will simply take over, as in the opening sequence of *Saving Private Ryan* or the battle scenes of *Braveheart*.

It is up to the director to give these areas guidance throughout the film, letting them know when it is "their turn."

Let's look at each piece of the sound puzzle separately.

DIALOGUE

Dialogue recorded on the set is called **set dialogue**. Am I going too fast? Unfortunately, it's pretty tricky to record dialogue on a set, especially if the set is on location or outdoors. Watch movie credits sometime and look for the line that says, "Filmed on location in Paris and Cairo and on the stages of Pinewood Studio, London." When James Bond turns that Paris street corner and enters the Maison de Sucre Patisserie, actor Sean Connery (is there any other Bond?) is actually walking off the streets of Paris and into a soundstage in London. There are lots of reasons to shoot in a soundstage, but the name of the place should give you a clue. Actually, it's not a soundstage, it's a sound*proof* stage.

When movies were silent, no one cared if the movie set was a noisy place. The director could talk the actors through the scene. Construction crews could be working right next door. An air-raid siren could go off . . . who cared? The movie was silent, so none of the ruckus was being recorded. Carl Laemmle, one of the pioneers of Hollywood, actually installed grandstands and charged admission to the general public, who egged on the hero and booed the villain at the top of their lungs. (Laemmle, who opened his studio on a chicken farm, also sold the audience eggs on the way out. His "studio tour" eventually grew up into the Universal Studios Tour and Theme Park, one of the biggest theme parks in the world, and the only one sharing space with a film studio.)

In any case, all of these sounds didn't become a problem until Al Jolson sang his way through *The Jazz Singer* in 1927, when Hollywood turned on its ear (literally), and, all of a sudden, film crews needed quiet places to shoot movies. Hence, the soundstages were built, so named because they were quiet enough to record sound along with the film.

Even in the soundstages, however, dialogue isn't always recorded perfectly. An actor may turn away at the wrong moment, or a background noise can cover a word or two. On location, the problem is exponentially worse. Besides the inevitable traffic and airplanes, the framing of the shot may prevent the boom operator from getting close to the actor without being seen.

In situations where the set dialogue is not clean enough to use, a postproduction crew will replace it, using **automated dialogue replacement**, or **ADR**. In the past, a dialogue editor would make a film loop of the portion of the scene containing the offending line and play it during the ADR session—thus, ADR's nickname of "looping." Nowadays, the ADR machine plays the line on videotape, then rewinds it lickety-split and plays it again. An ADR session progresses line by line. Sound tedious? It can be. The actor stands in a soundproof room, called a **dubbing stage**, watching herself on a monitor, trying to recreate her own performance. The dialogue editor adds a series of four beeps into the scene to cue the actor when to speak. Beep. Beep. Beep. BEEP. Start talking.

As the scene loops over and over again, the actor repeats the line until her performance matches the movement of her lips on-screen. Once it is recorded, she moves on to the next line.

There are a lot of downsides to ADR. Besides the extra cost of the dubbing stage and the actor's time, it is difficult to get the same emotional intensity that existed on the set when you are standing in a phone booth, listening to beeps. ADR has a tendency to sound sterile. Still, it is a real lifesaver when the set dialogue is muddied and unusable.

If you listen closely to modern movies, particularly low-budget ones, you can sometimes hear the difference between the set dialogue and the ADR. The ADR sounds cleaner, almost too good. It takes a real talent to match up set dialogue and ADR, both on the part of the actor and the dialogue editor. Editing dialogue is one of those jobs best done by someone who enjoys being invisible—if he does his job right, no one will know he was there.

ADR sessions are also used to create background sound for crowd scenes. In this case, a small group of people, known as a **loop group**, will stand on the stage and mumble, talk, and laugh amongst themselves. A good loop group can create a whole room full of talking, laughing people without saying anything intelligible. That's a good thing, because intelligible speech would detract from the written dialogue. This is known as creating **wallah**, because when you play it back, it sounds like "wallah-wallah-wallah…" When crowd scenes are shot on set, extras are frequently told to mime talking and laughter so the dialogue can be recorded cleanly. All of their noise is added later by the loop group. (Sometimes, the extras will be asked to record wallah on the set, once the principal filming is done. This saves time later.)

The ADR stage is used for any type of voices needed for a film: narration, public address announcements, television shows playing in the background, a couple fighting or making love in the apartment upstairs, and so on.

Sometimes, dialogue may need to be recorded that will clarify the story. One famous example is the movie *Casablanca*, whose ending was in doubt right up to the last few days of shooting. Director Michael Curtiz had already shot the classic final scene showing Humphrey Bogart and Paul Henreid walking away into the fog at the airport, but it was some time later before screenwriters Julius and Philip Epstein settled on the now-famous last line "This could be the beginning of a beautiful friendship." No problem: Humphrey Bogart drove over to the studio and dubbed the line in. It was hardly the only liberty the film took with reality. As Henreid reminds Bogart earlier in the film, "Casablanca is in a desert." And there's no fog in a desert.

One interesting side note: Not all ADR is done by the actor who originally played the scene. In commercials, performers are sometimes hired for their looks alone, while their voices are supplied by actors who sound great but might not be as photogenic. Not only that, but a busy star may not be available for an ADR session, so the production company will bring in someone who can imitate him. There are several actors in Hollywood who are kept busy providing the voices of A-list stars who are too busy for ADR sessions. This trend is changing, however, with the advent of worldwide digital connections. These days, an actor shooting a movie in London can step into a studio there, connect live with California, and do ADR for her previous film in postproduction in Hollywood, using digital phone or Internet connections.

MUSIC

Music used to be fairly simple—there were two kinds: ***source music*** and ***background music***. Source music is ostensibly created on the screen: a dance band backing up Tommy Dorsey, music coming out of a radio, the intergalactic cantina band in *Star Wars*—that sort of thing. The source music tended to be popular songs, while the background music was generally orchestral. Of course, in some cases, it was both, like "As Time Goes By" in *Casablanca*, which becomes a constant refrain in the background music after Sam sings it live. Besides source and background, movies also had **visual vocals** (an on-screen singer) and **background** vocals (an offscreen singer).

With film becoming more of a multimedia experience, however, the importance and complexity of music is increasing. As studios are grouped together with television and record companies in huge conglomerates, executives are always looking for ways to link their film products to their music products. These days, a film's sound track can be as important (and profitable) as the film itself. The sound tracks for *American Pie*, *The Matrix*, and *Shrek* contain a steady stream of pop music used as background music. In any case, as pop tunes are used more frequently as background music, the line between source music and background music is being blurred. Regardless of the style or format, however, music exists in film for the same reason as the acting, the editing, and the script: to tell the story.

Source Music

Source music is usually arranged by a **music supervisor**, someone with a good music-biz Rolodex. The music supervisor is in charge of gathering songs that would be appropriate for the film. Besides suggesting songs and schmoozing musicians, the music supervisor helps put together the complicated deals that determine the availability and cost of the rights. As pop songs have become more important to movies, the cost of using those songs has gone up. As one catalog of music becomes popular, the cost climbs. Motown songs, for example, have tripled in the last ten years. Many a director has added a song to a film only to discover later that the rights were prohibitively expensive or unavailable.

Rights must be arranged for any use of any song, even if it isn't the original recording. When Stanley Kubrick asked Malcolm McDowell to sing a song while beating up his victims in *A Clockwork Orange*, all McDowell could think of was "Singin' in the Rain." Kubrick loved the idea, stopped filming immediately, and ran to his office to call MGM. Once he had secured the rights (God only knows what he told them he was going to do with the song), he returned to the set, and McDowell began happily singing and beating up tourists.

Background Music

The process of creating background music (a.k.a. the **score**) starts with a viewing of the film. It is best if the composer can sit down and watch the film from beginning to end, without interruption. That way, he can get a feel for the pacing and personality of the film. This initial screening of the film may be a rough, unfinished cut, but it is enough for the composer to begin generating ideas.

Sometimes a director and a picture editor will assemble a **temp track** before the composer starts to work. A temp track might be used to set a mood for the picture editing or to dress up a rough cut being shown to potential investors. A director might also use the temp track to communicate his intentions to a composer. A temp track can create pitfalls, however, most often because the director falls in love with the temp score before the actual score is completed. The most bombastic example of this was Stanley Kubrick's hiring Alex North to write the score for *2001: A Space Odyssey*. Kubrick had already compiled a temp score containing the vocal compositions of Hungarian composer György Ligeti, as well as music from two Strausses: Johann's "The Blue Danube" and Richard's *Thus Spake Zarathustra*, with its famous three-note intro. North recorded a complete score for the film, but Kubrick never relinquished his original temp track. North found out his score had been dropped when everyone else did, sitting at the New York premiere with his wife.[32]

When a final, "locked" cut becomes available, the director and composer will sit down and watch it more microscopically in a **spotting session**. They may stop and start, rewind and rewatch, tearing the scenes apart and deciding what kind of music should go where. Each chunk of music is called a **cue**. Within a cue, there may be several different thematic moments, so the music can run the gamut of emotional content, depending on the scene.

The spotting session will usually be attended by the film editor, music editor, and, just to keep everybody honest, the producer. After this session, the music editor takes a copy of the film on time-coded video and prepares a **music timing sheet**. This list shows the exact number of frames in each shot of the scene, giving the composer exact timings for each piece of music.

---

[32] Fortunately, North's beautiful score was rediscovered and recorded by film composer Jerry Goldsmith in 1993, after North's death. The resulting album gives tremendous insight into how film composers interpret temp scores.

The composer takes this list and begins to write the score. These days, the score is often created first on a computer, using **MIDI**. The Musical Instrument Digital Interface is a computer language that allows a PC to control all manner of musical electronics, including keyboards, synthesizers, and drum machines. A modern film composer will create the score using a computer and his digital orchestra, working out the details of the music, first alone, then with the director. The days of the composer sitting at the piano, playing tunes for the director, are gone. Now, the director sits in the composer's home studio, listening to a computerized orchestra play the score while he watches his movie on a video screen. In this intimate, flexible environment, the two of them can make changes at will, cutting and pasting and shifting music around until it fits perfectly.

Once the score is finalized, however, the process is much the same as in years gone by. Computerized orchestras are fine for conceptual work, but, as of this writing, no one has succeeded in capturing the nuances of live performance in an electronic box. And really, why would you want to?

On a large feature, the composer gives his score to an **orchestrator**, who writes out the score for the orchestra. Even if the score has been fully orchestrated on a computer system, it is still faster to write out the parts by hand, especially as the orchestrator must interpret the computerized version into something the players can actually read. The players are assembled on a **scoring stage**, which is, basically, a very large recording studio with a movie screen on one wall. The composer may or may not actually conduct the orchestra. (This decision often has more to do with the composer's schedule than with his talent.)

There are two ways of recording music for film. The first method, called **free timing**, assembles the musicians in a studio to play under a large movie screen. Standing in a large studio, the conductor faces the orchestra, watching the film over their shoulders. Working through the film, cue by cue, he shapes the performance of the orchestra to the film. Of course, the film may have changed since he saw it last, so it is up to him to make it all fit.

He may have to cut and paste on the spot (no small trick with eighty expensive musicians sitting and watching) or adjust tempo to accommodate new shots, new edits, or new scenes. Scoring sessions are thrilling examples of talent at work. In many ways, it is quite close to the old process of conducting orchestras for silent films, the old "rides, rapes, and romance" school of musical accompaniment. Recording with free timing is more expensive and takes more time, but it gives the composer the opportunity to follow the flow of the film more organically, tying the emotion of the music more closely to the story.

In order to cue the conductor when the music must start, the film editor will add long red lines, called **streamers**, to the film two seconds before the cue. These lines used to be drawn on the film with a red marker. Nowadays, they are added electronically to a videotape. The streamer begins to appear on one side of the screen a few seconds before the cue. When it reaches the other side, it is time to play.

The cheaper, more efficient method involves a **click track**, a sort of metronome. The composer chooses a precise tempo for the music ahead of time. During the session, the click track plays in the conductor's headphones, keeping the orchestra on tempo. In this case, there is no need to watch the film—adherence to the click track guarantees that the final piece will fit in the time allotted. It does not allow the conductor to indulge in those tiny changes in tempo that give the score added life, but it is quicker and more precise.

The orchestra is recorded onto a multitrack tape, which is then brought to the final editing session to be mixed together with the dialogue and sound effects. Even though the film will eventually be mixed down to a small number of tracks, the orchestra recording may consist of dozens of different tracks—percussion, strings, woodwinds, and so on. These tracks are not mixed together until they are played against the film, because it is impossible to know which instruments will interfere with dialogue or effects. That lovely oboe melody may have to go if it interferes with Julia Roberts's dialogue.

For a television show, the process is necessarily streamlined. Most of the scores for modern television shows go straight from that computerized home studio to the final picture edit. There simply isn't time or money to have a full orchestra lay down a score for a weekly show. *The Simpsons* is a delightful exception, even though their orchestra is quite small.

The canyons around Los Angeles are dotted with home studios where composers crank out the music you hear every week on television. It goes like this: Videotapes have time code or SMPTE recorded on them along with the picture. The composer uses that same time code to "lock up" his computer to the tape. Then, he creates whatever musical cues the show requires, adding underscoring during the scenes or theme music at the beginning and end. The producers and director stop by and everyone drinks Evian while they watch the show with the music. Notes are given, some of which can be handled right there, some of which need more time. When everyone is happy, the composer records that music onto a multitrack tape containing the same SMPTE time code. He sends the tape back to the studio, where it is married up to the picture and broadcast to the universe.

Of course, it's never quite that simple, and many inches of stomach lining are still lost trying to meet impossible production schedules, but that's the theory. One of the biggest hang-ups still seems to be getting the audio and video synchronized. The many varieties of time code are one problem. If you are coordinating this kind of process, make sure that the composer talks to your editors so they can agree on one format.

Composer Jonathan Wolff had a great gig for years doing the slap bass and finger popping scores for *Seinfeld*. Because humor is based very much on timing, the little hits and bumpers that separate the scenes had to be done fresh every week.[33] Wolff would get a tape from the editing suite on Thursday, then spend a day crafting new bits of music to go before and after each scene. Using time code, he would sync his music up to the video, then ship the tape out Friday and relax until the following Thursday. Nice work if you can get it. Okay, maybe it wasn't quite that easy.

EFFECTS

Most people don't realize that virtually every sound you hear in a movie was added after the scene was shot. Every car door, footstep, sucker punch, gunshot, and siren was added by a team of audio wizards. While the basic technology of the picture hasn't fundamentally changed since

---

[33] Wolff spent a great deal of time listening to Jerry Seinfeld's comedy routines and he realized that the comedian had a very noticeable tempo—about 110 beats per minute. Thus, all his musical cues run at that tempo.

its invention, the technology of sound changes drastically every decade or so, and nowhere more than in sound effects. The world of effects is roughly divided into **sound effects** and **foley**.

Sound Effects

Airplane engines, car doors, wind in the trees, Tyrannosaurus footsteps; these are just a few examples of the thousands and thousands of sounds that are added to a modern-day film. Sound-effect houses have vast storehouses of sounds used to provide effects tracks for film and TV. Some of the larger houses have computer networks that link several sound studios to a central server loaded with thousands, or hundreds of thousands, of sounds. Postproduction sound companies (the so-called **post houses**) guard these libraries jealously, although budget-challenged filmmakers can buy partial libraries that are still high quality.

In some cases, even these huge catalogs of sound don't provide all the necessary pieces. The sound designers for *U-571*, for example, flew out to Chicago to play around inside the German submarine on display at the Museum of Science and Technology. For three nights, they banged on pipes, slammed watertight doors, and twisted knobs on old German control panels, creating a huge library of sounds they could use to create a realistic environment. It must have worked—they won an Academy Award.[34]

Sound designers don't always have this kind of time, however. Sound is the last thing added to a film, and it always seems everyone upstream of the sound designers uses up the extra time in the schedule. It is not uncommon for a film to be in production for three years, only to land in the sound effects studio just a few weeks before its scheduled opening day. For this reason, most sound designers depend heavily on their in-house libraries.

For science fiction and fantasy movies, however, those libraries may not be of much use, at least in their current form. Ever since Gary Rydstrom raised the bar with the sound effects for *Star Wars*, the expec-

---

[34] People who bet on Academy Award office pools are sometimes confused by the two awards for sound—sound design and sound effects editing. Briefly, sound effects editing covers the creation and choosing of sound effects, while sound design covers the whole sound package: dialogue, music, and effects. *U-571* won for sound effects editing.

tation has been that fantastical films would come complete with their own otherworldly audio environment. Rydstrom is a master of adapting existing sounds into sci-fi realities. Listen to the light saber fights from *Star Wars*, *The Empire Strikes Back*, and *The Return of the Jedi*, for example. Rydstrom took a metal bar out and whacked it against tightly strung telephone lines to create the twanging, grating metallic sounds of a light-saber fight. Chewbacca, the Wookie, uses growls and moans from a whole menagerie of animals.

But sound effects design isn't only important in otherworldly movies. A sound designer can create an entire subtext of ideas, based on what sounds he picks for everyday objects. Take Westerns, for example. In movies like *Silverado* or *Pale Rider*, the gunslinger is viewed as a hero, using his weapons to drive away villains and restore peace and order. Listen to the guns as they are loaded, closed, or fired. They sound slick and smooth, light and fast. Compare that to *Unforgiven*, a movie that shows gunfighters and the violence they create in a less favorable light. Here, people die slowly when shot, crying and begging for water. One "good guy" shoots a villain sitting on a toilet, a decidedly unheroic act. The guns sound completely different—heavy and clunky, awkward and rough. When Clint Eastwood tosses his gun on a table, it sounds like chunks of an old automobile transmission. The sound designer can put his own commentary into the sound track, as clearly as the actors or the writer.

Do audiences notice this kind of thing? Yes and no. No, they don't go out of the theater talking about the gun sound effects in the third reel, but yes, they do pick up the emotional implications of the sounds, and these variations do affect their experience of the film.

A modern film may have thousands of discrete sound effects, especially now that computers have taken over in the sound studio. The industry standard is a program called **Pro Tools**, by Digidesign. Pro Tools allows a designer to record his sounds digitally and then move them around as easily as a writer uses a word processor. Don't like the sound of steam coming off the griddle? Reach back into the hard drive and pull out seven others. Play around until you like it, then save the new sequence. The designer can lock up the computer to the film using SMPTE time code and play with it endlessly until the sound track is a thing of beauty, he is out of time, or both.

Foley

The distinction between "sound effects" and foley is vague, but, basically, foley is any sound created by the movement of the actor. Shut your eyes and listen to a film sometime. You hear that rustle of clothing that happens when an actor shifts his position on the sofa? That's foley, and it is performed by a *foley artist*.

Foley is named after Jack Foley, a sound effects wizard who developed the art at Universal Studios over many years. Foley was directing silent films for Universal when *The Jazz Singer* ushered in the talkies. With a small team of technicians, Foley held the first sound-effects session—what would later be known as a "foley session" —in 1929, for the hitherto silent film *Showboat*. The music and sound effects were added at the same time on Stage 10 at Universal. Try to imagine a forty-piece orchestra playing along on one side of the stage while a small group of sound-effects artists on the other side threw in footsteps, laughter, and anything else they could think of, making up a new art form as they went along. Amazing, when you consider the microscopic way this art is practiced today.[35]

Foley stages are the quietest places in the world. It's a little spooky, at first. After being in a foley stage for awhile, you begin to realize how noisy a normal office is. In a foley stage, there is no noise from air conditioning or fluorescent lights or traffic or *anything*. These stages are totally, 100 percent *quiet*. Graveyards are deafening, by comparison. A foley stage must be completely silent because the sounds being recorded can be quite soft and subtle. The microphones are so sensitive that actors must be careful not to breathe toward them (unless, of course, they are recording the sound of the actors' breathing).

A large portion of the floor is divided into a number of different surfaces (called *pits*)—concrete, gravel, dirt, and so forth—to allow the artists to do all kinds of footsteps. (Foley artists carry around a lot of different shoes.) Around the room are hundreds of objects that the artists use to create every sound you can think of, from the jingling of keys to a bone-crunching punch to a romantic kiss. It generally looks like a

---

[35] Jack Foley was known for adding all of the sound effects to a reel in one take. He used a cane so he could do the footsteps for two or three people at once, while keeping scraps of fabric in his pockets for the clothing sounds.

The foley walker.

garage in need of a yard sale. Of course, nothing here is ever actually filmed, so the objects that make the sounds may bear no resemblance to the things they are supposed to sound like. The life of a foley artist is a constant search for objects that make interesting noises. The talent of a foley artist is the ability to distinguish between what something looks like and what it sounds like. Close your eyes and listen to bacon frying sometime. Do you hear the rain on an empty street?

Even though much of the world of sound effects has been computerized, foley is still one area where the sounds are produced by real people. It is still faster and cheaper for artists to watch actors on the screen and follow their motions in the foley stage. For one thing, human movements are irregular and hard to program. The best way to imitate a human is with another human.

Foley sounds are broken into three general groups: ***clothing moves***, ***footsteps***, and ***specifics***.

Clothing Moves. Find a very quiet room (no small trick in this noisy world) and walk around in it. Sit down. Turn your body from side to side. Cross your legs. Stand up again.

If you listen closely, you will hear a constant stream of sound coming from your clothing. As you walk, sit, turn, or move in any way, your clothing makes a rustling sound. This sound, when added to a movie sound track, creates a kind of subconscious white noise that draws the listener into the film. Because these sounds would be heard in real life only if you were close to someone, your brain creates an artificial intimacy and convinces you that you are actually sitting right next to the actor. This rustling noise also creates a background bed of sound that helps tie the sound track together, camouflaging gaps in the sound effects and the slight differences between set dialogue and ADR. Without this track, the film starts to sound distant and sterile, especially now that modern audiences are so used to hearing it.

A foley artist records a "moves" track by sitting in a chair in front of a microphone holding a scrap of fabric. What kind of fabric he holds will depend, naturally, on what kind of clothing (denim, wool, or leather, for example) the actor is wearing in the film. As the foley artist watches the screen, he rustles the fabric, swings it around, and even rubs it against his body to simulate the sounds of the actor on-screen. Smoothness and instinct are the key. A good Foley artist can anticipate the actor on the screen, minimizing the number of takes required.

Footsteps. A foley artist is often called a foley walker because the sound of footsteps is one of the most common things he provides. Good footsteps are rarely recorded on the set, and, even if they are, they will be lost if the actor's dialogue gets replaced by ADR. For this reason, most footsteps are redone in foley.

Footsteps are quite a trick because they must all be done standing in one place. The microphone must remain stationary during recording, and the actor must maintain a constant distance from it. The pits around the studio provide all the different surfaces. The walker must provide his own shoes. The recording process is fairly straightforward— pick a pair of shoes, pick a pit, watch the screen, and try to put your feet down when the actor does—but really good footsteps take years to perfect.

A good foley walker can imitate steps by people of all different sizes and genders. Yes, a 250-pound man can walk like a 120-pound woman (as long as he is wearing a good pair of pumps) with practice. The footsteps are divided into three general groups: men, women, and background. The men and women are divided into two groups so that the mixers can provide the proper EQ (see below) for each. The background feet consist of layers of footsteps, mixed together to sound like a crowd, a sidewalk full of people, or a charging platoon of soldiers.

Specifics. Anything that isn't covered under clothing moves or footsteps is a specific. Specifics are why you need all those props in the foley stage. These sounds could be anything from a handshake to a kiss to a punch to a body falling down a flight of stairs. When Harrison Ford breaks into the tomb in the opening scene of *Raiders of the Lost Ark*, listen as he picks the idol off the altar. You can actually hear the clink of his gold ring hitting the idol. You can bet that wasn't recorded on the set.

Foley artists use time-tested tricks, like cornstarch in a leather pouch (footsteps in crunchy snow), a ball of audiotape (walking through tall grass), and yes, coconut shells for horse hooves. Unlike the squires in *Monty Python and the Holy Grail*, however, they don't bang them together. They fill them with padding and pound them on a soft surface, like a bed of sawdust.

THE MIX-DOWN

By now you probably realize that it takes hundreds of different sounds to create the sound track of a movie. All of these different sounds—dialogue, ADR, source music, the score, sound effects, and foley—are all brought together into a ***mixing stage***, where they are combined into the final sound track. A mixing stage is the size of a movie theater, just like the one you go to at the multiplex. After all, the filmmakers need to know what the movie will sound like in a theater, not in a small recording studio. These mixing stages have mixing boards that stretch all the way across the room, with hundreds of tracks, and mixing sessions can be interminable. The mixing board is divided into three sections—

dialogue, music, and effects—and a different mixing engineer operates each one. Behind this massive panel of lights and knobs stands the sound designer, looking like the captain of a starship. The back of the room has comfy chairs for the other members of the production staff who drop by from time to time.

The movie plays on a full-size screen on the far wall while the engineers tweak and fiddle with each track until it lays down in a beautiful bed of sound. There are a vast number of tricks the engineers can play to manipulate the sound, the most popular of which are *EQ* and *reverb*.

EQ

EQ stands for "equalization," and it allows an engineer to increase or decrease certain frequencies in a sound. It is kind of like the treble and bass knob on your stereo, although much more precise. EQ allows the sound designer to slip different sounds into different parts of the audio spectrum, keeping a low-frequency machine, for example, from drowning out a deep-voiced actor.

Reverb

When a sound goes out into a large space, it tends to echo off different surfaces. These collected echoes are known as "reverberation," and they are very specific to each space. A bus station has a completely different reverberation pattern than an office, for instance. An electronic reverb device comes preprogrammed with settings like "Cathedral" and "Large Hall," but any sound mixer worth his knobs will program his own settings.

When dialogue is recorded, whether on the set or on a dubbing stage, the microphone is placed as close as possible to the actor's mouth. Therefore, the mic will not pick up very much of the reverb in the room. This is actually a good thing—it is best to record an actor as "dry" as possible. Then, you can add whatever kind of reverb you want later. Once you've recorded reverb onto a vocal track, you can never get it out. Better to record the voices dry and add reverb in post.

Like the camera team on the set, a production mixing team tends to stick together for years, learning one another's talents and quirks. With this kind of complication and time pressure, it helps to have a familiar face sitting next to you.

SOUND TRACK FORMATS

Movies existed quite happily in mono for many years, until stereo sound really took off in the 1950s. When the stereo format first appeared, sound mixers would put an actor's dialogue in the speaker on his side of the screen. If he was standing on the right side, they would mix his voice into the right-hand channel. This led to some peculiar effects, particularly if a new shot suddenly appeared with the same actor on the other side of the screen. His voice would jump abruptly from one side to the other, causing a head-spinning nausea in the listener. The movie *Cleopatra* is famous for being the zenith of this really bad idea. Eventually, mixers figured out that it was best to put the dialogue dead center no matter where the actor was, and let the rest of the sound effects move from side to side. Thus, three-channel sound was born: left, right, and center. If you look behind a movie screen, you will see three stacks of speakers. The screen itself is perforated with thousands of tiny holes, making it functionally transparent to the sound.

Three-channel sound was the standard for many years until George Lucas's production company began to push the envelope of sound. Gary Rydstrom, the resident sound designer at Lucasfilm, began to be frustrated that all the careful work he was putting into his films was

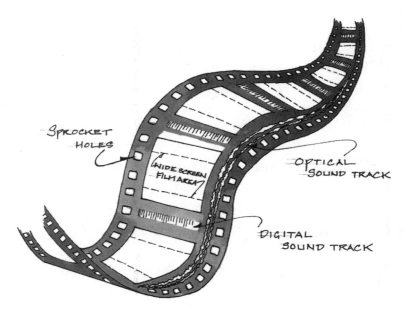

Where the sound tracks are.

being lost in theaters with poorly designed sound systems. Thus, THX was born. The new sound format was named after Lucas's first film, *THX 1138*. THX was not only a piece of equipment, but also an advise-and-review process that each theater would go through with the Lucasfilm designers. Theaters would install THX's magic electronics, make any changes to the layout of the theater that these designers deemed appropriate, and, when it sounded like love in a basket, Lucasfilm would allow the theater owner to advertise the theater as "THX-equipped." The magic box was basically an audio processor that split a movie's sound into six different channels—center, left, right, surround left, surround right, and a **subwoofer**. The first three were nothing new, but the surround speakers were quite an innovation. These are the speakers that you see hanging from the side of the theater and behind you. Using these speakers, sound designers could now make sounds travel around behind you. Besides letting them create fun novelties like planes that fly around the theater, it made it possible to create a more immersive atmosphere, putting the audience in the center of a battle, an earthquake, a football field, or whatever.

The last piece of the equation, the subwoofer, allowed the sound system to play back very low frequency sounds. When a subwoofer is really doing its job, you don't hear it so much as feel it. This six-channel

Five point one (5.1) sound.

format became known as "five point one" sound (generally written **5.1 sound**), to distinguish the subwoofer from the rest of the channels. It has become the industry standard, even though THX has been replaced by other technologies.

The technology used to put the sound physically onto the film has changed, as well. Sound used to be printed on the film as an optical sound track. If you actually pick up a piece of film and look at it, the optical sound track looks like two jagged white lines running next to the frames. These jagged lines operate much like the groove on a vinyl record. The groove on the record varies continually in width. The skinnier places push the needle up, while the fatter places let it slide back down. This variation in width is interpreted by a magnet and turned into an electrical signal. The same concept applies with an optical sound track. The varying width of the white lines reproduces the varying sound of the movie. An optical reader follows this line and turns it into sound.

But what about our 5.1 format? With a film only having room for two optical tracks, how do we imprint six tracks? Answer: technical magic. Audio engineers have figured out a way to collapse six tracks into two, and then have a computer sort it all out on the other end. This doesn't lead to the best audio quality, however, so the push to convert film playback to a digital medium has been very strong. For the digital 5.1 formats, the data is printed onto the film in chunks that are read by a computer at the other end.

As of this writing, there are three major digital formats—Dolby SR-D, DTS, and SDDS.[36] Plus, there are a host of theaters (particularly overseas) that are still playing the optical track. Therefore, it is not unusual for a film to be imprinted with four different sound tracks, so it can be played by any theater it might get sent to. This is just one reason why releasing films has gotten so darn expensive.

---

[36] DTS = Digital Theater Systems; SDDS = Sony Dynamic Digital Sound.

AFTERWORD

Words are powerful. Language is important. The Buddhists say, "An enlightened person helps people with his mouth." The failure of words can lead to anger, disillusionment, and even violence. The success of words can create harmony, love, and some darn fine movies.

This book is all about words. It's about learning a language to communicate with those around you who share your passion and your trade: film and television. And while you may be on the outside looking in, your face pressed against the glass of the industry like a kid at FAO Schwarz, you don't have to run a hazing gauntlet to get in—you just have to be willing to be ignorant, to ask questions, to feel silly. For awhile. A short while.

Ignorance, like your appendix, only has to be removed once. When you own up to not knowing and *ask*, you will find dozens, if not hundreds, of friendly faces in the wilderness. My hope is that the knowledge in this book will embolden you to ask, to delve, and to practice. The entertainment industry, in all its forms, from billion-dollar studios to high-school science projects, is full of gentle souls who want nothing more than to share their knowledge and build yours.

Yes, there are a few weenie-heads out there who will lord your ignorance over you. But they gain power through your fear, not through their knowledge. Fear them not, and they will leave.

Thanks for taking this trip with me through the world of film and TV. Let me know how you do.

BASIC THINGS: TEN TO KNOW AND SEVEN TO OWN

TEN THINGS EVERY FILM AND TV PERSON SHOULD KNOW

The difference between a grip and a gaffer. These two job descriptions intertwine on the set, but they are quite distinct. Gaffers deal with electrical things. Grips move scenery and set up C-stands.

Sequence doesn't matter. It never matters what order you shoot things in. If it is in the can, it is available to the editor. Of course, actors like to shoot things in sequence because it helps them maintain an emotional through-line, but when it comes to the final product, it doesn't matter if you shoot the opening scene on the very last day.

Why continuity is important. See the previous item. With everything shot out of sequence, it is vital that everyone on the set keeps continuity in mind. Every prop, costume, beam of light, or drop of blood must match from shot to shot, or you will give the audience unconscious clues that this story isn't real.

The West Virginia Law. See the lighting chapter for details, but here's the bottom line: When it comes to electrical circuits, it's Watts = Volts x Amps.

Are we shooting film or video? The difference in light sensitivity and media cost between these two formats will determine everything on the set, from the size of the lighting kit to the amount of time the camera is rolling.

Quiet, quiet, quiet. When the camera is rolling, any extraneous noise can ruin the shot, costing everybody time and money. When you come onto a set, turn your cell phone and pager OFF. Having your cell phone ring during a shot will get you ejected from a set, so don't say I didn't warn you. Once you see the sound light start to flash, stop, be still, and do not talk until it stops.

Safety yells. On a well-run set, people will call out to each other when any menace to safety appears. The most common is the yelled, "**Hot Points!**" when you are coming through a crowd of people with anything hot or sharp—most commonly yelled when bringing in a lighting instrument or a stand. There are also courtesy calls to be aware of. "Crossing!" means you are about to cross in front of the camera. This warns people staring at the monitor. You'd be surprised how disconcerting it is for the image to suddenly go black. "Flashing!" means you are about to take a flash photo. If the electricians see a flash, they will start searching for the bulb that has burnt out.

Order of commands. When a shot is being laid down on film, there is a predictable order of shouted commands that accompanies each take. Some crews vary them slightly, but they are fairly consistent throughout the industry. In order, they are:

"*Picture is up!*" (from the 1st AD. This is not a rehearsal. We are shooting.)
"*Settle please!*" (1st AD. Stop moving and talking. Be where you are supposed to be.)
"*Last looks!*" (1st AD. Everyone check that your area is ready to shoot.)
"*Roll Sound!*" (1st AD. Start the audiotape deck.)
"*Sound Speed!*" (from the sound mixer. I'm rolling.)
"*Roll Camera!*" (1st AD. Start the camera.)
"*Speed!*" (from the camera operator. I'm rolling.)
"*Marker!*" (1st AD to the camera assistant. Mark the shot.)
"*Action*" (from the director. Do the scene.)

And then, after the scene:

"*Cut!*" (from the director. Stop the scene.)
"*Back to one!*" or "*Check the Gate. Next Setup!*" (1st AD. We're either doing it again or moving on to the next shot. If we are moving on, the camera crew should check to make sure the inside of the camera is clean.)

What's up. The attention on a set is usually focused to one area or another. That area (rehearsal, lighting, camera, etc.) is "up."
What's in frame. "In frame" means crucial and deserving attention. "Out of frame" means we don't care. Know what is in the shot and what isn't.

SEVEN THINGS EVERY FILM AND TV PERSON SHOULD OWN

A Leatherman or the equivalent. It is the everything tool: pliers, knife, screwdriver. Beefier than a Swiss army knife and much more useful.

Alligator clips. We are forever trying to attach things to other things on movie sets. I recommend a small collection of clipping things, from clothespins to small 'gator clips to one or two big ones.

Gloves. You never know when heavy lifting or hot lights are going to become part of your job description.

LA 411 or the local equivalent. The essential guide to the industry. *LA 411* lists local businesses and individuals that serve the needs of the industry. Every major city in the United States has a version of it. Sometimes called the *Reel Guide*.

A cell phone. While I do not recommend the use of a cell phone while driving or eating in a restaurant, it has become an essential tool for film and TV production. The general assumption is, if you cannot be reached, you do not want the job.

A Thomas Guide. There is a time for brand loyalty, and this is it. No one, but no one, makes a map as good as the Thomas Guide. In Los Angeles, it is considered so ubiquitous that location directions often give the page number of the Thomas Guide where the address can be found.

A deck of cards. On a set, moments of high stress alternate with long periods of inactivity. Learn to play gin or, if you want to be really cool, euchre. Magic tricks are good, too.

Appendix B:

GLOSSARY

1st AD (First Assistant Director): Manages the flow of work on the set. Keeps the shoot on schedule by keeping the cast and crew on schedule during the shoot. Assists the director and DP in planning the shooting schedule.

2nd AD (Second Assistant Director): Assists the 1st AD in running the shoot by moving cast and crew into position, dealing with extras and background action, and communicating with the crew.

2nd 2nd AD (Second Second Assistant Director): Assists the 1st and 2nd AD in running the shoot.

5.1 Sound: A theatrical audio setup with five normal channels of sound (center, left center, right center, left surround, and right surround) and one subwoofer channel that carries only low frequency sound.

AatonCode: A form of time code specifically designed for Aaton cameras and printed directly on the film negative.

ADR (Automated Dialogue Replacement): The process of replacing badly recorded dialogue by recording the actor while she watches her own performance on-screen. Also known as looping.

Amperage: The amount of power flowing past a given point. Also known as current.

Anamorphic Lens: A lens that "squashes" the image horizontally while leaving it unchanged vertically. The method of making a wider image fit on a skinnier piece of film.

Answer Print: See Composite Answer Print.

Apple Box: A strong wooden box used to hold up just about anything on a set. So called because it resembles a box of apples in size and shape.

Arriflex Mount: A style of camera mount consisting of a round ball resting in an identically shaped bowl.

ASA (ISO): How light sensitivity is rated for film stock. The higher the ASA number, the more sensitive (or "faster") the film is.

Aspect Ratio: The ratio of the width of a film or television image to its height.

Autofocus: The control on a video camera that scans the image and automatically moves the camera lens to bring that image into focus.

Axial Magazine: A style of camera magazine where the supply and take-up reels are placed parallel to one another, i.e., on the same axis.

Baby Stand: A small lighting stand used for instruments mounted close to the floor.

Background Music: Musical sound track elements that do not contain vocals.

Background Vocal: Musical sound track elements that contain vocal elements, but the singer is not seen on-screen.

Balanced Line: An audio cable that contains three cables, allowing noise to travel to both ends at once, and thereby, cancels itself out.

Barn Doors: The swinging doors on the front of a light that allow the electrician to cut off a portion of the light beam.

Bates Plug: A plug with three round pins placed on the same axis. The most common version is 60 amps and is used as a feeder cable for lighting.

Beadboard: Known to many by the brand name Styrofoam, it is a soft, pebbly board used to bounce and diffuse light.

Best Boy: The first assistant to either the gaffer or the key grip.

Best Light Transfer: The fastest, cheapest, and lowest quality way to make a telecine transfer from film to video. Every scene is given the same balance of red, green, and amber light. Also known as a one light transfer.

Bit Depth: The number of bits of information that are used to describe a color. More bits means a more precise color. Used to describe video images.

Bit Rate: The number of pieces of information that a digital audio deck records per second. More bits means better sound.

BNC Connector: A style of push-and-turn connector often used on professional video cables.

Boom: A long pole, often on wheels, that holds the microphone over the set.

Boom Shadow: The shadow caused by the boom operator moving the boom over the set and under the lights.

Border Light: A light composed of a string of lightbulbs, all mounted side by side. Used for cycs and drops.

Bounceboard: A board covered with a silvered surface, used to bounce light beams at an actor.

Boundary-Level Mic (PZM): A type of microphone that is mounted on a hard surface (such as a floor or wall) and uses the sound reflections off that wall to increase the volume of the sound.

Broad Light: A type of lighting instrument that produces a wide, diffuse light, covering a large area.

Bus: An electrified metal bar in an electrical panel. Electricians use it to attach fuses and cables.

C-47: A clothespin.

Cable: Any long piece of rubberized wire that carries power. Generally used to describe a wire carrying a large amount of power, as opposed to a zip cord or a stinger.

Camcorder: A camera that also contains a recording deck.

Camera Body: The part of the camera where the film gets exposed to the light.

Camera Film: A type of film specifically designed for use on the set, as opposed to in the lab.

Camera Speed: The rate at which film is pulled past the lens. Normally twenty-four frames per second.

Cam-Lok Plug: A large and very tough style of plug used to connect large feeder cables to distribution boxes. Distinguished by its single pin and push-in-and-twist installation.

Cardioid Mic: A microphone with a heart-shaped pickup pattern.

Caterer: The person on the set who provides meals, as opposed to crafts services, who provides snacks.

CCD (Charge-Coupled Device): A light-sensitive computer chip that is the heart of all video cameras.

Changing Bag: The lightproof bag used by the camera assistant to reload the camera magazine.

Checking the Gate: The process of opening the camera and making sure no dust or hair was in front of the film during the previous shot.

Circuit Breaker: An electrical device that cuts off power to a circuit in the event of a short-circuit or power overload.

Clapper: See Marker Slate.

Click Track: An audible clicking sound used during recording sessions so the conductor and musicians can hear the proper tempo.

Close-Up: A shot that includes only the head and shoulders of an actor.

Clothing Moves: The sounds created by foley artists to imitate the sound of an actor's clothing when he moves.

Color Correction: 1) The process of altering the colors in an image to fulfill the artistic intentions of the director and the DP. 2) The process of correcting the color of a light source to match the color of other light sources on the set.

Color Temperature: The relative "warmth" or "coolness" of a light source, which translates to a light that is more orange or more blue.

Color Timer: The person in charge of the color balance when prints are made from original negatives.

Colorist: The person who runs the da Vinci color correction system during the telecine process, controlling the color balance of the video output.

Combo Stand: A large light stand on wheels. Also useful as a large stand for grip equipment.

Component Video: A video signal that sends each of the colors (red, blue, and green), as well as the luminance (brightness), separately.

Composite Answer Print: A print made from the original negatives and sent to the client to check color balance, sequence, and other questions.

Composite Video: Video that contains all the colors (red, blue, and green) as well as information about their relative luminance (brightness).

Conforming: Assembling the original negative and the sound track to match what is created in the editing suite.

Contact Printing: Creating a print from a negative by actually pressing the two pieces of film together.

Continuity: Making sure that details from one shot (e.g. props, costumes, and gestures) match those in successive shots.

Continuity Error: When props, costumes, gestures, or other elements do not match from shot to shot.

Contrast Ratio: The ratio between the brightness of an area lit by fill and key light to an area lit by fill light alone.

Courtesy Flag: A solid flag put up over the director and cameraman to keep them out of the hot sun.

Coverage: The collection of shots that depict a scene from a variety of angles.

Crab Dolly: A dolly that can move forward and backward, as well as sideways.

Craft Services: The person on the set who provides snacks between meals.

Crane: A camera platform that can rise up in the air, carrying the cameraman and the director, as well as the camera itself.

Crash Zoom: A fast zoom-in, used to bring sudden focus to a particular character or thing.

Cribbing: Small pieces of wood, used to level out the dolly track, among other things.

Crosscutting: An editing technique that involves cutting quickly back and forth between two different stories, allowing the audience to follow both simultaneously.

C-Stand: A three-legged metal stand with a rotating arm attached to the top. Used to hold up all kinds of grip equipment.

CT filter: Stands for "Correct To." A filter used to correct the color temperature of a light source to that of another source.

Cue: 1) A command to do something, like say a line or change the lighting. 2) A piece of music that goes with a particular scene or moment in a film.

Cup Block: A block of wood with a spherical hole cut out of the top. Used to protect delicate floors from the legs of tripods and C-stands.

Cuts-Only Edit: A version of the film with no dissolves or fancy transitions.

Cutter: A solid flag that blocks out (or "cuts") some of the light.

Cyc: A large, solid piece of fabric used to imitate the sky. Short for "cyclorama."

Cyc Foots: The lights that illuminate the bottom half of the cyc.

Cyc Heads: The lights that illuminate the top half of the cyc.

Cyc Light: A particular style of light, designed to give a wide, even light that fills the entire cyc.

DP: The director of photography, a.k.a. the cinematographer. Responsible for the lighting and the cinematography.

Dailies: The video or film prints made straight from the original negatives and shown to the production team the next day.

DAT (Digital Audio Tape): A type of high-quality tape that uses computerized numbers to record sound.

Da Vinci Color Corrector: A computer used during the telecine process that can alter the colors of the original image.

Day-for-Night: The process of shooting a scene during the day and making it look like nighttime on film.

Deep Focus: A situation when the actor can move a great distance toward or away from the camera and still be in focus. Also known as wide depth of field.

Depth of Field: The amount of space in front or behind the point of focus where the actor will still be in focus.

Destination Deck: See Master Deck.

Diffusion: Any substance used to spread out the light and reduce hard shadows.

Digitizing: Playing film or video into a computer and changing it from a tape-based format to a computer-based format.

Displacement Magazine: A camera magazine where the space created by the unspooling of the raw film is filled up by the incoming exposed film.

Dissolve: A smooth fade from one image to another.

Distro Box: Short for "distribution box." The piece of electrical equipment that takes large, powerful electrical lines and breaks them down to smaller plugs that can be used by individual lights.

DME: Dialogue, music, and effects—the three categories of sound in the film world.

Dolly: A rolling platform containing a place to mount the camera, as well as a place for the cameraman to sit.

Dolly Grip: The technician responsible for pushing the dolly during the shot.

Dolly Shot: Any shot that uses a rolling camera platform.

Dolly Track: The railroad track that the dolly rolls on during the shot.

Dot: A small, round flag used to create a dark spot in the middle of a beam of light.

Double Scrim: A cloth or metal filter used to reduce the intensity of a light beam. Slightly thicker than a single scrim.

Double-System: The process of recording picture and sound separately.

Dresser: The person responsible for getting clothes on the actors.

Dubbing Stage: A room where dialogue is recorded for voice-over or ADR.

Edge Numbers: Frame numbers printed on the edge of a piece of film. Also called keycode.

Edit Decision List (EDL): The list of shots put out by the editing software, showing the final order and length of all the shots in the film.

Editing Controller: The electronic device that controls video decks in linear editing.

Editor's Cut: The first version of the film produced by the editor before the director becomes involved in the editing process.

ENG: Electronic news gathering, the process of shooting news footage in the field.

EQ (Equalization): The process of controlling how much of each frequency will be heard in the audio track.

Exposure Index: The number showing how sensitive a piece of film is to light.

Exposure Latitude: The number showing the range of light levels a film can record.

Extreme Close-Up (ECU): A shot that only shows a very small area, such as a portion of an actor's face.

Eye Cup: The rubber cup on the end of the viewfinder.

Eye Light: A small lighting instrument, placed so it creates a point of light in the actor's eyes.

Eye Line: 1) In editing, the direction the actor appears to be looking out of frame. 2) On the set, the place where the actor actually is looking on the set.

Far Cyc: A lighting instrument specifically designed to mount above a cyc and throw light all the way down it.

Field: In video, one trip down the screen by the electron gun that is creating the image. Normal video in the United States has sixty fields every second.

Fill Light: Soft, diffuse light that fills in the shadows and softens the image.

Film Speed: A measure of a film's sensitivity to light. Films that are very sensitive are said to be "fast," while "slow" films are less sensitive and require more light.

Film Stock: Raw film that has not yet been exposed.

Filter: Anything put over the lens to change the look and feel of the image.

Final Cut: A privilege extended to well-known directors, giving them final approval of the film, without which it cannot be released.

Fine Cut: An edit of the film where small changes are made and small details are altered. The opposite of a "rough cut."

Finger: A long, slender flag, used to get rid of a long, slender bit of light.

Firewire: A system of cables, plugs, and software used to move video in and out of a computer.

Fish Pole: See Boom.

Flag: A rectangular piece of fabric mounted on a metal frame. Used to block, diffuse, or reduce light.

Flatbed: See Moviola.

Flex File: The computer file produced by a computerized telecine system listing the position, length, and time-code number of each clip.

Flicker: A disagreeable "strobing" effect visible on exposed film when a mismatched HMI lamp is in use.

Floating Camera: A camera mounted on a wearable harness that reduces shakes and wobbles.

Flooding the Lamp: Moving a lamp closer to a fresnel lens, creating a wider beam of light. The opposite of "spotting."

Fluid Head: A type of tripod head that uses oil to smooth out the movement of the camera.

Foamcore: A white, slightly flexible board used to redirect and diffuse light.

Focal Length: The length of the path that light follows through a lens.

Focus Puller: The person who monitors and changes the focus of the camera.

Fogging: A white haze that appears on photographic film when it has been inadvertently exposed to light.

Foley: Sound effects that imitate the sounds caused by the movements of an actor.

Foley Artist: A performer who imitates the movements of an actor on-screen, creating the sounds the actor would create.

Foley Walker: See Foley Artist.

Format: The size, shape, and type of media used by a project.

Four-by-Four: A solid flag that is four feet wide by four feet high.

Free Timing: Recording music without a click track, with the tempo being controlled by the conductor.

Fresnel: A type of lighting instrument containing a fresnel lens—a stepped lens with a pebbled back.

Friction Head: A type of tripod head that uses the friction between two surfaces to keep the head from rotating.

F-Stop: A number that describes the size of the iris opening in (and, thus, the amount of light allowed through) a lens.

Full Body Shot: A shot that shows the entire body of an actor.

Gaffer: The head of the electrics crew.

Gate: The opening in a camera that allows light to hit the film.

Geared Head: A type of tripod head that uses gears to turn the tripod and, thus, create smooth movement.

Generator: A gas- or diesel-powered motor that creates electricity.

Gimbal Mount: A tripod mount that keeps the camera upright even when the floor underneath the tripod is moving.

Graduated Filter (Grad Filter): A filter that allows more light (or a different color of light) through the bottom than through the top.

Greenbed: A temporary catwalk that hangs underneath the permanent grid in a soundstage.

Griffolyn: A large, white fabric used to diffuse or bounce light.

Grip: A crew member who moves scenery, lays track, and adjusts some kinds of nonelectric lighting equipment.

Ground Glass: A precision-built piece of glass that reflects the image from the lens into the viewfinder.

Groundrow: See Cyc Foots.

Half-Double: A scrim with a double scrim over half the light and nothing over the other half.

Half-Single: A scrim with a single scrim over half the light and nothing over the other half

Hard Matte: A metal picture frame placed in the matte box to mask out unwanted portions of the image.

Hazeltine Color Analyzer: A computerized system that alters color when making a print from a negative.

Head (on a C-Stand): The round clamp on a C-stand that holds the piece of grip equipment.

Heads: A grip's word for lighting instruments.

Hemispherical Light Collector: The white ball on a light meter that collects light from the sides, as well as from directly in front.

High Definition Television (HDTV): A video format that has a much greater resolution than standard formats.

Hi-Hat: A tripod that allows a camera to be mounted very close to the floor.

HMI: A type of powerful lighting instrument that can imitate natural light without color correction.

Hot Points: A safety warning telling everyone that a piece of equipment is being carried to or from the set.

Hypercardioid Microphone: A microphone with an elongated heart-shaped pattern.

Image Stabilizer: An electronic feature in some video cameras that stabilizes the image and removes some of the "jitters."

Impedance: The amount of resistance to a signal in a piece of sound equipment. Used to match up microphones, cables, speakers, and so forth.

In Point: Where an edited shot begins.

Incident Meter: A light meter that measures the general level of light coming from the lights.

Insert Car: A car specially equipped to carry a camera and crew to do shots while driving.

Intercut: The editing technique of cutting together shots of two characters who are in different places, such as two characters who are talking on the phone.

Internegative: A negative print of the film made from the interpositive and used to strike final prints.

Interpositive: A positive print of the film made from the original negative, allowing a new negative to be created, thus protecting the original negative.

Iris: 1) A set of louvers that create a circular opening inside the lens. Used to control the amount of light hitting the film. 2) An editing technique using a circular wipe to create a transition between two scenes.

ISO: See ASA.

Jam Sync: Synchronizing two devices so their time-code numbers match.

Jib Arm: A long, moveable arm with a camera mount at the end.

Key Grip: The chief of the grip crew.

Key Light: The most powerful light in any scene. Where the light is supposedly "coming from."

Key Makeup Artist: The chief of the makeup crew.

Keykode: See Edge Numbers.

Lab Transfer: A type of color correction used during telecine. Cheapest and lowest quality.

Laboratory Film: Film specifically designed for laboratory operations, like creating interpositives.

Lavalier (Lav) Microphone: A small, eraser-sized microphone designed to clip to clothing.

Lenser: A flag put over the lens to keep glare and flares off it.

Light Meter: An electronic device that measures the amount of light on the set.

Limpet Mount: A rubber mount that allows cameras to be attached to metal surfaces (like the outsides of cars) using only a vacuum effect.

Line Level: An audio signal level used to move audio signals from one piece of electronic equipment to another.

Lock-Off: A shot where the camera does not move.

Loop Group: A group of voice actors who provide background voices.

Lowboy: A camera mount that allows the camera to be put right at ground level.

Lowell Kit: A lighting kit used for mobile setups, such as ENG.

Lunchbox: An electrical distribution box that provides outlets for lighting equipment and anything else electrical.

M and E tracks: A movie sound track that contains only music and effects (i.e., no dialogue). Used when movies will be dubbed into foreign languages.

Magazine: The part of a camera where the film is stored.

Mains: The large cables that bring power into your house or into a soundstage.

Marker Slate: The slate held in front of the lens before every shot, showing the shot number, take number, and other useful information. Also contains the clapper, the board on top that is slapped down onto the slate to synchronize the audio.

Martini: The last shot of the day.

Master Deck: In a linear editing system, the deck that contains the final product.

Matching: See Continuity.

Mic Level: An audio signal level produced by a microphone.

MIDI (Musical Instrument Digital Interface.): A computer language that allows electronic instruments to be controlled by a computer.

Mitchell Mount: A means of mounting a camera to a tripod. Considered the strongest and most stable mount.

Mixing Stage: A soundstage specifically designed to allow sound designers to mix the final sound track for a film.

MOS Shot: A shot that has no sound track, just the picture. Stands for "Minus Optical Stripe."

Moviola: A film-editing machine that allows the editor to screen several reels of film at the same time, choosing shots from each one.

Music Supervisor: The person who arranges for the use of songs in a film.

Music Timing Sheet: The list of sound track cues in a film, showing the length and placement of each one.

Nagra Tape Deck: While Nagra actually makes all kinds of tape decks, this term is generally applied to an analog, 1/4" open-reel tape deck made by the Nagra company.

Negative Cutter: The person who takes the edit decision list and actually cuts the original negative into the finished film.

Negative Film: Film that, when exposed, creates a negative image that must be printed to be viewed.

Nets: Loosely woven fabric pieces used to diffuse light.

Neutral Density Filter: A filter that reduces the intensity of light hitting the film without changing the color.

Nonlinear Editing: Computer-based editing that allows the editor to add shots to the middle of a sequence without destroying other shots in the sequence.

Nook Light: A tiny soft light that can be stuck into a small place.

NTSC: The video format used in the United States.

Offline Editing: Editing a program together without complicated effects and at a lower resolution.

Omni Microphone: A microphone that picks up sound equally in all directions.

One Light Transfer: See Best Light Transfer.

Online Editing: Editing a program at high resolution and with all the final effects. The last step before distribution.

Open-Ended Silk: A piece of silk fabric mounted on a three-sided frame. Used for diffusing light without a visible edge.

Open-Face Light: A category of lighting instrument without a lens.

Optical Printing: Making a print from a negative using an optical printer. More flexible and expensive than contact printing.

Orchestrator: The person responsible for turning a piano score into a piece of music playable by an orchestra.

Out Point: Where an edited shot ends.

Over-the-Shoulder (OTS): A style of shot where the camera peeks over an actor's shoulder in order to shoot the face of a second actor.

PA: Production Assistant. Someone who assists the producer on the set. An entry-level position.

PAL: The video standard used in Europe.

Pan-and-Scan: A technique of adapting widescreen movies to a 4 x 3 television screen. The image is moved left and right across the film to catch the most important part of the frame.

Panning Shot: A shot where the camera swings on the tripod.

Parabolic Mic: A microphone with a parabolic reflector attached. Used to pick up sounds from a long distance away.

Parallel Editing: See Crosscutting.

PBG Plug (Parallel Blade Ground.): The standard household electrical plug with two parallel prongs and a U-shaped ground plug.

Perms: The permanent catwalk in a soundstage.

Persistence of Vision: The tendency of the human eye to retain an image for a short moment after it has disappeared. Why film appears continuous.

Phono Plug: A 1/4" wide plug commonly used to plug in audio equipment. So called because it was invented for telephone switchboards.

Photo Flood: A lightbulb that has a high color temperature and can match tungsten or daylight fixtures.

Pickup Pattern: The area around a microphone where sound can be detected by the microphone.

Pickup Shot: A shot that begins in the middle of a planned shot (i.e., a shot that only covers a portion of what it should).

Picture Car: Any vehicle that actually appears on-screen.

Picture Lock: When the visual part of an edited film is considered complete.

Pixel: Short for "Picture Element." One of the tiny points of light that makes up an image.

Polarizing Filter: A filter that separates the light beams into those that face a particular direction and those that do not. Used over a lens.

Post House: See PostProduction House.

Postproduction House: A business that specializes in postproduction— e.g., dubbing, editing, and sound tracks.

POV (Point-of-View) Shot: Any shot that imitates the point of view of a character in the scene.

Practical: A lighting instrument, such as a bedside lamp, that appears on-screen and actually works.

Preamp: An electronic amplifier that raises a microphone-level signal up to line level.

Pressure Plate: The flat plate that pushes the film against the gate at the moment of exposure.

Prime Lens: A lens that only has one possible focal length. Opposite of a zoom lens.

Print Film: Film specially designed for printing the final product of a movie.

Product Shot: In a commercial, the shot of the item we are selling.

Propmaster: The person in charge of obtaining or building props mentioned in the script.

Pro Tools: A computer program used to edit sound.

Pulldown Hooks: The hooks inside the camera body that reach up and pull down the film against the gate.

Putt-Putt: A small, portable generator.

PZM Mic: See Boundary-Level Mic.

Quarter-Inch Plug: See Phono Plug.

Raw Stock: Film that has not yet been exposed.

Register Pins: Inside the camera, the pins that stick through the sprocket holes and hold the film in place while it is being exposed.

Release Prints: Prints of the film that are destined to be released to theaters, as opposed to answer prints.

Remote Focus Unit: A remote control unit that allows the camera to be focused from some distance away.

Resolution: The degree of detail in an image.

Reverb: The echo effect created by sound bouncing around a room. Also can be created electronically to imitate such a room.

Reversal Film: Film that produces a positive image when exposed, like slide film in still cameras.

Riser: In a tripod, light stand, or C-stand, the vertical poles that nestle one inside the other. Can be extended to increase the height of the stand.

Room Tone: The sound of an empty room, without voices or movement.

Rough Cut: An early version of a film, without effects or a finished sound track. Not intended for release.

Runout: What happens when you run out of film in the middle of shooting a scene.

Rushes: See Dailies.

Sampling: Using a computer to electronically record something, thereby turning it into digital data that can be manipulated.

Sandbag: A bag of sand.

Scene-by-Scene Transfer: The best and most expensive quality of color-correction used during telecine.

Score: The music that plays under a film.

Scoring Stage: A stage specially designed to record an orchestra.

Scrim: 1) A lightweight fabric used to diffuse light. 2) A large drop made out of this fabric, used to partially hide a person or scenery.

Script Supervisor: The person who keeps track of which scenes were shot and how they were shot, and who watches for continuity.

SECAM: The video standard in most of Asia.

Set Dialogue: Dialogue that is recorded on the set.

Shallow Focus: A situation in which an actor cannot move toward or away from the lens without being out of focus.

Shooting Ratio: The ratio between how much film is shot and how much ends up in the film.

Short Ends: Small portions of unexposed film left over from high-budget shoots.

Shotgun Microphone: A microphone with a long, very slender pickup pattern. Used to pick up sound right in front while rejecting all sound to the sides.

Show Card: A piece of white card used to bounce light. Civilians call it "poster board".

Shutter: The piece of metal in a camera that opens when the film has landed against the gate, allowing light to hit the film.

Shutter Angle: The amount of the shutter that will be used for a shot. Normally, a shutter is a half-circle or 180 degrees, but other angles are possible in some cameras.

Side-by-Side Magazine: A magazine in which the supply and take-up reel stand edge to edge, like Mickey Mouse ears.

Signal Level: The strength of an audio signal—usually mic, line, or speaker level.

Silicone Spray: A slippery spray used to grease up dolly track.

Silk: A finely woven fabric used to diffuse light.

Silverboard: See Bounceboard.

Single Scrim: A cloth or metal filter used to reduce the intensity of a light beam. Slightly less dense than a double scrim.

SMPTE Time Code: A system of numbers used to time all types of media. Created by the Society of Motion Picture and Television Engineers.

Snap-On Matte Box: A cheaper style of matte box than the swing-away style. Used to hold filters and hard mattes in front of a lens.

Snot Tape: Sticky tape that can be rolled into balls and used to hold up gel, scrims, and so forth.

Softlite: Any of a range of lighting instruments that bounce light off an internal, reflective surface, thereby diffusing and softening it.

Solid: A flag made of solid, black fabric, usually Duvateen.

Sound Effects: Any sound that must be added to a scene after the fact, but usually used to describe sounds not made by a human being (those are called Foley).

Source Deck: In a linear video editing system, the tape deck that holds the raw, unedited footage.

Source Music: Any music that appears to be created on-screen, such as the music from a band playing in the movie.

Speaker Level: The strongest level of audio signal—the one fed into a speaker.

Spot Meter: A light meter that measures light reflecting off a specific spot on the set (or on an actor).

Spotting Session: A meeting between the director and the composer in which they decide the length, location, and style of the musical cues.

Spotting the Lamp: Moving a lamp further away from a fresnel lens, creating a narrower beam of light. The opposite of "flooding."

Spreader: The three-arm piece that connects the three legs of a tripod and keeps the legs from kicking out.

Spyder Dolly: A dolly that has legs that can be bent into nonstandard shapes, allowing the dolly to fit in strange corners.

Stage Pin: A style of plug with three round plugs, all placed in a straight line.

Stand-In: A person who sits or stands where a star will be, allowing the lighting crew to adjust the lighting without keeping the star on set.

Star Filters: Filters that turn points of light into starbursts.

Steadicam: See Floating Camera.

Step-Down Transformer: An electronic device that changes electricity from a higher voltage to a lower one.

Sticks: See Tripod.

Stinger: An extension cord that runs a single light.

Streamers: Long, red lines drawn onto a film. They help the conductor of the orchestra know a cue is coming.

Striping the Tape: Putting time code onto a videotape.

Subwoofer: A speaker designed to reproduce very low frequencies.

Sun Gun: A portable HMI lighting instrument.

Supply Reel: Inside the camera magazine, the reel that holds the unexposed film.

S-Video: A format of video that separates the luminance (how bright) from the chroma (what color), producing a higher quality image.

Swing-Away Matte Box: The metal case that attaches to the front of the lens and holds filters and hard mattes.

Switcher: The control panel for a multicamera video shoot. Used by the director to select which camera shot will be seen on-screen.

Taco Cart: On a film set, the cart that holds the grip equipment.

Tail Slate: An image of the marker slate, photographed at the end of a shot instead of at the beginning.

Take-Up Reel: In a camera magazine, the reel that holds the exposed film.

Telecine: The process of transferring the film image to video.

Telephoto Lens: A lens with a long focal length and, therefore, a narrow image. Any lens with a focal length over 100mm is generally considered a telephoto.

Temp Track: A set of temporary musical cues assembled by the director to give the composer an idea of what the director wants.

Three/Two Pulldown: During telecine, the process of converting twenty-four-frame-per-second film to thirty-frame-per-second video.

Three-Point Editing: Choosing an edit point based three places in the footage—two "in points" and one "out point," or one "in point" and two "out points."

Tie-In: The process of connecting the show's power distribution box to the building's power supply.

Tilting Shot: A shot in which the camera bends over forward, backward, or sideways.

Time Code: See SMPTE Time Code.

Topper: A flag placed mostly above the light beam, in order to get rid of the top part of it.

Translight: A translucent drop, lit from behind, used as a background for a set.

Transportation Captain: The person in charge of all the transportation (trucking, limos, etc.) on the set.

Tripod (Sticks): That three-legged thing holding up the camera.

TRT (Total Running Time): The total time of a program from the first frame to the last frame.

Twist-Lok: A style of electrical plug used for loads under 20amps. So-called because you must twist it to lock two plugs together.

Two-shot (Three-Shot, Four-Shot, etc.): A shot containing the stated number of people (two people in a two-shot, etc.)

Unbalanced Line: An audio line that contains only a single signal line plus a shield. Useful only for line-level signals.

Video Assist: The electronic device that converts the image in the viewfinder into one viewable on a video monitor.

Viewfinder: The piece of the camera you look into.

Visual Vocal: A singer who is singing on-screen, as opposed to a background vocal.

Voltage: How hard an electrical power source is pushing the power.

Wallah: A wash of background voices where no one voice or words can be identified.

Wardrobe Supervisor: The person who supervises the costumes on the set.

Wattage: How much power a particular electrical device is consuming.

Wedge: A wedge-shaped piece of wood used to level out dolly track.

White Balance: The process of "educating" a video camera about what sort of light it is shooting under.

Wide-Angle Lens: A lens with a short focal length. Any lens with a focal length under 25mm is considered wide-angle.

Wigwag: A rotating beacon that comes on whenever the soundman is rolling tape on a set.

Wild Lines: Dialogue recorded without picture.

Wipe: An editing transition where one image is replaced by another from side to side.

XLR plug: A three-pronged plug used for balanced audio lines.

Zip Cord: Small electrical cable used for very low-wattage electrical devices.

Zoom Lens: A lens for which the focal length can be changed.

Appendix C:

BIBLIOGRAPHY

You could build a mountain out of all the books written about the entertainment industry. The following is a sampling of the books that have been most helpful to me, both in my work and in the creation of this book.

PRODUCING FILM AND TELEVISION

Daniels, Bill, David Leedy, and Steven D. Sills. *Movie Money: Understanding Hollywood's (Creative) Accounting Practices.* Los Angeles: Silman-James Press, 1998. A useful (and funny) window into the way Hollywood handles money.

Donaldson, Michael C. *Clearance and Copyright.* Los Angeles: Silman-James Press, 1996. An excellent once-over about these sticky legal issues.

Gaines, Phillip and David J. Rhodes. *Micro-Budget Hollywood.* Los Angeles: Silman-James Press, 1995. A guide to making movies for $50,000 to $500,000.

Goodell, Gregory. *Independent Feature Film Production.* New York: St. Martin's Press, 1998. A superb guide to producing film from beginning to end.

Stubbs, Liz and Richard Rodriguez. *Making Independent Films.* New York: Allworth Press, 2000. A very readable guide to film production.

DIRECTING AND CONCEPTUALIZING

Boorstin, Jon. *Making Movies Work: Thinking Like a Filmmaker.* Los Angeles: Silman-James Press, 1995. A great way to train yourself to see the world with a filmmaker's eye.

Katz, Steven. *Film Directing, Shot by Shot.* Studio City, Calif.: Michael Wiese Productions, 1991. A guide to the basics.

Lumet, Sidney. *Making Movies.* New York: Alfred A. Knopf, 1995. Part memoir and part how-to guide, Lumet's book is a must for anyone who wants to be in the business.

Murch, Walter. *In the Blink of an Eye,* 2d ed. Los Angeles: Silman-James Press, 2001. A superb meditation on filmmaking from the only person to ever win both the sound-effects and the film-editing Oscars™ in the same year (for *The English Patient*).

SPECIFIC TECHNICAL GUIDES

Box, Harry C. *Set Lighting Technician's Handbook,* 2d ed. Woburn, Mass.: Focal Press, 1997. This book covers the basics for anyone wanting to work as a gaffer.

Holman, Tomlinson. *Sound for Film and Television.* Woburn, Mass.: Focal Press, 2002. A beautiful work on the topic.

Kenny, Tom, ed. *Sound for Picture.* New York: Mix Books, 2000. A collection of articles from the pages of *Mix,* the industry trade magazine for sound designers and engineers.

Malkiewicz, Kris. *Film Lighting.* New York: Prentice-Hall Press, 1986. A series of interviews with cinematographers that sheds a great deal of light (sorry) on the subject.

Miller, Pat P. *Script Supervising and Film Continuity.* Woburn, M.A.: Focal Press, 1999. This book covers the basics for anyone wanting to work as a script supervisor.

Ohanian, Thomas A. *Digital Nonlinear Editing: Editing Film and Video on the Desktop.* Woburn, Mass.: Focal Press, 1998. A well-written how-to guide for desktop editors.

Reisz, Karel and Gavin Millar. *The Technique of Film Editing.* Woburn, M.A.: Focal Press, 1995. The standard guide on the subject. First published in 1966 and recently republished. As much a conceptual guide as a technical one.

Samuelson, David W. *Motion Picture Camera & Lighting Equipment,* 2d ed. Woburn, Mass.: Focal Press, 1980. This book covers the basics for anyone wanting to work as an electrician or camera assistant.

Taub, Eric. *Gaffers, Grips, and Best Boys.* New York: St. Martin's Press, 1994. An excellent guide to who's who around the set.

Uva, Michael G. and Sabrina Uva. *The Grip Book.* Woburn, Mass.: Focal Press, 1997. This book covers the basics for anyone wanting to work as a grip.

CINEMATOGRAPHY

Grotticelli, Michael. *American Cinematographer Video Manual,* 3d ed. Los Angeles: American Society of Cinematography, 2001. The videographer's bible. Just as essential and technical as her big sister, above.

Hummel, Rob. *American Cinematographer Manual,* 8th ed. Los Angeles: American Society of Cinematography, 2002. The cinematographer's bible. Essential but highly technical.

Mascelli, Joseph V. *The Five C's of Cinematography*. Los Angeles: Silman-James Press, 1965. The Five C's, in case you are curious, are Camera Angles, Continuity, Cutting, Close-ups, and Composition. An essential text.

Malkiewicz, Kris. *Cinematography*. New York: Simon & Schuster, 1989. Malkiewicz is a celebrated cinematographer from Poland, the land that seems to spawn more great DPs per capita than any other country in the world.

FILM TRIVIA

Craddock, Jim, ed. *VideoHound's Golden Movie Retriever 2002*. Farmington Hills, Mich.: Visible Ink Press, 2002. The best of the video guides.

Gordon, William A. *Shot on This Site*. New York: Citadel Press, 1995. Much information about where hundreds of films were shot.

Robertson, Patrick. *Film Facts*. New York: Billboard Books, 2001. The most exhaustingly comprehensive guide to film trivia anywhere.

THIS CRAZY INDUSTRY

Davis, Hadley. *Development Girl: The Hollywood Virgin's Guide to Making It in the Movie Business*. New York: Doubleday, 1999. Often derided as shallow, this book tells it like it is, Prada shoes and all. A very funny account of how the industry works, seen from the development trenches.

Dunne, John Gregory. *Monster: Living off the Big Screen*. New York: Vintage Books, 1997. Dunne writes masterfully about writing, moviemaking, and the business.

Grey, Ian. *Sex, Stupidity and Greed*. New York: Juno Books, 1997. A very funny (and scary) guide to how Hollywood really works. Offbeat and irreverent.

Goldman, William. *Adventures in the Screen Trade*. New York: Warner Books, 1983. Goldman, who wrote (among many others) *Marathon Man* and *Butch Cassidy and the Sundance Kid*, muses on all things Hollywood. Funny and very insightful.

Obst, Lynda Rosen. *Hello, He Lied*. New York: Broadway Books, 1997. Obst is one of Hollywood's most successful female producers. One of the best books on the industry by anyone of either sex.

Phillips, Julia. *You'll Never Eat Lunch in This Town Again*. New York: Signet, 1992. Funny, raw, and a little frightening. Phillips trashed her entire Rolodex in her memoir, giving us an inside view of a no-holds-barred industry. Made poignant by her recent passing.

Rodriguez, Robert. *Rebel Without a Crew*. New York: Plume, 1996. Rodriguez became famous for parlaying a $7,000 film into a Hollywood career. This is how he did it.

Steel, Dawn. *They Can Kill You but They Can't Eat You*. New York: Simon and Schuster, 1993. Sadly out of print after her death, Dawn Steele's book is as much about women in corporate America as it is about the entertainment industry.

INDEX